ISBN 978-1-331-63414-0
PIBN 10215760

English
Français
Deutsche
Italiano
Español
Português

www.forgottenbooks.com

Mythology Photography **Fiction**
Fishing Christianity **Art** Cooking
Essays Buddhism Freemasonry
Medicine **Biology** Music **Ancient**
Egypt Evolution Carpentry Physics
Dance Geology **Mathematics** Fitness
Shakespeare **Folklore** Yoga Marketing
Confidence Immortality Biographies
Poetry **Psychology** Witchcraft
Electronics Chemistry History **Law**
Accounting **Philosophy** Anthropology
Alchemy Drama Quantum Mechanics
Atheism Sexual Health **Ancient History**
Entrepreneurship Languages Sport
Paleontology Needlework Islam
Metaphysics Investment Archaeology
Parenting Statistics Criminology
Motivational

THE
CHRISTIAN ANNUAL

Containing the Proceedings of

THE SOUTHERN CHRISTIAN CONVENTION

and of

The Several Conferences Composing the Convention, with all Auxiliary Bodies, for 1930

Volume Fifty-nine

THE

CHRISTIAN ANNUAL

* * *

Containing the Proceedings of the

SOUTHERN CHRISTIAN CONVENTION

and of the

Various Conferences and Auxiliary Bodies for 1930

* * *

VOLUME FIETY-NINE

* * *

CENTRAL PUBLISHING CO., INC.
RICHMOND, VIRGINIA
1930

Edited by

I. W. JOHNSON, *Secretary*

Southern Christian Convention

Proceedings of the Twenty-Ninth Regular Session of the Southern Christian Convention.

HELD AT UNITED CHURCH
RALEIGH, N. C., APRIL 29TH TO MAY 2, 1930.

FIRST DAY—AFTERNOON SESSION.

Raleigh, N. C., April 29, 1930.

The Southern Christian Convention met in Twenty-ninth Regular Session and was called to order at 2 o'clock by Dr. L. E. Smith, President.

Song service in charge of Rev. J. F. Morgan. Hymn, "All Hail the Power of Jesus' Name."

Worship conducted by Dr. J. Edward Kirbye, pastor of the United Church, Raleigh, N. C.

Prayer led by Dr. N. G. Newman, Holland, Va.

Address by Dr. J. Edward Kirbye, "The Spirit of Unity."

The following delegates were enrolled:

ENROLLMENT OF DELEGATES.

Virginia Valley Central Conference—Ministers: B. J. Earp, A. W. Andes, R. L. Williamson, W. B. Fuller; laymen: J. A. Kagey and John Dean.

Georgia and Alabama Conference—

Alabama Conference—Ministers: G. D. Hunt, George Staley Hunt; laymen: V. E. Kitchens, J. W. Lane, C. J. Hester; S. L. Beougher, ex officio, president Piedmont Junior College.

Eastern Virginia Conference—Ministers: M. F. Allen, J. W. Fix, H. S. Hardcastle, W. D. Harwood, I. W. Johnson, F. C. Lester, J. F. Morgan, J. E. McCauley, N. G. Newman, O. D. Poythress, H. E. Rountree, W. W. Staley, L. E. Smith, E. B. White, C. E. Gerringer, T. N. Lowe, H. C. Caviness, C. C. Ryan, W. C. Hook, W. H. Denison; laymen: Dr. J. W. Manning, Col. E. E. Holland, M. W. Hollowell, E. T. Holland, R. C. Norfleet, Mrs. J. M. Raby, Mrs. I. W. Johnson, Mrs. B. D. Jones, Mrs. C. C. Rawles, Mrs. J. W. Fix, A. M. Johnson, Mrs. L. W. Stagg, Mrs. W. H. Andrews, J. A. Williams, Mrs. Dora Pierce, J. T. Kernodle, J. M. Darden, J. E. West.

North Carolina and Virginia Conference—Ministers: J. O. Atkinson,
S. A. Bennett, G. C. Crutchfield, P. H. Fleming, Stanley C. Harrell,
W. M. Jay, P. T. Klapp, J. W. Patton, A. W. Hurst, J. L. Neese,
C. H. Rowland, J. S. Carden, C. E. Newman, R. A. Whitten;
laymen: W. B. Truitt, W. E. Cook, Mrs. W. A. Harper, Mrs.
C. H. Rowland, C. D. Johnston, Mrs. C. V. Dunn, T. J. Earp,
Mrs. J. R. Foster, Mrs. W. P. Lawrence, Elbert Tolley, W. T.
Dunn; W. A. Harper, ex officio, President Elon College.

Western North Carolina Conference—Ministers: G. O. Lankford,
G. R. Underwood; laymen: W. R. Sellars, J. H. Harden, W. H.
Smith, Miss Essie Cotton.

Eastern North Carolina Conference—Ministers: J. A. Denton, W. C.
Wicker, H. E. Crutchfield, J. Lee Johnson, T. F. Wright; laymen:
L. L. Vaughan, Edward Branch, Mrs. T. F. Ayscue, J. A. Kimball,
M. J. Carlton, J. Walker Kelley, W. A. Newman.

It was moved and carried that the Secretary be authorized to send
a telegram of greeting to Rev. H. W. Elder.

APPOINTMENT OF SPECIAL COMMITTEES.

The President announced the appointment of the following special
committees:

Credentials—E. T. Holland, M. W. Hollowell, T. F. Wright.

Press—C. M. Cannon, P. J. Kernodle, L. L. Vaughan.

Auditing—W. R. Sellars, J. P. Dalton, Dr. W. H. Boone.

Nominations—J. E. West, Mrs. C. H. Rowland, Mrs. L. W. Stagg,
Rev. J. Lee Johnson, Rev. A. W. Andes.

Resolutions—Rev. J. W. Fix, Jesse F. West, Jr., Dr. J. W. Manning.

Apportionments—Dr. W. W. Staley, W. B. Truitt, K. B. Johnson.

Request made for an addition to the Board of Education to take
the place of Rev. J. G. Truitt. E. E. Holland appointed.

It was moved and carried that the program submitted by the Executive Board be adopted, subject to change by the Convention.

Rev. A. W. Sparks, Home Mission Secretary of the General Convention, was introduced to the Convention.

It was moved and carried that the President appoint a committee
to confer with a similar committee from the Woman's Missionary Convention concerning the matter of the time of holding the session of
the Woman's Missionary Convention. S. C. Harrell, J. E. McCauley
and C. D. Johnston, committee.

It was moved and carried that the Board of Christian Education
be requested to make definite recommendations concerning the work
of the young people.

Convention adjourned until the evening session. Benediction by
Rev. S. A. Bennett.

FIRST DAY—EVENING SESSION.

After a delightful banquet of the Woman's Board of Missions, the Convention met at 8 o'clock, Dr. J. Edward Kirbye presiding.

Song service conducted by Rev. J. F. Morgan.

Devotionals led by Dr. W. M. Jay. Scripture lesson, Heb. 1st chapter. Anthem, "The Lord is Great," by the choir.

Address, "The Function of the Church," Dr. Chas. E. Burton, secretary National Council Congregational Churches.

Address, "The Persecution of the Church," Dr. L. E. Smith, President.

Convention adjourned until 9 o'clock A. M. Wednesday. Benediction by Dr. W. C. Wicker.

SECOND DAY—FORENOON SESSION.

Raleigh, N. C., April 30, 1930.

Convention met and called to order at 9 o'clock. Devotions by Rev. J. Lee Johnson.

Roll call, minutes read and approved, enrollment of delegates.

Report of Treasurer read by Dr. W. C. Wicker, Treasurer, and referred to the Auditing Committee.

Report of Executive and Finance Committee was read by I. W. Johnson. It was moved and carried that the report be carried over until Thursday, as provided by the program.

Report of the Board of Superannuation was submitted. On motion, the report was referred back to the Board of Superannuation.

The report of Orphanage Board was read by Mr. J. M. Darden, chairman.

Address by Mr. J. M. Darden.

Address by Mr. Chas. D. Johnston, superintendent.

On motion, the report of the Orphanage Board was adopted, as follows:

REPORT OF THE CHRISTIAN ORPHANAGE.

The Christian Orphanage was chartered under the private laws of North Carolina, 1905, chapter 183, and was established for the purpose of giving a home, care and training to children who had the misfortune to lose father and mother, or either father or mother, or who were helpless and needed a home and care. Since the Orphanage opened its doors on January 1, 1907, it has cared for 341 children.

During its twenty-three years of service in ministering to the fatherless and motherless children who have come to abide under its loving care, the friends of Orphanage children have stood by it and have made it possible for it to lend a helping hand where the need was the greatest and the appeal worthy.

In rendering a service to orphan children all these years, it has not been for the purpose of giving a helpless child a home just because it had no home and to let it grow to young manhood or womanhood, but it has had a still higher aim and purpose. It has tried to build character, and has sent out boys and girls who have been so trained that they may make worthy citizens. While a small number have not done as well as we had wished for them, the larger percentage of our children have made good, and we feel proud of them.

The board of trustees has purchased land from time to time until it now has 204 acres in its farm. This has been made possible by special donations of loyal friends. The last addition of five acres of splendid wheat land was donated by Bro. P. J. Carlton, of Richmond. We are trying to develop our farm in such a way as to produce our bread, meat, potatoes and milk. And for the two years past we have succeeded fairly well along this line.

The Carlton farm in South Carolina, which is being developed for the Christian Orphanage by our good friend and brother, H. A. Carlton, of Raleigh, is a very great help to us. During the last two years we have received from this farm more than $4,000 worth of corn, oats, potatoes, etc.

This Convention owes Bro. Carlton a debt of gratitude for this most noble gift for the assistance of needy humanity.

The Orphanage suffered quite a loss during the fall of 1929 in the destruction by fire of its large feed barn, with practically all of the crop of hay stored during the year 1929. While it was partly covered by insurance, the real loss was several thousand dollars.

It was most unfortunate that the misfortune came soon after the hay crop was stored, and left our cattle out in the weather, with just a temporary shelter. The weather set in very cold and rough, and the stock suffered greatly. The board of trustees met in special session and made arrangements to rebuild, and the new barn built on a modern plan now takes the place of the old one.

In the latter part of October, our superintendent was in Wadley, Ala., attending the Conference, and while there was stricken with appendicitis, came home, went to the hospital, and underwent a serious operation. He was confined in the hospital nearly a month. Unfortunately, his trouble came right in our special Thanksgiving campaign for the Orphanage, and he not being able to attend the Conference and be in the field any during the campaign, the offerings fell short of the usual amount. This will make us financially short this year.

The Orphanage has three buildings for children, and all of them are well filled. The board, several years ago, set the maximum number of children at any one time at 120, and has never exceeded that limit at any one time.

We want to thank the good women of our Church for their loyal support. They have been exceedingly kind to make and send us dresses for the girls and little suits for little boys. They are also very mindful at Thanksgiving and Christmas to see to it that our children have a good dinner on these two occasions.

We want to thank the members of the Southern Convention for their loyal support for all these years, and we trust we will always have your co-operation in this a most worthy service to help humanity.

FINANCIAL REPORT.
January 1, 1928, to December 31, 1928.
Income.

Brought forward, Jan. 1, 1928	$ 6,181.06
Sunday Schools	6,525.36
Special	9,605.49
Willed	273.68
Northern Sunday Schools	59.32
Thanksgiving	7,679.33
Endowments	3,667.12
Total income, 1928	$33,991.36

Expenses.

Administration $5,304.29
Household 10,648.22
Health 474.74
Education 1,070.22
Plant operation 2,657.58
Farm, dairy and garden............................... 4,448.67
Capital expenditures 1,270.87
                                                    ————— 25,874.59

Balance on hand, Dec. 31, 1928................................... $ 8,116.77

To the Board of Trustees of the Christian Orphanage:

We, your auditing committee, have this day checked the books of Chas. D. Johnston, secretary-treasurer of the Christian Orphanage, and find the following:

Brought forward, Jan. 1, 1928.................................... $ 6,181.06
Income, Jan. 1 to Dec. 31, 1928................................. 27,810.30

Total $33,991.36
Expenses from Jan. 1, 1928, to Dec. 31, 1928.................... 25,874.59

To balance on hand, Jan. 1, 1929............................... $ 8,116.77

We beg to say that we have checked the vouchers with the voucher record, and checked the paid checks with the vouchers, and checked the checks with the check stubs, and find the additions were correct.

We also checked the income book for the year 1928 and found 'it to total with the grand total income and with the monthly reports.

This January 31, 1929.

H. C. SIMPSON,
JOHN R. FOSTER,
Committee.

————

From January 1, 1929, to December 31, 1929.

Income.

Brought forward, Jan. 1, 1929.................................... $ 8,116.77
Sunday Schools and Churches 17,662.10
The Duke endowment 2,520.79
Lawrence Holt endowment 900.00
Alamance County 300.00
Friends 5,311.40

Total $34,811.36

Expenses.

Administration $5,583.63
Paid salaries for matrons 2,503.25
Paid for food 4,932.14
Clothing 2,721.45
Laundry 552.99
Household supplies 499.37
Recreation 70.40
Transportation 117.48
Health 493.06
Education 1,188.32
Plant account 49.00
Fuel, light and water 1,344.31

Repairs 754.86
Hospital bills .: 169.00
Farm and dairy expense............................ 5,350.59
Capital investment 2,685.52
                                              ————— 29,029.37

Balance cash on hand, Jan. 1, 1930........................... $ 5,785.99

To the Board of Trustees of the Christian Orphanage:

We, your auditing committee, have this day checked the books of Chas. D. Johnston, secretary-treasurer of the Christian Orphanage, and find the following:

Brought forward, Jan. 1, 1929.................................. $ 8,116.77
Income for year 1929 .... 26,694.59

Total $34,811.36
Expenditures for year 1929................................... 29,029.37

Leaving balance on hand, Jan. 1, 1930........................ $ 5,785.99

We beg to say that we checked the vouchers with the voucher record, compared the checks with the voucher record, and compared the additions, and find the same to be as stated above.

This March 10, 1930.

> JOHN R. FOSTER,
> MARY MURRY,
> *Committee.*

> Very respectfully submitted,
> J. M. DARDEN, *President,*
> *Board of Trustees.*

The following is the report of the Treasurer:

REPORT OF TREASURER.

COLLECTIONS FROM CONFERENCE.

1928.

Sep.	19.	Samuel Earman, Treas. ....$	1,211.59	
	25.	Samuel Earman, Treas.	12.10	
Nov.	14.	J. W. Payne, Treas.	391.58	
	27.	O. D. Lawrence, Treas.	1,312.00	
		I. W. Johnson, Secy.......................	7,217.00	
Dec.	7.	W. W. Boone, Treas........................	4,390.55	
	11.	W. J. Ballentine, Treas.....................	1,481.38	
	13.	H. B. Floyd, Treas.........................	286.81	
	17.	Superannuation Fund	......	$ 2,000.00

1929.

Jan.	7.	Convention Fund	......	2,000.00
		Publications Fund	......	4,000.00
		College Fund	......	7,263.56
Feb.	1.	J. W. Payne, Treas.........................	156.65	
	4.	College Fund	......	1,196.09
Oct.	21.	J. W. Payne, Treas.........................	292.58	
	26.	H. B. Floyd, Treas.........................	50.26	
Nov.	21.	I. W. Johnson, Secy.......................	6,825.00	
	26.	Samuel Earman, Treas.....................	913.66	
	29.	O. D. Lawrence, Treas.....................	1,025.00	
Dec.	6.	W. Waldo Boone, Treas....................	3,559.76	

1930.
Jan. 15. W. J. Ballentine, Treas.................... 1,000.00
Feb. 4. Superannuation Fund 3,000.00
         Convention Fund 2,000.00
         Publication Fund 4,000.00
         College Fund 4,666.26

                                          $30,125.91 $30,125.91

1928.   COLLEGE FUND.
Apl. 26. Balance ....$ 2.00
Nov. 13. W. C. Simpson, Treas..................... 700.00
1929.
Jan. 7. Convention collections 7,263.56
     10. T. C. Amick, Treas., Draft No. 409........ ...... $ 7,265.56
         T. C. Amick, Treas., Draft No. 408........ .... 700.00
Feb. 4. Convention collections 1,196.09
         S. L. Beougher, Pres., Draft No. 507........ ...... 361.06
         S. L. Beougher, Pres., Draft No. 508........ ...... 835.03
1930.
Jan. 7. T. C. Amick, Treas., Draft No. 644........ ...... 3,217.42
         S. L. Beougher, Pres., Draft No. 645........ . ... 348.84
Feb. 7. Convention collections 4,666.26
Apl. 7. Balance 1,100.00

                                          $13,827.91 $13,827.91

1928.   MISSIONS.
Apl. 26. Convention missions .... $ 456.92
         Missions ....$ .81
         Foreign missions 254.00
Sep. 22. H. C. Simpson, Treas. 350.00
Nov. 14. H. C. Simpson, Treas...................... 275.00
     20. H. C. Simpson, Treas., check protested....... ...... 826.50
Dec. 3. O. D. Lawrence, Treas.................... 250.00
     31. H. C. Simpson, Treas.................... 1,005.53
1929.
Jan. 4. J. O. Atkinson, Draft No. 500.............. ...... 250.00
May 31. J. O. Atkinson, Sec., Draft No. 619.......... ...... 93.92

                                          $ 1,881.34 $ 1,881.34

1928.   SUPERANNUATION FUND.
Apl. 26. Balance (overdraft) .... $ 1.00
Dec. 18. Convention collections ....$ 2,000.00
         J. W. Fix, Treas., Draft No. 406........... ...... 2,000.00
1929.
May 31. From Convention 1.00
Dec. 4. J. O. Atkinson, Draft No. 639.............. ...... 1,800.00
1930.
Feb. 4. Convention collections 3,000.00
Apl. 10. Balance 1,200.00

                                          $ 5,001.00 $ 5,001.00

1928.   MINISTERIAL EDUCATION FUND.
Apl. 26. Balance ....$ 175.00
May 31. T. C. Amick, Custodian, Draft No. 620...... ...... $ 175.00

                                          $ 175.00 $ 175.00

1928.   CHRISTIAN EDUCATIONAL FUND.

Apl. 26.	Balance ....$	392.00		
May 24.	C. H. Stephenson, Draft No. 375............	......	$	392.00
		$ 392.00	$	392.00

1928.   BENEVOLENCE FUND.

Apl. 26.	Balance ....$	381.44		
May 5.	E. P. Jones, Treas..........................	125.00		
	E. P. Jones, Treas..........................	175.00		
14.	T. C. Amick, Treas.........................	......	$	125.00
	T. C. Amick, Treas.........................	......		156.00
June 9.	E. P. Jones, Treas..........................	200.00		
Aug. 20.	J. O. Atkinson, Sec., Draft No. 377.........	......		375.00
1929.				
May 31.	J. O. Atkinson, Sec., Draft No. 619..........	......		225.44
		$ 881.44	$	881.44

1928.   WALTERS' ACCOUNT.

Apr. 26.	Balance ....$	324.70		
May 5.	P. J. Carlton	2,000.00		
7.	American National Bank	2,996.90		
31.	J. O. Atkinson, Sec., Draft No. 382..........	......	$	4,593.15
Dec. 1.	C. D. Johnston, Supt., Draft No. 388.........	......		451.70
	C. C. Ryan, Draft No. 387.................	......		277.75
1929.				
May 31.	From Convention Fund	1.00	·	
		$ 5,322.60	$	5,322.60

1928.   ORPHANAGE FUND.

Nov. 13.	H. C. Simpson, Treas......................$	350.00		
1929.				
Jan. 28.	C. D. Johnston, Draft No. 503..............	......	$	350.00
		$ 350.00	$	350.00

1928.   CONVENTION FUND.

Apr. 26.	Overdraft	......	$	142.18
	First National Bank ....$	79.02		
May 5.	L. E. Smith, Pres...........................	27.65		
14.	Geraldine Belsham, Draft No. 373...........	......		50.00
15.	I. W. Johnson, Sec.........................	1,230.00		
21.	W. C. Wicker, Sec., Draft No. 376..........	......		50.00
30.	C. C. Ryan, Draft No. 377.................	......		4.30
	I. W. Johnson, Sec., Draft No. 378.........	......		65.50
June 2.	Central Publishing Co., Draft No. 380.......	......		29.00
4.	Mrs. C. J. Rollings, Draft No. 379..........	......		25.00
14.	C. H. Rowland, Draft No. 386.............	......		15.20
19.	First National Bank, Draft No. 383.........	......		79.02
20.	Geraldine Belsham, Draft No. 389...........	......		50.00
July 2.	L. E. Smith, Draft No. 370.................	......		52.10
	Dr. Jason H. Pierce, Draft No. 371..........	......		13.60
23.	Geraldine Belsham, Draft No. 373...........	......		50.00
Aug. 20.	H. C. Simpson, Treas., note for col..........	2,225.00		
22.	Geraldine Belsham, Draft No. 379...........	......		50.00
27.	H. C. Simpson, Treas.......................	211.13		
	H. C. Simpson, Treas., check protested......	......		212.63
	H. C. Simpson, Treas.......................	211.13		

Sep.	1.	H. C. Simpson, Treas.....................	1.50	
	14.	H. C. Simpson, Treas., note returned........	......	2,235.00
	20.	G. O. Lankford, Draft No. 382..............	......	9.62
	22.	H. C. Simpson, Treas.....................	550.00	
	25.	Geraldine Belsham, Draft No. 380..........	......	50.00
Oct.	2.	B. J. Earp, Draft No. 383..................	......	13.41
	11.	A. R. Flowers, Draft No. 384..............	......	10.90
	20.	Louise Patrick, Draft No. 388..............	......	50.00
Nov.	20.	Louise Patrick, Draft No. 391..............	......	50.00
Dec.	6.	West & Withers, Draft No. 402..............	......	127.34
	27.	Louise Patrick, Draft No. 404..............	......	50.00

1929.

Jan.	7.	Convention collections	2,000.00	
	23.	Teagle & Little, Inc., Draft 502.............	......	16.00
		Louise Patrick, Draft 501...................	......	50.00
Feb.	6.	L. E. Smith, Pres., Draft 509..............	......	10.86
	15.	Louise Patrick, Draft 600...................	......	50.00
Mar.	15.	Louise Patrick, Draft 604...................	......	50.00
Apr.	5.	Warren H. Dennison, Sec., Draft 605........	......	500.00
May	13.	Mrs. Louise Marshall, Draft 616...........	......	50.00
	20.	W. C. Wicker, Treas., Draft 617............	......	50.00
	27.	West & Withers, Draft 618..................	......	62.50
	31.	To balance other funds	......	2.00
June	10.	L. E. Smith, Pres., Draft 622..............	......	52.55
		Mrs. Louise Marshall, Draft 624...........	......	50.00
Apr.	22.	Mrs. Louise Marshall, Draft 608...........	......	50.00
July	15.	Mrs. Louise Marshall, Draft 625...........	......	50.00
Aug.	16.	L. E. Smith, Pres., Draft 629..............	......	50.00
Sep.	12.	L. E. Smith, Pres., Draft 632.............	......	50.00
Oct.	16.	Emily H. Miller, Draft 634.................	......	50.00
Nov.	11.	Emily H. Miller, Draft 635.................	......	50.00
Dec.	12.	L. E. Smith, Pres., Draft 643..............	......	50.00

1930.

Jan.	18.	P. J. Kernodle, Draft 627..................	......	259.00
		L. E. Smith, Pres., Draft 647..............	......	50.00
	27.	Warren H. Denison, Sec., Draft 651.........	......	750.00
Feb.	4.	Convention collections	2,000.00	
	25.	L. E. Smith, Pres., Draft 653..............	......	50.00
Mar.	14.	L. E. Smith, Pres., Draft 655..............	......	50.00
Apr.	10.	Balance	......	2,607.72

$ 8,535.43	$ 8,535.43

1928.   WOMAN'S MISSION BOARD.

Apr.	26.	Balance ....$ 4,156.80		
		R. W. Malone, check....................	......	$ 972.02
May	14.	Mrs. H. S. Hardcastle, Treas..............	250.00	
	29.	Mrs. W. V. Leathers, Draft 374.............	......	250 00
Apr.	26.	J. O. Atkinson, Sec., Draft 367.............	......	1,491.00
		J. O. Atkinson, Sec., Draft 366.............	......	1,248.07
	27.	C. D. Johnston, Draft 368.................	......	31.95
June	18	J. O. Atkinson, Sec., Draft 384.............	......	413.76
Aug.	9.	Mrs. H. S. Hardcastle, Treas..............	902.67	
		Mrs. H. S. Hardcastle, Treas..............	214.52	
		Mrs. H. S. Hardcastle, Treas..............	704.84	
		Mrs. H. S. Hardcastle, Treas..............	74.16	
		Mrs. H. S. Hardcastle, Treas..............	261.82	
		Mrs. H. S. Hardcastle, Treas..............	85.00	

		Mrs. H. S. Hardcastle, Treas.	29.85	
		Mrs. H. S. Hardcastle, Treas.	159.51	
	14.	Mrs. W. V. Leathers, Draft 376	......	159.51
	20.	J. O. Atkinson, Sec., Draft 375	......	1,117.19
		J. O. Atkinson, Sec., Draft 374	......	1,155.67
Oct.	28.	Mrs. H. S. Hardcastle, Treas.	65.65	
Nov.	10.	J. O. Atkinson, Sec., Draft 389	......	65.65
	14.	Mrs. H. S. Hardcastle, Treas.	1,871.86	
		Mrs. H. S. Hardcastle, Treas.	919.42	
		Mrs. H. S. Hardcastle, Treas.	28.00	
		Mrs. H. S. Hardcastle, Treas.	730.76	
		Mrs. H. S. Hardcastle, Treas.	500.86	
		Mrs. H. S. Hardcastle, Treas.	130.71	
		Mrs. H. S. Hardcastle, Treas.	759.06	
		Mrs. H. S. Hardcastle, Treas.	280.49	
	21.	J. O. Atkinson, Draft 392	......	1,871.86
		J. O. Atkinson, Draft 394	......	28.00
		J. O. Atkinson, Draft 395	......	730.76
		J. O. Atkinson, Sec., Draft 396	......	500.86
		J. O. Atkinson, Sec., Draft 397	......	759.06
		J. O. Atkinson, Sec., Draft 399	......	280.49
		J. O. Atkinson, Sec., Draft 393	......	919.42
		J. O. Atkinson, Sec., Draft 400	......	130.71

1929.

Feb.	1.	Mrs. H. S. Hardcastle, Treas.	597.23	
		Mrs. H. S. Hardcastle, Treas.	825.33	
		Mrs. H. S. Hardcastle, Treas.	731.66	
Jan.	26.	J. O. Atkinson, Sec., Draft 505	......	825.33
		J. O. Atkinson, Sec., Draft 504	......	597.23
		J. O. Atkinson, Sec., Draft 506	......	731.66
Apr.	27.	Mrs. H. S. Hardcastle, Treas.	975.83	
		Mrs. H. S. Hardcastle, Treas.	454.55	
		Mrs. H. S. Hardcastle, Treas.	589.71	
		Mrs. H. S. Hardcastle, Treas.	322.23	
		Mrs. H. S. Hardcastle, Treas.	243.54	
		Mrs. H. S. Hardcastle, Treas.	15.00	
		Mrs. H. S. Hardcastle, Treas.	50.00	
		J. O. Atkinson, Sec., Draft 609	......	589.71
		J. O. Atkinson, Sec., Draft 610	......	1,430.49
		J. O. Atkinson, Sec., Draft 611	......	322.23
		J. O. Atkinson, Sec., Draft 612	......	243.54
		J. O. Atkinson, Sec., Draft 613	......	15.00
		J. O. Atkinson, Sec., Draft 614	......	50.00
July	26.	Mrs. H. S. Hardcastle, Treas.	1,538.95	
		Mrs. H. S. Hardcastle, Treas.	657.83	
		Mrs. H. S. Hardcastle, Treas.	39.70	
		Mrs. H. S. Hardcastle, Treas.	783.72	
		Mrs. H. S. Hardcastle, Treas.	573.56	
		Mrs. H. S. Hardcastle, Treas.	516.53	
	20.	Mrs. H. S. Hardcastle, Treas.	1,009.72	
Sep.	20.	Mrs. H. S. Hardcastle, Treas.	670.87	
		Mrs. H. S. Hardcastle, Treas.	14.50	
		Mrs. H. S. Hardcastle, Treas.	768.61	
		Mrs. H. S. Hardcastle, Treas.	592.30	
		Mrs. H. S. Hardcastle, Treas.	4.00	
July	30.	J. O. Atkinson, Sec., Draft 628	......	4,110.29
Sep.	19.	J. O. Atkinson, Sec., Draft 633	......	3,100.00

Nov. 21.	I. W. Johnson, Sec........................	18.94		
	I. W. Johnson, Sec........................	50.25		
1930.				
Jan. 27.	Mrs. H. S. Hardcastle, Treas..............	259.75		
	Mrs. H. S. Hardcastle, Treas..............	897.21		
	Mrs. H. S. Hardcastle, Treas..............	112.24		
	Mrs. H. S. Hardcastle, Treas..............	228.35		
	Mrs. H. S. Hardcastle, Treas..............	20.00		
	J. O. Atkinson, Sec., Draft 649...........	......	259.75
	J. O. Atkinson, Sec., Draft 650...........	......	360.59
	J. O. Atkinson, Sec., Draft 648...........	......	897.21
Mar. 29.	Mrs. H. S. Hardcastle, Treas..............	50.00		
Apr. 10.	Balance		

$25,778.20	$25,778.20

1928. **PUBLICATION FUND.**

Apr. 26.	Balance ....$	311.00	
30.	L. E. Smith, Pres..........................	198.50	
May 8.	P. J. Kernodle, Draft 369.................	......	$ 138.50
	P. J. Kernodle, Draft 370.................	......	554.00
June 16.	L. E. Smith, Pres.........................	164.75	
13.	P. J. Kernodle, Draft 385.................	......	692.50
July 6.	L. E. Smith, Pres.........................	84.87	
14.	Loan, First National Bank.................	500.00	
17.	P. J. Kernodle, Draft 372.................	......	554.00
28.	L. E. Smith, Pres.........................	150.00	
Aug. 19.	P. J. Kernodle, Draft 378.................	......	554.00
Sep. 8.	L. E. Smith, Pres.........................	118.95	
18.	L. E. Smith, Pres.........................	94.00	
25.	Central Publishing Co., Draft 381..........	......	692.50
Oct. 8.	L. E. Smith, Pres.........................	341.63	
9.	C. D. Johnston, Draft 385.................	......	53.35
16.	First National Bank, Draft 387............	......	7.50
25.	Central Publishing Co., Draft 386..........	......	554.00
Nov. 14.	L. E. Smith, Pres.........................	276.50	
17.	P. J. Kernodle, Draft 390.................	......	554.00
3.	L. E. Smith, Pres.........................	390.75	
12.	Central Publishing Co., Draft 402..........	......	692.50
14.	First National Bank, Draft 405............	......	505.00
1929.			
Jan. 10.	L. E. Smith, Pres.........................	453.80	
7.	Convention collections	4,000.00	
12.	P. J. Kernodle, Draft 407.................	......	415.50
Feb. 8.	P. J. Kernodle, Draft 601.................	......	692.50
15.	L. E. Smith, Pres.........................	148.00	
Mar. 4.	L. E. Smith, Pres.........................	425.27	
4.	P. J. Kernodle, Draft 602.................	......	554.00
	C. D. Johnston, Draft 603.................	......	75.00
Apr. 8.	L. E. Smith, Pres.........................	198.00	
	P. J. Kernodle, Draft 606.................	......	554.00
30.	L. E. Smith, Pres.........................	137.75	
May 11.	P. J. Kernodle, Draft 615.................	......	554.00
June 10.	L. E. Smith, Pres.........................	338.48	
10.	P. J. Kernodle, Draft 623.................	......	692.50
July 20.	L. E. Smith, Treas........................	150.33	
	P. J. Kernodle, Draft 626.................	......	554.00
29.	P. J. Kernodle, Draft 627.................	......	259.00

Aug.	16.	L. E. Smith, Pres..........................	158.75	
Sep.	12.	L. E. Smith, Pres..........................	91.00	
		P. J. Kernodle, Draft 630..................	......	554.00
		P. J. Kernodle, Draft 631..................	......	692.50
	16.	Loan, First National Bank.................	750.00	
	30.	L. E. Smith, Pres..........................	266.50	
Nov.	12.	L. E. Smith, Pres..........................	390.00	
		First National Bank, note, Draft 636........	......	757.50
	30.	P. J. Kernodle, Draft 637..................	......	554.00
		P. J. Kernodle, Draft 638..................	......	554.00
Dec.	6.	C. D. Johnston, Draft 640..................	......	100.00
		L. E. Smith, Pres..........................	271.35	
	14.	P. J. Kernodle, Draft 641..................	......	138.50
		P. J. Kernodle, Draft 642..................	......	554.00
1930.				
Jan.	7.	L. E. Smith, Pres..........................	78.00	
	18.	Draft 627, charged to Conference Fund......	259.00	
		Central Publishing Co., Draft 646..........	......	415.50
	27.	L. E. Smith, Pres. (Aug. 29)..............	178.05	
Feb.	4.	Convention collections	4,000.00	
		L. E. Smith, Pres..........................	250.00	
		P. J. Kernodle, Draft 652..................	......	692.50
Mar.	11.	L. E. Smith, Pres..........................	423.83	
		P. J. Kernodle, Draft 654..................	......	554.00
Apr.	10.	Balance	......	140.81

$15,609.66 $15,609.66

RECAPITULATION OF BALANCES.

April 10, 1930.

College Fund ....$	1,100.00	
Superannuation Fund	1,200.00	
Convention Fund	2,607.72	
Woman's Mission Board	119.19	
Publication Fund	140.81	
Balance in bank	......	$ 5,167.72

$ 5,167.72 $ 5,167.72

Draft No. 656, in favor of J. O. Atkinson, Secretary, from the Woman's Mission Board, is not included in this report, but will be paid when presented.

Draft No. 657, in favor of P. J. Kernodle, amount of $554.00, is in my hands, with insufficient balance in the Publication Fund to pay it.

As is my usual custom, I am giving an exhibit of the funds which I have handled during my tenure of office, as follows:

1914-1916 ....$	15,791.98
1916-1918	27,478.60
1918-1920	84,169.22
1920-1922	88,585.37
1922-1924	74,854.85
1924-1926	68,353.11
1926-1928	70,108.14
1928-1930	107,880.49
Total ....$	537,221.76

From this amount should be deducted the Convention collections, amounting to $30,125.91, leaving a net balance of $507,095.85.

In closing my report, I wish to express my keen appreciation for the confidence reposed in me by electing me to the high office of Treasurer of this Convention consecutively for sixteen years. The service I have rendered has been a genuine pleasure, as it gives me opportunity to express my love for the general work of the Convention.

Respectfully submitted,

WALTON CRUMP WICKER,
Treasurer, Southern Christian Convention.

The ministers and laymen of the Congregational Church were introduced to the Convention and invited to have seats as deliberative members.

Sermon, "Pentecostal Celebration," by Rev. Alfred W. Hurst, Elon College, N. C.

Communion in charge of Dr. John Brittain Clark and Dr. W. W. Staley.

Convention adjourned for lunch. Benediction by Dr. J. B. Clark.

SECOND DAY—AFTERNOON SESSION.

Convention met and was called to order at 2 o'clock. Worship in charge of Rev. M. F. Allen, Newport News, Va.

Report of Mr. W. E. MacClenny, Convention Historian, was read and adopted, as follows:

REPORT OF HISTORIAN.

Your Historian regrets that circumstances over which he had no control has rendered it impossible to do any research work during the past two years, and for that reason has very little to report at this session.

In the first place, we are now assembled in the capital city of North Carolina, and a Christian Church was the first religious edifice erected in this city. We quote from Dr. Kemp P. Battle's "History of Raleigh, N. C.," prepared in 1892; on page 64 and following, we find the following:

"As early as 1805 or 1806, William Glendenning, a native of Scotland, removed to Raleigh and established a grocery store on Newbern Avenue, opposite the present (1892) Episcopal rectory. He had been a preacher of the Methodist Episcopal Church, but seceded with James O'Kelly. He built the first Church in the city, on Blount Street, between Morgan and Hargett, and called it Bethel. He became insane and was called the "Crazy Parson," and of course made little impression on the community. . . . For many years there was only one Sunday School in the city, at first held in Glendenning's Church, Bethel, and afterwards in the Academy."

Rev. William Glendenning built his Church in Raleigh before 1807, as a "general meeting" of the Christians was held in the city in that year. This shows that the Christians were the first on the ground in the city of Raleigh.

So far as we know, the first foreign missionary to be ordained and sent out under the auspices of the Christian Church in the United States was ordained in Raleigh, on August 29, 1852. He was Isaac Scott, a negro, and was preparing to sail in the following November for work in Liberia, Africa. On that occasion, the ordination sermon was delivered by Dr. J. B. Hinton, the prayer was made by Rev. H. B. Hayes, while Rev. Isaac N. Walter, of Ohio, delivered the charge and presented the Bible. His Excellency Governor Reid was present and witnessed the ceremonies.

So far as we are informed, the North Carolina Conference of the colored Christians was the first Church organization composed entirely of colored people to be organized in the South after the War Between the States. This body was organized in the city of Raleigh, N. C., in 1866. Rev. William B. Wellons, President of the Southern Christian Convention, and Rev. H. B. Hayes and Rev. James W. Wellons were present at and assisted in the organization of that Conference. Rev. Wm. M. Hayes was the first President.

Since the last meeting of this body, the monument on the campus at Elon College to the memory of Rev. James O'Kelly, the early leader of the Christians in the South, has been erected and unveiled, with appropriate ceremonies, on October 16, 1929, one hundred and three years after his death. For that occasion, your Historian prepared a paper on the life of the great leader, which was read at the unveiling and later published in *The Christian Sun*.

Since the last meeting, there has been a merger made with the Congregational Church, with which all are familiar.

Again the attention of the body is called to the necessity of gathering up all of the remaining original documents bearing on the history of the Christian Church in the South and placing the same in the fireproof library building at Elon College for the use and instruction of coming generations.

It is time that we had a "Historical Society" in the Convention to stimulate interest in our history. This has been of great benefit to other denominations, and we believe it would greatly help us.

All of which is respectfully submitted.

W. E. MacCLENNY,
Convention Historian.

Report of the Mission Board was read by Colonel J. E. West, chairman, Suffolk, Va., and adopted, as follows:

REPORT OF MISSION BOARD.

Since our last report, closing March 31, 1928, we have collected, through our Secretary, and turned over to the Treasurer, the following amounts:

RECEIPTS FROM ALL SOURCES.

April, 1928—S. S. regular, $320.40; specials, $75.85; individual and Church collections, $1,219.83; mountain work, $2.10; Woman's Board, $2,739.07—total, $4,357.25.

May, 1928—S. S. regular, $393.02; specials, $802.54; individual and Church collections, $1,403.40; mountain work, $406.05—total, $3,005.01.

June, 1928—S. S. regular, $259.34; specials, $399.56; Church and individual collections, $1,222.79; mountain work, $5.00; Woman's Board, $5,006.91—total, $6,893.60.

July, 1928—S. S. regular, $320.76; specials, $652.69; individual and Church collections, $1,210.18; mountain work, $5.00—total, $2,188.63.

August, 1928—S. S. regular, $315.94; specials, $339.12; Church and individual collections, $950.42; Woman's Board, $2,187.86—total, $3,793.34.

September, 1928—S. S. regular, $336.57; specials, $325.29; individual and Church collections, $433.03; mountain work, $17.50—total, $1,112.39.

October, 1928—S. S. regular, $363.29; specials, $73.55; reconstruction fund, Porto Rico, $112.81; mountain work, $5.00; individual and Church collections, $118.56—total, $673.21.

November, 1928—S. S. regular, $403.91; specials, $319.15; reconstruction fund, Porto Rico, $217.76; mountain work, $137.00; individual and Church collections, $99.35; Woman's Board, $5,221.16; loans, $5,000—total, $11,398.33.

December, 1928—S. S. regular, $303.90; specials, $606.04; mountain work, $5.00; individual and Church collections, $47.00—total, $961.94.

January, 1929—S. S. regular, $461.49; specials, $911.54; mountain work, $120; individual and Church collections, $101.68; Woman's Board, $2,154.22; Conference home missions, $250.00—total, $3,998.93.

February, 1929—S. S. regular, $271.05; specials, $226.19; individual and Church collections, $304.72—total, $801.96.

March, 1929—S. S. regular, $404.68; specials, $115.18; individual and Church collections, $294.40—total, $814.26.

April, 1929—S. S. regular, $488.12; specials, $1,033.51; individual and Church collections, $3,790.46; mountain work, $84.90; Woman's Board, $2,650.97—total, $8,047.96.

May, 1929—S. S. regular, $464.45; individual and Church collections, $1,945.60; specials, $24.50; mountain work, $5.00—total, $2,439.55.

June, 1929—S. S. regular, $363.98; individual and Church collections, $332.69; specials, $195.56; mountain work, $5.00—total, $897.23.

July, 1929—S. S. regular, $495.40; specials, $2,672.56; individual and Church collections, $691.26; mountain work, $5.00—total, $3,864.22.

August, 1929—S. S. regular, $473.72; specials, $1,790.40; individual and Church collections, $1,898.25; Woman's Board, $4,110.29—total, $8,272.66.

September, 1929—S. S. regular, $568.88; individual and Church collections, $1,014.96; Woman's Board, $3,100.00; specials, $192.63—total, $4,876.47.

October, 1929—S. S. regular, $448.04; individual and Church collections, $103.99; specials, $115.34—total, $667.37.

November, 1929—S. S. regular, $358.61; individual and Church collections, $159.14; specials, $200.87; Conference home missions, $500—total, $1,218.62.

December, 1929—S. S. regular, $357.11; individual and Church collections, $13.06; specials, $196.84; Conference home missions, $100; loans, $500; mountain work, $6.05—total, $1,173.06.

January, 1930—S. S. regular, $358.66; individual and Church collections, $82.00; specials, $316.28; mountain work, $150; loans, $1,500; Woman's Board, $1,517.55—total, $3,924.49.

February, 1930—S. S. regular, $309.93; individual and Church collections, $29.82; specials, $54.50; Conference home missions, $400—total, $794.25.

March, 1930—S. S. regular, $427; individual and Church collections, $60.04; specials, $168.41—total, $655.45.

Grand total receipts, March 31, 1928, to April 1, 1930, $76,830.18.

DISBURSEMENTS.

The fiscal year for appropriations and disbursements of the Mission Board begins October 1st, since the Mission Board meets in annual session on or about September 15th. It is, therefore, necessary, in order to make this report clear, to give appropriations from October 1, 1927, to October 1, 1929, and those voted by the Board are being made for the present fiscal year ending October 1, 1930.

To Home Missions.

The following places received appropriations during the two years ending October 1, 1929:

Mountain work, Carroll County, Va.	$ 3,928.77
Elm Avenue, Portsmouth, Va.	1,070.00
Richmond, Va.	5,194.91
Franklinton, N. C.	25.00
Winchester, Va.	650.00
Roanoke, Ala.	600.00
First Church, Portsmouth	1,200.00
Raleigh, N. C.	4,506.46
South Norfolk, Va.	5,000.00
Lynchburg, Va.	500.00
Paid notes in banks	15,300.00
Total	$37,975.14

Appropriations voted for the present year now in course of payment are:

First Church, Portsmouth, Va.	$ 600.00
Hopewell, Va.	500.00
South Norfolk, Va.	1,500.00

Winchester, Va.	200.00
Lynchburg, Va.	300.00
Bethel Church (Valley Virginia)	100.00
Elm Avenue, Portsmouth	100.00
Mountain work	1,300.00
United Church, Raleigh (conditional)	2,500.00
Ocean View, Va.	1,200.00
Salisbury, N. C.	900.00
Cypress Chapel (conditional)	540.00
Total	$ 9,740.00

Foreign Missions.

Since our last report, we have paid for foreign missions, through the office of Dr. W. P. Minton, Foreign Missions Secretary, $34,064.23. Our disbursements to foreign missions, October 1, 1927, to October 1, 1928, were $17,221.18; and those October 1, 1928, to October 1, 1929, were $16,843.05. These amounts were administered from the Dayton office to Japan and to Porto Rico. In the former field, we have as our missionaries at the present time Rev. and Mrs. C. P. Garman, Dr. and Mrs. A. D. Woodworth, Dr. E. C. Fry, Rev. and Mrs. Wm. Q. McKnight, Miss Martha Stacy, and Miss Angie Crew, and fourteen native pastors, sixteen kindergarten teachers, a dozen other national workers, sixteen organized Churches with a membership of 1,966, and twenty-three Sunday Schools with an enrollment of 1,629. In Porto Rico, our missionaries are Rev. and Mrs. D. P. Barrett, Miss Victoria Adams, five native pastors, a Bible woman, a kindergarten teacher, and a number of part-time and volunteer workers. We have seven organized Churches, with a membership of 450; ten outposts, thirteen Sunday Schools enrolling over a thousand, and several young people's societies, with over two hundred active members.

We have not increased the number of our missionaries on the foreign field the past biennium except through a united effort with the Congregationalists. Under their auspices and by their generosity, Dr. and Mrs. M. J. W. White, Jr., were sent to the Philippine Islands. Dr. White is a graduate of Elon College and of the Medical College of the University of Virginia, a member of Christian Temple, Norfolk, and has gone out as a well-equipped medical missionary. Reports indicate that he is rendering great service at a place of great need, with a splendidly equipped hospital, in the Philippines.

By agreement and merger in our foreign work with the Congregationalists, we are to have a part in the work of foreign missions in Japan, Africa, China, India, Greece, Turkey and the Philippines; and, through our Foreign Board, are to have a voice in the administration of missions in these fields. The Congregationalists merged with us in the work in missions in Japan and Porto Rico, thus becoming one in the work of building up the kingdom to the uttermost parts. This constitutes a challenge to our liberality and to our devotion for the upbuilding of the kingdom of our Lord on earth. The enlarged opportunity and fields demand enlarged liberality for the work, and entails upon us a larger and a more weighty responsibility for world-wide missions.

Mountain Work.

We have been carrying on a much-needed work in Carroll County, Va., both in the field of education and evangelization. We have had two week-day schools, two Sunday Schools, and regular preaching at two Churches. Rev. S. E. Madren is the pastor in charge, and, in addition to preaching each Sunday, has assisted in school work the past year, having been located in the parsonage at Elk Spur since his graduation from Elon College in 1929. We have two Churches, both of which belong to the North Carolina and Virginia Christian Conference—Elk Spur, with 59 members, and Rocky Ford, with 48 members.

The value of these Church buildings is $6,400, and the parsonage is valued at $1,500. Both of these Churches contribute to the general enterprises of the Church and have come to be a part of us in Christian name and polity.

Sunday School Missions.

One of the most gratifying features of our mission work is the increasing interest in missions on the part of our Sunday Schools. With the exception of a very few, our active and progressive Sunday Schools have adopted the plan ratified by this Convention of giving one offering per month for missions. This creates interest in missions where it will do most good in the future, and so we urge that this plan be continued and emphasized in all our schools. The donations from the Sunday Schools during the past biennium amounted to $9,468.25. During the biennial period preceding, they amounted to $7,065.34, an increase of $2,402.91. This is exceedingly gratifying, since it indicates increasing interest in missions in the Sunday Schools, the very place where missionary education and information can, with greatest efficiency, be given. We will have a missionary Church only when we have missionary education in our Sunday Schools and among our young people.

THE WOMAN'S MISSIONARY WORK.

The Woman's Board will make its own report to the Convention. During the previous biennium, the Woman's Board raised $17,858.57. During the present biennium they have turned over to this Board $28,688.03—an increase of $10,829.46.

The woman's annual missionary conferences and their one-day schools of missions continue to grow in interest and in attendance. Frankly, we do not know what would have happened to the missionary cause of the Christian denomination in the South if it had not been for the splendid work of the Woman's Board. Our grateful thanks are hereby recorded.

MISSIONARY INTEREST INCREASING.

This Board has every indication of a constantly increasing interest in missions in the Churches composing the Conferences of this Convention. One indication of this is evidenced by an increase of income to missions the past biennium from $65,029.26 (amount reported two years ago) to $76,830.18, a total increase of income for the past two years of $11,800.92. This increase is the more hopeful and promising because it represents an increase from each of the various sources of income to missions. During the past biennium the appeal has been carried direct to the people in the Churches and Sunday Schools and to individuals. We are of opinion that the Convention acted wisely in its decision two years ago of taking missions out of the budget and of carrying the appeal for missions and also the educational work of missions directly to the people. It has taken time and effort for this readjustment, and many of the Churches have not yet fully adjusted themselves to this schedule, but our faith in the method is greatly strengthened by the results achieved even in so brief a period. The plan to urge all Sunday Schools to take at least a monthly offering for missions and then give all the membership of all the Churches an opportunity to contribute to missions at or about Easter time, with an opportunity of individual gifts from time to time, seems, in the light of facts and two years' experience, to be the best method at present for financing our missionary enterprise. Since the Board goes on the assumption that our people and Churches, when not otherwise designated, wish their money to go one-half for home and one-half for foreign missions, we ask that four months—March, April, May and June—of the year be designated as mission months, having in mind two months for home and two months for foreign missions, though taking only the one offering, as has been done the past two years, from the Churches during this time.

NEW PROJECTS.

While the Mission Board is carrying on its work of building up the home base in our Christian constituency, as heretofore, united projects with the Congregationalists at points of promise are welcome, but each is considered on its individual merit. Where possible, and when deemed advisable by agreement, Christians and Congregationalists, where there are members of both communions, will work together in developing these places. We have, for example, a united undertaking now begun at Salisbury, N. C., where the Congregationalists had property and members and where Christians have members but no Church building or organization. The Congregational Board and the Christian Board have united with the local Church in calling Rev. W. T. Scott to the work, who begins the pastorate there May 1st, with the Church under the title of "United Church (Congregational-Christian)." We have also united in a similar way in Birmingham, where both have members but no property. We are holding services unitedly in the Y. M. C. A. building and trying out the situation for a few months, and if by this experiment and investigation there seems prospect of permanent work, the boards will unite in securing a pastor for a united effort there.

By the assistance of the Woman's Board, we have a permanent pastor at Ocean View, Va., giving all his time to the work, and the prospect seems promising for building up a strong Church there.

We have recently made a survey of Winston-Salem and find over fifty members and ex-members of Christian Churches living in that city, and there seems to be an invitation and an opening as well as a demand and opportunity for a Christian Church in that city. No organization is yet formed.

For the past two years, strenuous effort was made to pay off our home mission obligations, which efforts were successful. On this account, however, we have not been able to enter the new fields desiring and demanding our services, and we are hopeful now and the prospects are that we can direct our attention to the establishment of Churches and congregations where there is great opportunity and urgent demand.

STEWARDSHIP.

We cannot close this report conscientiously without giving emphasis to the great need of stewardship teaching throughout the Churches. As a people, we occupy an unenviable position in the matter of giving to missions and to other Church enterprises. We need to realize that God is the Owner of all and that we are His stewards; more than this, that we are His trustees and under obligation to use our trusteeship for the upbuilding of His kingdom. We are in imperative need of definite, continuous, constructive teaching in stewardship. We urge that every Conference composing this Convention give place in its annual program for the discussion of stewardship and that the Conference secretaries of stewardship be continued, with a committee on stewardship working in conjunction with the said Conference secretary.

J. E. WEST, *Chairman.*
J. O. ATKINSON, *Secretary.*

Address by Col. J. E. West.

Address: "The Burden and Weight of a Missionless Church," Dr. C. H. Rowland.

Address: "Making a Church Missionary," Dr. G. O. Lankford.

Address: "Financing Missionary Work," Mr. J. M. Darden.

Address: "Our Missionary Program," Dr. J. O. Atkinson, Mission Secretary.

The report of the Committee on Evangelism was read by Rev. H. C. Caviness, Portsmouth, Va., and adopted, as follows:

REPORT OF COMMITTEE ON EVANGELISM.

The cross of the Lord Jesus Christ presents a challenge to His Church which is eternally exemplified in evangelism, and the extent of our evangelistic fervor is the evidence of our love for our Lord. He said, "If you love me, keep my commandments"; and the challenge of His great commission ever confronts us: "Go ye into all the world and preach the gospel to every creature." Again He said, "Ye are my witnesses," ever rendering a testimony for or against the Christ of Calvary, a barren life through fruitlessness, or blessed through fruit-bearing, for said He, "Ye have not chosen me, but I have chosen you, and ordained you, that you should go forth and bring forth fruit, and that your fruit should remain." A Church represented by those therein who go not "forth" in fruit-bearing for God is a barren thing, divested of blessing or benefaction to life. "Every tree that bringeth not forth good fruit is hewn down and cast into the fire, wherefore by their fruits ye shall know them."

The cross of our Lord Jesus Christ presents also a challenge to the wisdom we possess, for wisdom is not altogether exemplified in the scholarship of college and university, important as this may be, for the wisdom of the cross is not in words but is expressed in winning souls through its eternal message of atonement to the children of man. The Word of God declares that "The fruit of the righteous is a tree of life, and he that winneth souls is wise." In the Revised Version, it is better translated perhaps: "He that is wise winneth souls." And the glorious rewards for such wisdom, while wisdom always repays those who seek diligently her paths, yet the award made those who exemplify the wisdom of the cross is set forth in those marvelous words: "They that be wise shall shine as the brightness of the firmament, and they that turn many to righteousness as the stars forever and ever."

We, your committee, find, upon diligently comparing the records of the Conferences which compose the Convention, the following facts, interesting, but we think extremely startling. In 1928 there were 227 Churches which rendered their reports to the seven Conferences which compose the Southern Christian Convention. Of that number, 105 Churches out of the total of 227 Churches so reporting reported additions to their respective Churches; 122 Churches out of the 227 Churches reporting reported no additions to their respective Churches, but in many instances reported a decrease in membership. The total membership in the Convention for 1927 was reported as composed of 30,893 members. For 1928, the report rendered shows a membership of 30,788—a decrease in membership for the year of 1928 of 95 members. Four of the seven Conferences composing the Convention reported decreases aggregating 422 members in their respective Churches, while three of the Conferences composing the Convention reported additions to their various Churches of 327 members for the year 1928.

In 1929 there were 227 Churches which rendered their reports to the seven Conferences composing the aforesaid Convention. Of that number, 115 Churches out of the 227 Churches reporting reported additions during the preceding year, and 112 Churches so reporting out of the total of 227 Churches composing the Conferences, reported no additions for the preceding year. But again, in many instances, decreases had occurred. The total membership as reported for 1928 was 30,798; for 1929 the membership was reported as numbering 32,117, which shows an increase of 1,319 members throughout the 115 Churches of the various Conferences composing the Convention, over the preceding year. There were two Conferences composing the Convention which reported decreases of 144 members for the preceding year, and five Conferences out of the seven Conferences composing the Convention reported over the preceding year of 1,363 members. So that we find in the reports, taken from THE ANNUAL for the past two years, that in each year since the Convention last met there have been over one hundred Churches in the various Conferences composing the Convention, which reported no additions to their Church registers. To be exact, 122 Churches in the year 1928, and 112 Churches in the year 1929, reporting no additions, and in many instances decreases in their Church membership.

The power of evangelism is a preachment of the Word of God. Paul cried out in the midst of paganism and persecution, "I am not ashamed of the gospel of Christ, for it is the power of God unto salvation to every one that believeth." "For the Word of God is quick and powerful and sharper than any two-edged sword, and is a discerner of the thoughts and intents of the heart."

The directing force of evangelism is the Holy Spirit, for God hath said: "It is not by might or power, but by Spirit, said the Lord." And His command to the Church is, "Be not filled with wine wherein is excess, but be ye filled with the Holy Spirit." The predicate of evangelism is the power of prayer as indicated by the Holy Ghost of God based upon the eternal promises of God which fail not. Again and again are we commissioned and commanded to pray. Never did the disciples, so far as the record discloses, ask Christ to teach them to preach, but they cried out, "Lord, teach us to pray." The glorious conquests which prayer insures constitutes the greatest heritage of the Church.

In the midst of His supreme crisis in the Garden of Gethsemane, Christ found His disciples aslumber. His question to them must have been the most profound rebuke of their ministry, "Why sleep ye?"

Oh! Lord, awaken us from our slumber of indifference; the lethargy of unspirituality; the tolerance of evil; and the dream of a civilization and progress builded upon a disobedience to God's commands.

Wherefore, your committee respectfully recommends the adoption of the following resolutions:

1. That the presidents of the various Conferences, together with their respective committees upon evangelism, be urged to adopt throughout the entire boundaries of the Convention an evangelistic program which embodies both the plan of mass and personal evangelism. This plan to become the paramount issue of the entire Convention.

2. That the Board of Editors directing the publication of *The Christian Sun* be urged to incorporate a department in *The Sun* to be known as "The Department of Evangelism," where from week to week timely and appropriate articles may appear upon the altogether supreme and important subject of evangelism.

3. That the Mission Board of the Southern Christian Convention be, and is, hereby urged to take under consideration the advisability of creating and directing an evangelistic effort throughout the boundaries of the entire Southern Christian Convention.

Respectfully submitted,

H. C. CAVINESS, *Ch'n*,
J. F. MORGAN,
O. D. POYTHRESS,
A. W. ANDES,
Committee.

Address on "Evangelism," by Rev. H. C. Caviness.

The committee to consider the matter of the time of the meeting of the Woman's Missionary Convention recommended that the present plan of meeting be continued, with the understanding that Tuesday, the first day, be given entirely to the Woman's Convention; the Southern Convention to have its first session on Tuesday night. Report adopted.

On motion, the Convention adjourned until 8 P. M. Benediction by Rev. R. L. Williamson.

SECOND DAY—EVENING SESSION.

Convention met and was called to order at 8 o'clock. Song service conducted by Rev. J. F. Morgan.

Devotions conducted by Rev. Stanley C. Harrell; Scripture, Matt. 18:16, 17.

Address: "Church Women and World Leadership," Mrs. John Ferguson, New York City.

The report of the Woman's Mission Board was read by Mrs. J. A. Williams, President, and adopted by a rising vote, as follows:

REPORT OF THE WOMAN'S BOARD.

The Woman's Missionary Convention submits the following report:

North Carolina Conference—42 Woman's Missionary Societies, with 893 members; 16 Young People's Missionary Societies, with 210 members; 6 Willing Workers' Missionary Societies, with 124 members; 11 Missionary Cradle Rolls, with 223 babies on roll; apportionment for biennium 1929-'30, $10,000; total amount raised, $9,385.94.

Virginia Valley Central Conference—7 Woman's Missionary Societies, with 163 members; 4 Young People's Missionary Societies, with 64 members; 2 Willing Workers' Missionary Societies, with 20 members; 6 Cradle Rolls, with 116 babies on roll; apportionment for biennium 1928-'30, $1,000; total amount raised, $1,008.50.

Alabama Conference—8 Woman's Missionary Societies, with 115 members; 3 Young People's Missionary Societies, with 22 members; 3 Willing Workers' Societies, with 38 members; 2 Cradle Rolls, with 17 babies on roll; apportionment for biennium 1928-'30, $750; total amount raised, $756.03.

Georgia and Alabama Conference—2 Woman's Missionary Societies; no young people's organizations; no Cradle Rolls; apportionment for biennium 1928-'30, $250; total amount raised, $124.38.

Eastern Virginia Conference—28 Woman's Missionary Societies, with 872 members; 26 Young People's Missionary Societies, with 608 members; 20 Willing Workers' Missionary Societies, with 383 members; 21 Cradle Rolls, with 409 babies on roll; apportionment for biennium 1928-'30, $13,000; total amount raised, $14,685.46.

The goal for the Woman's Missionary Convention for biennium 1928-'30 was $25,000; total amount raised, $26,004.01.

DISBURSEMENTS.
Foreign Missions.

Japan	$ 9,116.64
Porto Rico	5,234.57
Ellen Guston	82.20
Indian work	5.00
Total	$14,438.41
Amount on hand for Raleigh Church	$ 895.80
Expense account	271.89
Total	$1,167.69

Home Missions.

Balance on hand May 1, 1928	$ 612.75
Richmond Church	3,151.11
Raleigh Church	1,573.56

Mountains of Virginia	3,163.25
Elon Orphanage	270.56
Special, Dr. Atkinson	85.00
Ocean View Church	712.64
Undesignated	768.61
Roanoke, Ala., Church	133.58
N. C. general purpose fund	130.00
Missionary endowment fund	490.00
Expense account	532.36
	11,010.66

Total home and foreign missions........................ $25,449.07

The following officers were elected, subject to the approval of this body: President, Mrs. J. A. Williams; Vice-President, Mrs. C. H. Rowland; Secretary, Mrs. L. W. Stagg; Treasurer, Mrs. H. S. Hardcastle; Corresponding Secretary, Mrs. E. L. Beale; Superintendent of Young People's Work, Mrs. S. C. Harrell; Superintendent of Cradle Roll, Mrs. I. W. Johnson; Superintendent of Spiritual Life, Mrs. W. H. Carroll; Superintendent of Life Memberships and Memorials, Mrs. M. J. W. White; Woman's Convention Editor, Mrs. W. M. Jay.

Just a forward look: we work by faith, not by sight; therefore, the goal for the Woman's Missionary Convention for the biennium 1930-'32 has been set at $27,000.

Christianity is a look forward. Its Founder, the Christ, was ever looking forward. Those about Him looked at the present and the past. They would not understand Him, and could not, because His whole life was a mirror of things to come. His eyes were set toward the future. Here, then, is the hope of our common task. The greater conquest for our Lord has not yet been achieved; the more glorious privileges and opportunities are yet before us.

In our missionary work, one and all, it doth not yet appear that we should be contented, for our God is leading on and calling us, not only to new tasks, but to new delights and more glorious visions.

There are two things that bear upon my heart today, and to which I seek to direct particular attention:

First, we must somehow interest our young people in missions. They are our hope. They have imagination and enthusiasm. There's a challenge in the missionary task, and charm also. This is the weakest part of our missionary work, as I see it today, is our failure to interest more of our young people in this, the most challenging task that a righteous God has given to a waiting and a bewildered world. In due course, the trusteeship committed to us will pass from our hands to theirs, and they will be prepared to discharge the duties of this trusteeship only as they have training preparation to bear forward the torch thus handed them from our more feeble hands.

The second item of deepest interest, and that upon which we must put emphasis, is that of furthering the cause of missions in our own ranks. None of our societies are yet measuring up to the high privilege, and there are many of our Churches in which there are yet no missionary organizations. The Woman's Missionary Society is to give the evangel of our Lord to those who haven't the good news of Him. Our Lord is leading us on, and we are pressing toward the mark of the high calling of God through Christ, looking forward to that day when the people of all tongues, tribes and nations shall acclaim "King of kings, and Lord of lords." It is a great and glorious task; it is the forward look that calls and challenges us, and we press forward, knowing that the Captain of our salvation will not lead us in vain or to failure, but will lead us, if we will be faithful and true, to a glad and glorious victory.

At a called meeting of the Woman's Board of the S. C. C.:

Raleigh, N. C., April 30, 1930.

In compliance with the request of the Mission Board, it was moved and carried that the Woman's Board of the Southern Christian Convention agrees to pay to the treasurer of the United Church, Raleigh, N. C., the sum of two thousand five hundred ($2,500) dollars annually for five years, making a total of twelve thousand five hundred ($12,500) dollars; provided:

1. That the amounts contributed by Congregationalists shall equal amounts contributed by the Mission Board of the Christian Church, to be applied on Church building debts, including Elon College mortgage, after other building obligations are met.

2. That the United Church in Raleigh put up one dollar every time we put up two dollars.

Also, that Dr. Kirbye remain pastor here, or that another minister just as strong as he be secured for this Church.

Respectfully submitted,

MRS. J. A. WILLIAMS,
MRS. L. W. STAGG,
Executive Committee.

Address by Mrs. J. A. Williams.

Convention adjourned until 9 o'clock A. M. tomorrow. Benediction by Chaplain H. E. Rountree.

THIRD DAY—FORENOON SESSION.

Raleigh, N. C., May 1, 1930.

Convention met and was called to order at 9 o'clock A. M. Devotions by Rev. C. C. Ryan.

Minutes read, and approved as corrected.

Moved and carried that a committee composed of Rev. A. W. Andes, Rev. Stanley C. Harrell and J. T. Kernodle, be appointed to revise Church letter-blanks.

Moved and carried that it is the sense of this Convention that the President should attend the Congregational Conference, at Bournmouth, England, this summer, and that the President of Convention be instructed to draw a draft in favor of Dr. L. E. Smith for $200, or such portion as may be necessary to cover expenses of trip.

The joint report of the Executive and Finance Committees, as presented Wednesday morning, was taken up for consideration and was adopted, by motion, as follows:

JOINT REPORT OF EXECUTIVE AND FINANCE COMMITTEES.

In January, 1929, your Executive Board was called upon to interpret the action of the last session of this Convention pertaining to Bethlehem and Elon Colleges.

In the opinion of your Executive Board, the Convention provided for the Sunday School offerings in Georgia and Alabama to be allotted to Bethlehem College, and the Sunday School offerings in North Carolina and Virginia should be sent to Elon College.

It was also agreed that the president, or legally authorized financial agents, of each institution should have the privilege of making personal solicitation for funds at any time and wherever opportunity should be found.

It was also agreed that funds for colleges should be allotted from available funds in the Convention treasury, on the basis of the notes and endowment bonds of the Convention held by said institutions.

Upon request of the board of trustees of the Christian Orphanage, we approved a change of the charter of the Orphanage, permitting an increase in the number of trustees, and elected the additional trustees nominated by the board.

The Finance Committee met in Suffolk, Va., December 30, 1929, at 10 A. M., jointly with the Executive Committee and heads of departments of the Convention.

The Committee took under consideration the recent financial condition of the Church, deploring the failure of the several Conferences to send to the Convention the full amount requested, and would remind the Conferences that it does not propose to regulate the funds spent within the Conferences, but that in interest of the Church as a whole they are respectfully requested to send the full amount of the Convention's asking to the Convention's Treasurer.

The committee advised the postponing of the "Million Dollar Campaign" for Elon College until conditions were more favorable. Dr. L. E. Smith was elected temporary chairman of the committee.

It was decided to instruct the Christian Temple to extend an invitation to the National Council of Congregational and Christian Churches to hold its biennial session 1932 in Norfolk, Va., pledging to the local Churches the Convention's financial support in this undertaking.

Financial goals for the various departments of the Convention were discussed and agreed upon, as follows: Missions, home and foreign, $50,000 annually; educational, $45,000; Orphanage, $30,000; Board of Religious Education, $4,500.

Also the committee recommends that the Church year for educational and financial purposes be divided and allocated as follows:

January and February, for schools and colleges; March, April, May and June, for missions (home and foreign); July, August, September, October, November and December, for Christian education (it being understood that the Board of Education is to share this period with the Board of Christian Education).

These departments of the Convention are to have access to individuals at all times, but are respectfully requested not to overlap each other in their appeals to the Churches.

We held a meeting with representatives of the Congregational Church concerning details of union of the Congregational and Christian official organizations. The results of that meeting will be presented to this Convention at the proper time.

We prepared a program for this session of the Convention, and voted to accept the invitation of the United Church of Raleigh to entertain the Convention. The program is submitted herewith for your consideration.

We had a number of other meetings during the past two years and considered many matters of interest to the work of the Convention. We presume that the various reports to be submitted to this body will formally present all the items of general interest to the work of the Convention.

We appreciate the trust you have committed to us, and we have carefully and prayerfully tried to be fair and faithful in the discharge of our duties. We have sought to avoid personal fear or favor, and have always tried to work for the larger interest of the kingdom.

Respectfully submitted,

L. E. SMITH.
I. W. JOHNSON.
W. W. STALEY.
E. E. HOLLAND.
J. A. WILLIAMS.
K. B. JOHNSON.

The Committee on Nominations reported as follows:

REPORT OF COMMITTEE ON NOMINATIONS.

Officers—President, Rev. L. E. Smith, D. D., Norfolk, Va.; Vice-President, Rev. N. G. Newman, D. D., Holland, Va.; Secretary, Rev. I. W. Johnson, D. D., Suffolk, Va.; Assistant Secretary, Mrs. Mary Andrews Rollings, Suffolk, Va.; Treasurer, Rev. W. C. Wicker, D. D., Elon College, N. C.

Trustees of Elon College—Hon. Ben T. Holden, Louisburg, N. C.; Dr. J. O. Atkinson, Elon College, N. C.; Rev. A. W. Andes, Harrisonburg, Va.; Hon. K. B. Johnson, Fuquay Springs, N. C.; Hon. J. H. Harden, Burlington, N. C.; Dr. I. W. Johnson, Suffolk, Va.; D. R. Fonville, Burlington, N. C.; Walter C. Rawles, Richmond, Va.; Floyd Hurst, Norfolk, Va.; J. L. Farmer, Rocky Mount, N. C.; W. S. Beamon, Suffolk, Va.; Herbert A. Carlton, Raleigh, N. C.; J. A. Kimball, Manson, N. C.; R. A. Larrick, Winchester, Va.; W. R. Sellars, Burlington, N. C.; Jesse F. West, Jr., Waverly, Va.; Mrs. John H. Barnwell, Burlington, N. C.; Mrs. J. B. Gay, Franklin, Va.; Mrs. J. T. Kernodle, Richmond, Va.; Mrs. R. J. Kernodle, Durham, N. C.-

Trustees of Piedmont Junior College—Rev. G. D. Hunt, Wadley, Ala.; T. J. Holland, Ambrose, Ga.; Wade Royston, Lafayette, Ala.; Rev. E. M. Carter, Youngsville, N. C.; S. C. Heindel, Demorest, Ga.; Rev. D. Witherspoon Dodge, Atlanta, Ga.; J. F. Blackburn, Atlanta, Ga.; Dr. H. M. Edmons, Birmingham, Ala.; Rev. Chas. W. Smith, Phoenix City, Ala.; Rev. Almon O. Stevens, Stearns, Ky.; Robert Sparks Walker, Chattanooga, Tenn.; Rev. G. H. Veazey, Roanoke, Ala.; Rev. Buckingham Mobray, Demorest, Ga.; Rev. Martin Luther Stinson, Atlanta, Ga.; Rev. George W. Blunt, Chattanooga, Tenn.; G. K. Tackler, Daisy, Tenn.

Trustees of Christian Orphanage—Mrs. W. H. Andrews, Suffolk, Va.; Mrs. M. L. Bryant, Norfolk, Va.; Mrs. Stanley C. Harrell, Durham, N. C.; Mrs. W. R. Sellars, Burlington, N. C.

Board of Religious Education—Rev. F. C. Lester, Waverly, Va.; E. T. Holland, Holland, Va.; Mrs. J. W. Patton, Elon College, N. C.; C. H. Stephenson, Raleigh, N. C.; Rev. J. F. Morgan, Route 3, Norfolk, Va.; W. H. Baker, Newport News, Va.; Rev. H. S. Hardcastle, Suffolk, Va.

Mission Board—Colonel J. E. West, Suffolk, Va.; Rev. G. O. Lankford, D. D., Burlington, N. C.; Mrs. John A. Williams, Franklin, Va.; Mrs. M. L. Bryant, Norfolk, Va.; J. A. Williams, Franklin, Va.; J. M. Darden, Suffolk, Va.; Rev. W. W. Staley, D. D., Suffolk, Va.; Rev. C. H. Rowland, D. D., Greensboro, N. C.; K. B. Johnson, Cardenas, N. C.; Mrs. C. H. Rowland, Greensboro, N. C.

Mission Secretary—Dr. J. O. Atkinson, Elon College, N. C.

Board of Publication—Prof. L. L. Vaughna, Raleigh, N. C.; Dr. E. L. Moffitt, Asheboro, N. C.; Rev. P. H. Fleming, D. D., Burlington, N. C.; Rev. N. G. Newman, D. D., Holland, Va.; Rev. Stanley C. Harrell, Durham, N. C.

Board of Superannuation—Rev. J. O. Atkinson, D. D., Elon College, N. C.; Rev. T. E. White, Graham, N. C.; Mrs. C. H. Rowland, Greensboro, N. C.; J. M. Fix, Burlington, N. C.; D. R Fonville, Burlington, N. C.

Editors of "The Christian Sun"—Rev. J. O. Atkinson, D. D., Elon College, N. C., editor-in-chief; Rev. W. W. Staley, D. D., Suffolk, Va.; Rev. Stanley C. Harrell, Durham, N. C.; Dr. W. A. Harper, Elon College, N. C.; Rev. J. E. McCauley, Norfolk, Va., contributing editors; Dr. W. C. Wicker, Elon College, N. C., news editor; Dr. P. J. Kernodle, Richmond, Va., managing editor; C. D. Johnston, Elon College, N. C., circulation manager.

Delegates to General Convention, Seattle, Wash. (1931)—Ministers: A. W. Andes, J. O. Atkinson, H. C. Caviness, B. J. Earp, J. W. Fix, P. H. Fleming, H. S. Hardcastle, Stanley C. Harrell, W. C. Hook, J. D. Dollar, I. W. Johnson,

J. Lee Johnson, G. O. Lankford, F. C. Lester, J. E. McCauley, J. F. Morgan, N. G. Newman, C. E. Newman, J. W. Patton, O. D. Poythress, C. H. Rowland, C. C. Ryan, W. C. Wicker, R. L. Williamson, G. D. Hunt.

Laymen: E. E. Holland, J. E. West, Miss Graham Rowland, Miss Jewel Truitt, J. A. Williams, W. V. Leathers, M. J. W. White, Mrs. M. J. W. White, Mrs. John A. Williams, Mrs. R. T. Bradford, Dr. J. E. Rawles, Mrs. W. V. Leathers, Mrs. M. L. Bryant, J. A. Kimball, K. B. Johnson, Mrs. J. H. Harden, F. F. Myrick, Mrs. C. H. Rowland, Mrs. W. A. Harper, C. D. Johnston, Mrs. S. C. Harrell, T. J. Holland, J. H. Abell, E. L. Moffitt, J. M. Darden.

Members of General Convention ex officio—W. A. Harper, W. W. Staley, L. E. Smith, W. H. Denison, G. O. Lankford, S. L. Beougher.

Joint Commission of Christian-Congregational Churches—Dr. W. W. Staley, Dr. J. O. Atkinson, Dr. W. A. Harper, Col. E. E. Holland, J. A. Williams, K. B. Johnson, Rev. F. C. Lester, Dr. I. W. Johnson, C. D. Johnston, L. L. Vaughan, Mrs. J. A. Williams, Dr. L. E. Smith.

Executive Board—Dr. L. E. Smith, Rev. I. W. Johnson, E. E. Holland, Dr. W. W. Staley.

RECOMMENDATIONS.

We recommend that during the next biennium—May 1, 1930, to May 1, 1932—$600 be appropriated from the Convention funds annually for secretarial help for the President of the Convention, to be paid in equal monthly install-ments.

> J. E. WEST,
> A. W. ANDES,
> MRS. C. H. ROWLAND,
> MRS. L. W. STAGG,
> J. LEE JOHNSON,
> *Committee.*

Special Committee of Twenty-four—Following are the twelve members from the Congregational Church: Dr. W. Knighton Bloom, Washington, D. C.; Dr. C. Rexford Raymond, Chattanooga, Tenn.; Dr. E. C. Gillette, Jacksonville, Fla.; Dr. J. E. Kirbye, Raleigh, N. C.; Rev. G. N. Edwards, Charleston, S. C.; Dr. D. W. Dodge, Atlanta, Ga.; Dr. C. A. Lincoln, Daytona, Fla.; Rev. A. O. Stevens, Stearns, Ky.; Mrs. E. W. Boshart, Raleigh, N. C.; Rev. Milo J. Sweet, Raleigh, N. C.; Dr. W. J. Campbell, Nashville, Tenn.; Dr. F. P. Ensminger, Chattanooga, Tenn.

Additional Trustees for Elon College (Congregational constituency)—Rev. Dwight Bradley, Newton Center, Mass.; Rev. J. Edward Kirbye, Raleigh, N. C.; Rev. R. E. Bowers, Cleveland, Ohio; Frank Robinson, Southern Pines, N. C.; Nelson Jackson, Jr., Tryon, N. C.; William Knowles Cooper, Washing-ton, D. C.; Rev. J. B. Thrall, Asheville, N. C.; Rev. J. B. Clark, Tryon, N. C.; Rev. E. W. Serl, Southern Pines, N. C.; Rev. George N. Edwards, Charleston, S. C.; Rev. Lewis T. Reed, New York City; Rev. Jason Noble Pierce, Wash-ington, D. C.

Moved and carried that the report of the Nominating Committee be adopted and that the Acting Secretary be instructed to cast the ballot of the Convention in electing nominees. The ballot was duly cast.

The report of the Committee on Christian Unity was presented, as follows, by the chairman, Dr. W. A. Harper:

REPORT OF COMMITTEE ON CHRISTIAN UNION.

At the Richmond session of the Southern Christian Convention, the "Recom-mendations Relating to the Organic Union of the Christian and Congregational Churches" were unanimously adopted by a rising vote. Previous to this action by the Southern Christian Convention, the several Conferences that are constituent members of this body had ratified these same recommendations.

The two commissions appointed by the Congregational and Christian Churches held several meetings for the elaboration of these general recommendations, and finally perfected what has now become the official "Plan of Union of the Congregational and Christian Churches," consisting of twenty-five articles. This "Plan of Union" has been published in our Church papers, also in pamphlet form, and is generally known and understood throughout our Church.

This "Plan of Union" was formally adopted by the National Council of Congregational Churches, in session in Detroit, Mich., on June 3, 1929, and by the General Convention of the Christian Church on October 29, 1929, in session at Piqua, Ohio. The name of the united body is "The General Council of Congregational and Christian Churches, Unincorporated." The plan leaves the local Church entirely independent, as it has always been. It may be known simply as a Christian Church, or a Congregational-Christian Church, or a United Church, or it may give itself any name which it may desire.

In communities where there are both Congregational and Christian Churches and where it may seem desirable to combine these Churches, a joint commission has been set up from both constituent bodies to advise as to methods of procedure. But here again the local Churches are the final arbiters of what steps should be taken in bringing about their organic union.

The same liberty which has characterized Conferences of the Christian Church will continue to be operative in the merged body. If it should be the desire of the two bodies in any State or section to keep their local Conferences separate and distinct, this can be done and will not be the occasion of any criticism, such Conferences being represented according to the agreed basis in the General Council.

We are particularly concerned as to the relationship of the Congregational Churches of the Southeast with our own Southern Christian Convention. At this session, a plan of merger of these two groups in this area will be submitted.

We are glad to report that the United Church is making considerable progress in all ways, with the most beautiful harmony in effectuating the "Plan of Union" as adopted in Detroit and Piqua. Christian Church representatives are now members of all the boards of the United Church. The *Herald of Gospel Liberty* and the *Congregationalist* have formally united under the title of *The Congregationalist and Herald of Gospel Liberty*, with Dr. F. G. Coffin and Mr. Hermon Eldredge as associate editors of the merged publication.

The Sunday School literature also of both constituent bodies is being merged as of October 1, 1930. The *Adult Quarterly*, edited by Dr. S. Q. Helfenstein, and the *Young People's Quarterly*, edited by Mr. Hermon Eldredge, are to be published for circulation in both constituencies. The quarterlies edited by Mrs. F. E. Bullock, for the Children's Division, will be discontinued after October 1st. All the Pilgrim Press publications for Sunday Schools are to be published with joint imprint for circulation in both bodies.

Through the use of "projects," the home and foreign missionary work of the two bodies is being brought into organic relationship. In the course of a brief time, the missionary work of the United Church will really be a United Church work.

In the field of Christian education, Miss Lucy M. Eldredge is recognized as assistant young people's secretary by the Educational Society of the General Council, while she serves as administrative secretary for Christian education in our own body.

All of these steps have been taken in the spirit of complete harmony and agreement, and they are set forth here as an evidence that not only has the merger been voted, but that it is actually functioning.

This committee does not presume it to be its function to submit the plan of union for the two constituent bodies in the South, but we record our supreme satisfaction in the effort which we believe will at this session be perfected for the future of the Church of Christ in America. The Christian Church, from the beginning, has stood for Christian union. James O'Kelly, in the very first volume of the *Herald of Gospel Liberty*, gave forty reasons for Christian union. It is a source of real satisfaction to our people that this preaching and teaching of more than a century has finally borne fruit in the actual bringing together in organic relationship of two Christian bodies in this country and that we are one of these bodies.

We summon the members of the Southern Christian Convention to earnest prayer and to wise statesmanship, that steps may be taken at this session to effectualize in our area this "Plan of Union, which is, in a real sense, the herald of that coming union of the followers of Christ in the world which will answer His prayer for the oneness of His followers and be the means of establishing His kingdom in the hearts of men.

Finally, we rejoice that the General Council of Congregational and Christian Churches has decided to merge the two commissions that worked out the "Plan of Union" which has brought our two bodies into union, and that for the future, as a merged body, they will approach other bodies of Christians with a common plea for Christian union. A new day has dawned for the cause of Jesus Christ, and we are on the threshold of a new movement and not at the end of our journey. We earnestly pray that these commissioners of the United Church may have wisdom and good success in their efforts to bring together into a single functioning whole the scattered members of Christ's kingdom in our country and in the world.

> W. A. HARPER,
> L. E. SMITH,
> W. H. DENISON,
> *Committee.*

Motion to adopt. Pending the adoption of report, addresses by Dr. C. Rexford Raymond and Dr. C. H. Rowland. By vote, the report was adopted.

The Joint Committee from Congregational and Christian Churches reported as follows:

REPORT OF JOINT COMMITTEE OF CONGREGATIONAL-CHRISTIAN CHURCHES.

1. That the Congregational Conferences of the Carolinas, Georgia, Florida, Alabama, Tennessee, and Kentucky (with any other State Conference that may be organized within the Southeast) united for fellowship and general direction in an unincorporated organization known as the Congregational Advisory Board of the Southeast, and for supervision being included in the territory of the Eastern Division of the Congregational Church Extension Boards, seek recognition by, and affiliation with, the Southern Christian Convention, each Conference and local Church to retain its corporate identity, thereby meeting necessary legal requirements. The name of the united body shall be "The Southeast Convention of Congregational and Christian Churches, Unincorporated."

2. That the Congregational Conferences referred to be entitled to representation in the Southeast Convention of Congregational and Christian Churches, Unincorporated, on the same basis as the Conferences of the Christian Church are represented in the Southern Christian Convention.

3. That the purpose of this new relation shall be to perform, on behalf of the united groups, the various functions dealing with a common service, and calling for unification of action, it being understood that where technical and legal questions may be involved, the action of the separate bodies shall be secured.

4. That this affiliated body shall meet biennially, in alternation with the General Council of the Congregational and Christian Churches, Unincorporated. It shall be promotional, inspirational, educational, and policy-determining.

5. That the territory included in the activities of the two Church groups being both administratively and geographically a unit, the regularly appointed official leadership of the Congregational and Christian Churches will naturally co-operate and direct the various interests involved.

6. That there be only one regional Church paper functioning for the united groups. It is, therefore, proposed that the *Southern Congregationalist* be discontinued, and that a plan be worked out whereby special Congregational interests be promoted through the use of at least two pages in *The Christian Sun* once a month. The matter of name, policy and other details are to be left to a joint committee, consisting of the editorial boards of both papers.

7. That a joint committee of twenty-four, of which twelve members shall be chosen by the Southern Christian Convention and the same number by the Congregational Advisory Board of the Southeast, be appointed as an executive committee of the Southeast Convention of Congregational and Christian Churches, Unincorporated.

W. KNIGHTON BLOOM,
J. EDWARD KIRBYE,
EDWIN C. GILLETTE,
C. REXFORD RAYMOND,
GEORGE N. EDWARDS,
Special Committee of Congregational Advisory Board of S. E.
L. E. SMITH,
W. A. HARPER,
W. W. STALEY,
J. O. ATKINSON,
E. E. HOLLAND,
I. W. JOHNSON,
Special Committee of the Christian Church.

On motion, the report was unanimously adopted.

On motion, Dr. D. A. Long and Rev. W. T. Scott were presented to the Convention and invited to seats as deliberative members.

Dr. G. O. Lankford, on behalf of the Woman's Convention, presented the banner for progress and efficiency, awarded to Conferences, to the Eastern Virginia Woman's Conference. The banner was received by Mrs. L. W. Stagg.

Dr. J. O. Atkinson, treasurer of Committee on Memorials, reported as follows:

REPORT OF COMMITTEE ON O'KELLY MEMORIAL.

As reported to the Convention two years ago, the Old Lebanon Memorial, near Surry Courthouse, Va., was completed and unveiled with appropriate exercises, and the same was paid for as reported.

Since the last Convention, the O'Kelly Memorial, consisting of an Egyptian marble statue of Rev. James O'Kelly, has been placed upon the campus of Elon College. This statue has been completed, erected and unveiled at the south front, in a conspicuous place on the campus, at Elon College. The memorial was unveiled on October 16, 1929, with appropriate exercises, in the presence of a large concourse of people. *The Christian Sun*, October 24, 1929, was a "James O'Kelly Edition" and carried the program and papers presented on the day of the unveiling. The contract price of the memorial was $1,275. Of this amount, we paid in cash $950. We have on hand $53.78. This leaves a balance due of $271.22. We wish that steps might be taken to raise this sum at once.

Since our last report, the honored and beloved chairman of this committee, Judge J. F. West, Waverly, Va., has passed away. This report covers the financial situation and status of transactions to date.

Respectfully submitted,

J. O. ATKINSON, *Treasurer.*

A collection was taken of pledges amounting to $140, and cash, $15; total, $155.

On motion, report of Committee on Memorials was adopted.

The President appointed Committee on Memoirs, composed of Dr. W. W. Staley, Dr. W. A. Harper, Dr. G. O. Lankford.

By motion, Convention adjourned. Benediction by Dr. D. A. Long.

At the noon hour, the Joint Committee of Twenty-four lunched together and perfected its organization. A central committee of seven was elected as follows: chairman, Dr. L. E. Smith; vice-chairman, Dr. W. Knighton Bloom; secretary, Dr. I. W. Johnson; co-secretary, Rev. George N. Edwards. Additional members: Dr. J. Edward Kirbye, Dr. W. A. Harper, and Col. E. E. Holland.

THIRD DAY—AFTERNOON SESSION.

Convention called to order at 2 P. M. Devotionals by Rev. G. D. Hunt.

The report of Committee on Social Service was presented by Rev. H. S. Hardcastle as follows:

REPORT OF COMMITTEE ON SOCIAL SERVICE.

"None of us liveth to himself." There are inevitable and inescapable special contacts which make it imperative that we learn the fine art of living together. Unless we can learn to live together harmoniously and helpfully, the situation is packed with dynamite. This applies not only to those who live actually with us and next to us, but to the peoples of other nations, for the world, due to modern means of communication and transportation, is fast becoming a neighborhood. The social relationships of life are, therefore, presenting more and more a challenge to the Church of Jesus Christ; for the Church, as the divinely appointed agency for establishing the kingdom of God on earth, must of necessity seek ways and means of applying and expressing the spirit of Christ in these social relationships. Nothing that concerns human life is foreign to it. It should be concerned with the problems involved in such things as family life, industrial and economic conditions, political life, both national and international, and other phases of social life, and it should seek to interpret and to apply the spirit of Christ to all these complex and baffling problems.

The committee recommends and urges that the Churches of the Southern Christian Convention give their hearty support to all movements and agencies that have as their object the application of the principles and spirit of Christianity to life in its social aspects. Pastors, in their teaching and their preaching, should emphasize the place and the importance of the Christian home and family, the advancement of social education, the application of the Golden Rule in industry and economic life, the maintenance of purity in sex relationships, the appalling prevalence of divorce and its evils, the seeming increase of disregard for the Lord's Day, the observance and enforcement of law, the application of Christian principles to political life, the abolishment of war and the promotion of peace, the practice of Christian principles in all our relations with other peoples and nations. The committee feels that the Churches should also take such action as is necessary and possible in an organized way to make all these things effective. Furthermore, if the Southern Christian Convention is to do any effective work, it must do it in a co-operative way. Our Congregational brethren carry on social service work in co-operation with the National Council Commission on Social Relations, and in this way they put into their education program such materials and methods as shall serve to inspire their Churches with the spirit of practical Christianity in all human relationships. The committee recommends that some steps be taken to relate our social service activities to this, or some such constituted body, to give definiteness to our activities.

The committee feels that some study should be given to the question of the movies. A recent series of articles in the *Christian Century*, by Fred Eastman, which were later published in pamphlet form and which can be secured from the *Christian Century* in quantities for 10 cents, presented some facts which are sobering and challenging. One thing is certain: there are many movies today which millions of people are seeing which are a menace to wholesome social life and which are ambassadors of misunderstanding and of ill will when sent to other countries.

In the light of the disappointing outcome of the London Naval Arms Conference, the committee feels that a new emphasis should be placed upon education for peace, and a new loyalty developed to the Paris Peace Pact outlawing war. War is mankind's collective sin against social welfare, and the Church must condemn it unequivocally and seek to develop and promote the spirit that will outlaw it in fact as well as in theory.

The industrial situation gives evidence, too, that the Golden Rule has not been made operative in all its phases. The industrialization of the South and recent events in some of the industries of the South constitute a challenge to the Church to interpret and apply the principles of Christ in industry.

Racial conditions have materially improved, it seems, but there is still a clear call for something more than pronouncements on brotherhood. There is a call for the practice of brotherhood. He who has broken down the middle wall of partition demands that we not only rejoice in the Fatherhood of God, but that we make operative the spirit of brotherhood.

H. S. HARDCASTLE,
F. C. LESTER,
B. J. EARP,
R. L. WILLIAMSON,
Committee.

Moved to amend that it is the sense of this Convention that there be no priority in distribution of Conference apportionments.

Moved and carried that item 4, page 2, and item 5, page 7, of report, together with the amendment, be referred to the Board of Finance, with request to report at this session of Convention.

Dr. Harper presented President Green, of the Country Life Academy, Star, N. C., who spoke of the plan and purpose of his institution.

Dr. S. L. Beougher spoke of the work of Piedmont Junior College.

Dr. Jenkins, of Piedmont College, and Dr. Campbell, of the Atlanta Foundation, Nashville, Tenn., each spoke of the work in their respective fields.

Dr. Harper spoke on the subject, "Our United Educational Plan."

Dr. Kirbye presented the position of the Congregational Conference of the Southeast.

Moved and carried that, with the exception of the articles referred to the Board of Finance, that the report on education be adopted.

Rev. E. C. Partridge, missionary to Alippo, Syria, was presented to the Convention.

The Auditing Committee reported as follows:

REPORT OF AUDITING COMMITTEE.

We, the Auditing Committee, have checked the receipts and disbursements of Dr. W. C. Wicker, Treasurer of the Southern Christian Convention, and find the same to be correct.

On account of the increased volume of work and expense of the office, we recommend that the Treasurer be paid $100 a year, to cover expenses and service.

We recommend that an auditing committee be appointed at this Convention, and that the report of the Treasurer be audited before it is presented to the Convention at the next session.

We recommend that the Treasurer of the Southern Christian Convention be required to countersign all drafts, so as to avoid overdrafts.

Respectfully submitted,
W. R. SELLARS,
J. A. KIMBALL,
Committee.

On motion, the report was adopted.

The report of apportionment was presented as follows:

REPORT OF COMMITTEE ON APPORTIONMENTS.

We, your committee appointed to apportion the twenty-five thousand dollars ($25,000) for the Convention, to the seven Conferences, submit the following:

Alabama Conference	$ 1,250.00
Georgia and Alabama Conference	1,000.00
North Carolina and Virginia Conference	7,500.00
Eastern North Carolina Conference	2,500.00
Western North Carolina Conference	1,500.00
Eastern Virginia Conference	10,000.00
Virginia Valley Central Conference	1,250.00
Total	$25,000.00

We recommend that pastors and Churches exert themselves prayerfully and earnestly to raise the sums apportioned to local Churches by the several Conferences.

W. W. STALEY,
W. B. TRUITT,
K. B. JOHNSON,
Committee.

Moved and carried that the report be adopted.

The report of the Board of Religious Education was presented by Rev. F. C. Lester, chairman, as follows:

REPORT OF BOARD OF CHRISTIAN EDUCATION.

During the biennium, your Board of Christian Education has been faithful in the discharge of duty. We have done our best in a difficult situation. We are glad to render an account of our stewardship, and receive our wages, if any be due.

At the annual meeting in July, 1928, the Board organized with the following officers: F. C. Lester, chairman; H. S. Hardcastle, vice-chairman; Mrs. J. W. Patton, secretary; C. H. Stephenson, treasurer (these officers were re-elected in 1929). Miss Pattie Coghill was continued as field secretary, and, under her leadership, the work continued as usual during 1928.

On January 1, 1929, at her request, and with the regrets of the Board, the resignation of Miss Coghill became effective. Since there were not sufficient funds available to justify the employment of another field secretary, the office, with all equipment, was moved to Waverly, Va., and the work continued by the chairman of the Board, with the assistance of an office secretary as needed. This arrangement continued until September 1, 1929, when Miss Jewel Truitt, a graduate of Elon College, class of 1929, became field secretary. Miss Coghill was in our employ for two months during the summer of last year to help with the summer schools.

TYPE OF WORK DONE.

Notes on the Sunday School lesson have been furnished to *The Christian Sun* each week by Rev. H. S. Hardcastle. The field secretary has furnished notes on the Christian Endeavor topic. News of religious education has been published. Suggestions for program on special days, such as Christmas, Easter, Mother's Day and "Rally Day," have been given, and suitable literature furnished to those requesting it. A gradually increasing library of books on religious education has been available to all those who desire to use such books, and several books have been loaned. Many leaders have been aided with their special programs of religious leadership. Daily vacation Bible schools have been held each summer in these Churches asking for a leader, and many other Churches have been furnished literature and suggestions to aid in putting on such schools. Leadership training schools have been held in local Churches wherever requested. The annual summer schools for leadership training have been held at Elon and Piedmont Junior Colleges. The Sunday School and Christian Endeavor Conventions have been assisted in making up programs, and a speaker has been furnished for most of these conventions. Several of the annual Conferences have been attended and the matter of religious education presented. This year a manual and guide containing the minutes of the Sunday School and Christian Endeavor Conventions was published in mimeograph form. Young people have been assisted with their congress work.

At the request of the Program Committee of this Convention, we have sponsored a banquet for young people in connection with this Convention.

STATISTICS.

During the biennium we have issued 168 certificates for leadership training. In addition to this, a school was held in Norfolk, Va., under the leadership of the General Board of Christian Education, in which 78 credits were given. Many who did not receive credits were in the training schools. Elon and Piedmont Junior also issued many credits. With an annual army of 123 trained leaders, in addition to those students who receive training as a part of their college work, going into our local Churches it seems that the time is not far away when every Church in our Convention will have trained leadership.

Two years ago the Sunday School enrollment was reported to be 23,061. The last report gives the enrollment as 25,119, or a gain of 3,058. Complete reports were received the past year from the Alabama, Eastern Virginia, North Carolina and Virginia, Western North Carolina, and Valley of Virginia Central Conferences. The average attendance of the Sunday Schools in these was a little less than 47 per cent. It cost three schools $11,266.63 to operate. This was 60 cents per enrolled member, or a little more than 1 cent per Sunday. But it was $1.28 for each member who really attended, or two and one-half cents per

Sunday for each person present in Sunday School. The records also show that these schools gave a little more for benevolences than they used for themselves. Incomplete records indicate that about 600 members of the Sunday Schools joined the Church last year. We feel that these figures indicate healthful growth.

RELATION TO THE GENERAL BOARD.

By a recent agreement with the General Board of Christian Education, at Dayton, Ohio, we now are responsible for all work in leadership training done in this Convention. All kinds of work done by the denominational board in the field of leadership training is done by this Board. We receive all requests for aid, even if they come via Dayton, and issue all credits. Complete records are kept in our office, and duplicates of credits are sent Dayton. We support the General Board financially to an amount equivalent to the services received. All moneys raised in the South go through our Treasurer. This plan is working quite satisfactorily to both boards. The agreement should be complied with by local Churches, and thus save the time of the office workers.

OUR DIFFICULTIES.

Our first and greatest difficulty has been, and is, financial. The Convention granted us a budget of $4,500 and directed us to the Sunday School and Christian Endeavor Conventions and to Sunday Schools and Christian Endeavor Societies to raise it. We presented the matter to the conventions and received their contributions in 1928. That fall we urgently appealed to the Sunday Schools for the modest sum of sixteen dollars from each school. Last year we carefully figured, on the basis of membership and previous records for giving, the amount that each Sunday School and Christian Endeavor Society would need to give in order to meet our budget, and presented this to the officers of all conventions, with a request that they seek to lead their people to undertake this matter. Then the chairman attended the five conventions in North Carolina and Virginia and pled for support on the budget basis. All the Conventions gave us all the money received except enough for running expenses, and the North Carolina and Virginia Convention increased its dues for this year, so it would have more to give. Our Treasurer's report attached hereto indicates the response received. We hope you will study the report.

With such a small amount of money to pay bills, it has been impossible to accomplish much. We are now paying Miss Truitt the disgraceful sum of fifty dollars ($50.00) per month. The chairman gives her board for services rendered in his Churches. Office room costs nothing. Most of the printing is done without cost. Every saving is made that seems to be possible. And yet the work is cramped, impeded, almost crushed. And the financial future seems no brighter, unless there is some radical change.

A second difficulty is the distance to be covered. One person cannot do effective field work in more than two hundred Churches scattered over an area of two hundred thousand square miles. The office work, attendance at Conventions and Conferences, the summer schools, and an occasional trip to local Churches is all that one person can do.

RECOMMENDATIONS.

In view of the foregoing, we respectfully submit the following recommendations:

1. That the various types of work undertaken by the Board be continued, and that summer student work be undertaken as soon as possible.

2. That the budget of $4,500 be continued, and that $2,500 of this amount come from Conference apportionments, the remainder to be secured from the Sunday School and Christian Endeavor Conventions and individuals.

3. That we seek an agreement with the Congregationalists of the South whereby field work for the two groups be divided according to areas.

4. That the young people, in their banquet this evening, be asked to elect a committee of three to work with this Board and the Congregational Extension Board in planning and promoting the work among young people.

5. That Miss Priscilla Chase be added to our Board.

Respectfully submitted,

F. C. LESTER, *Ch'n*,
H. S. HARDCASTLE,
MRS. J. W. PATTON,
C. H. STEPHENSON,
E. T. HOLLAND,
J. F. MORGAN,
W. H. BAKER.

Committee.

FINANCIAL STATEMENT OF BOARD OF RELIGIOUS EDUCATION.
August 1, 1926, to August 1, 1927.
Receipts.

Balance in bank	$ 29.36
Conventions	1,054.40
Conferences	378.00
Sunday Schools and Churches	373.69
Miscellaneous, loans, etc.	448.75
Total	$2,284.20

Disbursements.

Salaries, $925 & $125	$1,050.00	
Office and traveling expenses	338.40	
Board meetings	15.00	
Miscellaneous	477.75	
Printing	157.50	
Chautauqua	164.98	
Balance in bank, 7-23-27	80.57	
		$2,284.20

August 1, 1927, to June 25, 1928.
Receipts.

Balance in bank, Aug. 1, 1927	$ 80.57
Sunday Schools and Churches	140.24
Conventions	1,391.67
Elon, advertising	100.00
Loan E. T. H.	295.50
Total	$2,007.98

Disbursements.

Salaries	$ 900.00	
Office and traveling expenses	187.11	
Miscellaneous accounts	306.25	
Printing	305.38	
Balance in bank, 6-25-28	309.24	
		$2,007.98

June 25, 1928, to July 30, 1929.
Receipts.

Balance in bank, June 25, 1929	$ 309.24
Sunday School and C. E. Conventions	1,334.78
Sunday Schools and Churches	193.52
Miscellaneous	241.80
Total	$2,079.34

Disbursements.

Salary and expenses, Miss Coghill	$1,147.35	
Salary and expenses, F. C. Lester	418.69	
Miscellaneous accounts	450.70	
Balance in bank, 7-30-29	62.60	
		$2,079.34

July 30, 1929, to April 25, 1930.
Receipts.

Balance in bank, July 30, 1929	$ 62.60
Conventions	902.47
Sunday Schools and Churches	295.23
Miscellaneous	60.59
Total	$1,320.89

Disbursements.

Expense account, F. C. Lester	$ 250.06	
Salary and expenses, Misses Coghill & Truitt	726.27	
Miscellaneous	166.61	
Balance in bank, 4-25-30	177.95	
		$1,320.89

Moved and carried that recommendation No. 2 be referred to the Board of Finance, with request to report to this session.

Moved and carried that the report, with the exception of article 2, be adopted.

The Custodian of Funds for Ministerial Education reported as follows:

REPORT OF CUSTODIAN OF FUNDS, MINISTERIAL EDUCATION.

1929.   RECEIPTS.

May 31.	Received from Dr. L. E. Smith	$ 175.00
Nov. 18.	Received on note of D. M. Spence	100.00
1930.		
Jan. 16.	Received on note of J. V. Knight	40.00
	Total receipts	$ 315.00

1929.   DISBURSEMENTS.

Mar. 25.	Loan to Silas Madren	$ 250.00
	Loan to George Robinson	250.00
	Loan to Gardner Underhill	200.00
1930.		
Jan. 31.	Loan to H. C. Hilliard	150.00
Mar. 1.	Loan to Carl Dollar	250.00
	Payments on notes of Silas Madren, note given but payment not made in full at Convention	40.00
	On note of Gardner Underhill, payment since last Convention, but note reported in full then	25.00
	Total disbursements since last Convention	$1,165.00

The total disbursements during this biennium exceed the receipts by $850. The Custodian has the following notes on hand:

W. H. Brewer	$ 100.00
R. F. Brown	145.00
E. Carl Brady	250.00
E. M. Carter	150.00
G. C. Crutchfield	900.00

H. E. Crutchfield	250.00
Jesse H. Dollar	875.00
C. Carl Dollar	500.00
Joe French	400.00
Hamilton J. Fleming	230.00
J. U. Fogleman	173.89
W. B. Fuller	125.00
H. T. Gray	100.00
W. C. Hook	50.00
W. J. B. Hines	125.00
W. J. B. Hines, authorized by Dr. J. O. Atkinson	15.00
G. S. Hunt	200.00
H. C. Hilliard	150.00
A. H. Hook	600.00
J. V. Knight	135.00
Siddie Latham	100.00
S. D. Lankford	250.00
S. M. Lynam	700.00
S. E. Madren	600.00
Joseph E. McCauley	225.00
M. A. Pollard	600.00
H. George Robinson	400.00
C. B. Riddle	255.00
D. M. Spence	300.00
W. T. Scott	700.00
W. B. Terrell	450.00
I. T. Underwood	140.00
Gardner Underhill	200.00
G. H. Veazey	450.00
W. L. Wells	310.00
L. L. Wyrick	25.00

Grand total in notes $11,178.89

In addition to the above, the Custodian has the following amount of funds on hand: Cash, in bank and in certificates, $1,725.00.

The present Custodian of the Ministerial Funds of the Southern Christian Convention is resigning his position as business manager of Elon College, the same to take place at the coming college commencement. He, therefore, respectfully requests that the Southern Christian Convention elect his successor in office, Mr. A. T. West, to the position of Custodian of the Ministerial Funds of the Southern Christian Convention. Mr. West is assistant business manager of Elon College at the present time, and the undersigned is resigning his position and asking that you elect at this meeting of the Convention the aforesaid A. T. West to succeed the present Custodian immediately.

Thanking the Convention for all courtesies, I am,

Fraternally,

THOMAS C. AMICK, *Custodian.*

Moved and carried that the report be admitted to record, that Dr. T. C. Amick's resignation be accepted, and that A. T. West be elected as his successor, and that Dr. Amick be thanked for his service.

Moved and carried that the Committee to Pass on Loans to Ministerial Students be re-elected, the committee being composed of J. O. Atkinson, W. A. Harper, C. D. Johnston.

The report of the Board of Education was presented by Dr. W. A. Harper, chairman, as follows:

REPORT OF BOARD OF EDUCATION.

The Liberal Arts College Conference, which assembled in Chicago, Ill., March 18-20, 1930, gave national emphasis to the importance of this typical American institution. Nearly three hundred colleges sent representatives to this conference, which was addressed by leading educators of the nation. The conference not only gave emphasis to the importance of the liberal arts college, but particularly emphasized the need for the Christian college in the American educational system.

It was voted to set up a steering committee of fifteen, who will undertake to impress the country with the need for financial support for the four-year liberal arts college to the extent of giving one billion dollars to these institutions individually. Each college will, of course, be responsible for its own financial campaign, but the prestige which this outstanding committee of fifteen will give to the united cause should prove a real asset for these institutions in securing the necessary funds for their maintenance and expansion. It is clear that American educators are not willing that the small college should be junked, nor that Christian education shuld cease its contribution to the development of character in American youth.

ELON COLLEGE.

1. *History.*—Elon College was chartered by the General Assembly of North Carolina, March 11, 1889, and opened its doors for students September 2, 1890. The college, therefore, this year completes its fortieth session, and has served the Christian Church in the preparation of leaders for pulpit and pew most effectively during these four decades. The place of its work for the future is most promising. Elon College evidently has filled a large and real place in the total program of the Christian Church in the South, and it is destined, in our judgment, to fill an even larger place in the total program of the United Church in this territory. It is true that the denominational college is the backbone of the denominational structure, not in that it strives to teach sectarianism nor to perpetuate it, but that leadership for denominational enterprises, experience teaches, comes almost entirely from this type of institution. This committee cannot too earnestly recommend Elon College to the support of the Congregational and Christian Churches in the South and the nation.

2. *Plant and Endowment.*—The Elon College plant, as inventoried and as carried on the books of the business manager, consists of the following items:

Buildings.	Value.
Alamance Building	$143,961.06
Alumni Building	107,000.00
Carlton Library Building	99,909.98
Duke Science Building	98,105.89
Mooney Christian Education Building	121,115.35
Whitley Auditorium	99,577.06
East Dormitory	15,500.00
West Dormitory	84,400.00
Ladies' Hall	30,500.00
Power Plant	12,000.00
Total of buildings	$812,069.34
Equipment in buildings and campus, with improvements	336,486.53
Grand total for plant	$1,148,555.87
The endowment of the college	530,896.81

The college carries insurance on the buildings and equipment of $599,800.

The friends of the college carry insurance on the president's life amounting to $200,000, payable to the college.

3. *Alumni.*—Those who hold the bachelor degree from Elon received during the last forty years, including the class of 1930, total 832 in number and are distributed in the following groups:

	Men.	Women.	Total.
Education	176	237	413
Ministry and missionary	114	4	118
Business	112	19	131
Home-makers (women)	..	81	81
Public service	26	11	37
Law	18	..	18
Medicine	18	1	19
Engineering	12	..	12
Fine arts	1	2	3
Total	477	355	832

It is easy to discern the type of institution which Elon College is from these vital facts regarding its graduate alumni.

4. *Current Finances.*—At the Richmond session of the Convention, it was voted to pay the interest on the note of the Convention which the college holds as endowment in the sum of $112,500, and on the bonds which it holds also as endowment in the amount of $100,000 out of the Convention apportionment. The interest on those two items amounts to $12,750 annually. In order to guarantee the integrity of the college endowment, it is necessary that the Convention should continue to pay this interest. The Finance Board ruled that certain items should take priority in the distribution of the Convention apportionment, and that has left the college to receive the payment only of the residue of the Conference apportionment. The first year there was paid on this account $7,265.56, and this year there was paid $4,317.42. The remainder to fill out the balance of the $12,750 for each of the past two years has been contributed by individual members of the Church. This committee recommends that the Convention, at this time, take steps that will insure the payment to the college of the interest charge of $12,750 annually on these endowment obligations through Conference apportionments.

The Richmond Convention also provided that, in addition to this endowment interest obligation, $24,000 should be raised each year in the bounds of the Convention as interest on the $400,000 of bonds given the college to offset its indebtedness. To meet this $24,000 item, it was provided that there should be voluntary offerings in the Sunday Schools on the fifth Sundays for the benefit of the college.

During these two years, eighty-four Sunday Schools have participated in this offering. It has been the means of keeping the college before our local constituencies and creating interest in the Sunday Schools for the college. The college, in co-operation with a generous layman, has provided two scholarships for each of the five constituent Conferences for that Sunday School in each Conference that raises the largest per capita amount through this fifth-Sunday offering, and also for the Sunday School that raises the largest gross amount. In this way, ten promising young people of the Christian Church are introduced to our college annually as representatives of the Sunday Schools. Though this plan has only been in operation for two years, it has amply justified itself, and it is hoped that the Convention will authorize its continuance.

Whatever sum should be required above the Sunday School offering to make up the $24,000, the college has been authorized to secure from individuals in the name of the Church. During the year which ended May 20, 1929, the full amount was raised. During the present year there is a spirit of co-operation between the college and the pastors of Churches which bids fair to secure the full amount again, despite the financial depression from which the Elon constituency has been suffering. The Church understands, we are sure, that the raising of this money is an absolute essential, and that it is even more necessary to raise this money in times of depression than in times of prosperity.

It is our judgment that the raising of the $24,000 for the next two years should be made the responsibility of the "Million Dollar Campaign" committee, and that they should undertake to raise this sum of money for current expenses and such a sum for each of the two years succeeding as, in their judgment, is wise, to apply to the general campaign, so that only one campaign will be proceeding at the same time. It is our further conviction that the plan of raising this money by pastors and local leaders is the only sure way of financing the college and of tying the constituency to it. We commend this cause heartily, and call upon our ministers and local leaders to co-operate fully not only this year but during the next two years.

5. *Congregational Trustees.*—The board of trustees of Elon College requests the Convention to authorize the amendment of its charter so as to permit the addition of six trustees from the Congregational constituency, and requests the Convention likewise to have twelve persons from the Congregational constituency nominated at this session, from whom, at the May session of the board, these six trustees may be chosen. Since Elon is designed to serve the United Church in the South, the reason for this recommendation on the part of the board of trustees is patent to all.

6. *Million Dollar Campaign.*—We recommend that the Convention endorse again the raising of a million dollars for Elon College, $400,000 of which shall be used to liquidate the debt of the college, for which the Convention gave its bonds; and that when this $400,000 has been raised, the college surrender these bonds to the Convention; the remaining $600,000 to be raised in the campaign, we recommend, to be added to the permanent invested funds of the college.

In the paragraph on current finances, above, we have recommended that the campaign committee set up by the college be authorized, in addition to raising the interest on these bonds, so as to obviate the necessity of conducting two campaigns for one enterprise at the same time. We reiterate our recommendation that in the raising of money for the interest on the $400,000 of bonds, as well as that to apply on the million dollar campaign, the campaign committee should utilize the pastors of Churches and local leaders.

We recommend that the number of years to be taken to raise this million dollars, the survey to be undertaken in connection with the campaign, the financial set-up of the campaign, and the manner of the campaign, be left to the college campaign committee, with full power to proceed. We are, however, of the opinion that this campaign committee should secure the approval of the Executive Committee of the Convention for its plans when they have matured.

We call upon the leaders of the Christian Church, assembled in this session of the Southern Christian Convention, to lend hearty support to the college and this campaign committee in its efforts to strengthen Elon College.

7. *Death of Trustee Watson.*—On March 4, 1930, Dr. Geo. S. Watson passed to his reward in his home in Elon College. Dr. Watson was a member of the committee on location for Elon College and a member of the original board of trustees. He had served as a member of the board of trustees from the beginning, and during forty years only missed one session, and that was when he was ill. Dr. Watson saw the need of a college for the Christian Church and espoused the cause with that enthusiasm for Christian enterprises which characterized his life throughout. In his passing in his eighty-sixth year, the Christian Church has lost a distinguished leader, and the college a most devoted and generous-hearted friend.

PIEDMONT JUNIOR COLLEGE.

1. *History and Purpose.*—Our denominational colleges were founded specifically to give a Christian education. Our fathers built the Church and college side by side, that the faith of the Church might permeate the college and the

intellectual development of the college might be given to the service of the Church. A Christian college is not one controlled by dogmatic tests and formulas, but one as free as the Church itself—free to interpret the ideals of the Nazarene and apply them to every problem of the age.

The founding of Bethlehem College, in 1922, grew out of the Men and Millions Movement of the Southern Christian Convention. It was born of the desire on the part of many earnest Christian men and women of Georgia and Alabama to see developed in their midst a higher and stronger type of ministerial and lay leadership and a higher type of Christian citizenship.

Educational development in this great section has been held back because of shortage of institutions of higher learning, shortage of funds for building up and operation of educational institutions, and lack of funds on the part of the boys and girls. The United States census shows that there are eight Southern States, with the highest percentage of native-born stocks, which have the poorest educational opportunities, facilities and development in America.

Great wisdom was shown by the locating committee in placing the college at Wadley, Ala., as it does not in any way duplicate the work of any other institution; its field is exclusive. It is in the center of an area of densely populated country, with a radius of seventy-five miles, practically untouched by other colleges, with high schools turning our hundreds of graduates every year that are unable financially to go a long distance to school or to pay the exorbitant price asked by other institutions for an education.

Piedmont Junior College has every reason which might be demanded for continued existence, but they are all contained in this statement: Offering an education to worthy Chrisitan Americans for Christian Americanism of very limited means at the lowest possible cost. We recommend that it continue its operations.

2. *Affiliation with Piedmont College.*—In anticipation of a final merger of the Congregational and Christian denominations, the boards of trustees of Bethlehem College and of Piedmont College, Demorest, Ga., voted on a basis of co-operation which was approved in principle by the Richmond Convention.

Bethlehem College was affiliated with Piedmont College in 1928, and its name changed to Piedmont Junior College. The educational co-ordination of these institutions has resulted in making Piedmont Junior College an accredited junior college, whose graduates are accepted readily by senior colleges. This plan was approved by the Executive Committee of the Convention at a meeting held in Suffolk, Va., January, 1929.

We recommend that this educational affiliation of Piedmont and Piedmont Junior Colleges be allowed to continue and terminate at their option, and that any other arrangements between the institutions which may further the cause of union and strengthen the colleges, which do not infringe on the rights of the Convention, be left in the hands of the board of trustees of Piedmont Junior College.

3. *Plant and Endowment.*

Administration building	$ 50,000.00
Dormitory	30,000.00
Grounds	5,000.00
Equipment	4,000.00
Library, laboratory, etc.	3,000.00
Endowment	35,000.00
Subscriptions and notes	20,000.00
Insurance	10,000.00
Total	$157,000.00
Indebtedness	25,000.00
	$132,000.00

4. *Alumni.*—For the first three years the school operated an academy in connection with the college. During this period, eighty-seven were graduated from the high school department. Including the graduation class of 1930, there will have graduated from the college sixty-six. Many have gone on and made good in other colleges and have received their bachelor's degree. Nearly all have entered the teaching profession; fourteen the ministry.

5. *Current Operating Funds.*—The Convention approved of raising $10,000 for current expenses, and divided it as follows:

On Convention note ....$ 750.00
Quarterly offerings from S. S. in Georgia & Alabama   250.00
From Churches in Georgia & Alabama Conference.. 1,000.00
From members S. C. C. outside Georgia & Alabama 5,000.00
From general public and students................. 3,000.00

The campaign to raise $50,000 for the college, which was approved at the last Convention, was started last year and yielded about $35,000 for indebtedness and endowment.

Piedmont Junior College must have better financial support; therefore, we would recommend that:

(1) The Convention approve of the raising of $25,000 in donations for the budget from September 1, 1930, to August 31, 1931, and the same for the following year.

(2) The raising of $35,000 to clear the college from debt, complete and equip its buildings and grounds.

(3) Also that it approve of a plan to begin July 1, 1930, to raise the standards along all lines, to beautify the grounds, and have the buildings to correspond with the grounds in all possible respects.

(4) The college must raise $600,000 for endowment.

(5) We recommend that Piedmont Junior College be written in the Convention's apportionments for $2,000 annually.

(6) We also recommend that Piedmont Junior College be allowed to raise $5,000 from members of the Christian Churches of the Conferences in Virginia and North Carolina.

(7) There have been two scholarships provided for our two Conferences in Georgia and Alabama of $100 each, a very generous layman making this possible, for that Sunday School in each Conference that raises the largest amount per capita through the fifth-Sunday offering, and another for the Sunday School that raises the largest gross amount. It will be a very great help to your young people, and we ask the Convention to authorize its continuance.

6. *A Change in Charter.*—We recommend that the Convention authorize a change in the charter of Piedmont Junior College to conform to the affiliation which now exists between the institution and Piedmont College, Demorest, Ga.; also to provide for as many trustees from the Congregational constituency as may be deemed best for the United Church. The terms of eight are expiring at this time, and we suggest that twelve be nominated from the Congregational constituncy.

W. A. HARPER, *Ch'n,*
W. W. STALEY,
E. L. MOFFITT,
S. L. BEOUGHER,
E. E. HOLLAND,
Board of Education.

On motion, the report was adopted.

On motion, the Convention adjourned. Benediction by Dr. C. R. Raymond.

THIRD DAY—EVENING SESSION.

Music by Elon College Choral Club..
Devotionals by Rev. S. A. Bennett.
Address: "The Place of Religion in Education," Dr. W. A. Harper.
Address: "At the Switch," Dr. John Brittain Clark.
Address: "The Meaning of Education," Dr. A. T. Allen, State Superintendent of Education.
Music by Elon College Choral Club.
Convention adjourned. Benediction by Rev. T. Fred Wright.

FOURTH DAY—FORENOON SESSION.

Raleigh, N. C., May 2, 1930.

Convention called to order at 9 o'clock. Devotionals by Rev. W. C. Hook.

The report of the Committee on Temperance was read by Dr. G. O. Lankford, chairman, and, on motion, adopted, as follows:

REPORT OF COMMITTEE ON TEMPERANCE.

Temperance is a subject upon which it is much easier to provoke discussion and to make resolutions than it is to arrive at definite, concrete and constructive action. It has been customary for a long while for Church gatherings, such as this or similar to this, to pass resolutions upon this subject and to engage in enthusiastic discussion of the same. It may be said also that such resolutions and discussions have largely, and in many instances, very quickly been forgotten. At the same time, it has been necessary through the years for those who wished to advance the cause of temperance or bring about reform in any other direction, to continue to stress most earnestly the measures advocated in the effort to reach the ends to be attained. The arrival at the results desired, if the realm of reform has been a matter of "precept upon precept, line upon line, here a little and there a little," until the truth stressed has been driven home to the hearts that are willing to take up the cause thus brought to them and to pass the same on to others. Thus it is that worthy and worth-while measures and movements have been handed down from one generation to another.

The temperance movement in our country and in the world has been one of gradual but certain growth and progress. This cause, moreover, has increased the number of its friends and advocates as the years have gone on, despite the facts that certain propagandists would have us think such is not the case. Contrary to what some would have us believe even at the present, the friends of temperance and supporters of the law are not decreasing, but rather the number is on the increase, although there is a deplorable amount of intemperance abroad in the land. And there is reason to believe that the friends of this cause, the advocates of temperance, law-observance and civic righteousness have no intention of deserting the field of action, but rather will they move fearlessly and relentlessly on until yet larger and completer victories have been won, and until higher and more righteous standards of living have been established in our land.

Be it, therefore, resolved:

1. That this Convention go on record as deploring the many forms of lawbreaking, vice and corruption that are so prevalent in our country, and that the friends of righteousness everywhere be called upon to denounce the flagrant

infringement upon the morals and the sanctities of life throughout the nation, and that every possible and constructive service be rendered to overcome the evil with the good.

2. That this body express its unqualified disapproval of the widespread disregard of the Lord's Day and of the many un-Christian activities to which large numbers are giving themselves upon that day, and that we do all that lies within our power to turn the tide of public sentiment to a more thoughtful and a more thoroughly Christian observance of the day.

3. That this gathering most earnestly deprecates the deceptive and misleading propaganda which is quite current in many of our publications throughout the country, and which is heard from many platforms of power and influence, as these agencies seek to prejudice the public mind against certain important moral issues which need to be faced impartially and solved for the good of all.

4. That this Convention register its attitude as unequivocally opposed to the modification or repeal of the eighteenth amendment to the Constitution of the United States, and that we pledge ourselves as heartily and unalterably in favor of the strict observance and enforcement of the same.

G. O. LANKFORD, *Ch'n,*
W. B. FULLER,
J. A. KIMBALL,
Committee.

Moved and carried that the matter of Congregational representation on the standing committees of the Convention be referred to the Committee of Twenty-four.

Moved and carried that the Convention authorize the payment of bills as follows:

I. W. Johnson, Secretary, salary	$ 50.00
I. W. Johnson, postage, stationery, etc., two years	5.00
Mrs. J. S. Rollings, Assistant Secretary, salary	25.00
Mrs. J. S. Rollings, expenses	8.00
Central Publishing Co., 1,000 report blanks	16.50
Central Publishing Co., 600 programs	11.20
Rent typewriter for session	2.50
Dr. L. E. Smith, supplies, etc., for printing	39.00
Total	$ 157.20

Moved and carried that the Convention request the compilation of committee reports for the next session in booklet form, and that the Convention express its thanks for the work done by the President in thus preparing reports for this session.

The Board of Publications reported, and, on motion, the report was adopted, as follows:

REPORT OF BOARD OF PUBLICATIONS.

We, your Board of Publications, wish to submit the following report:

The Christian Sun, as of April 1st, had a total mailing list of 2,769. Of this number of subscribers, 1,118 have paid up to 1930, 1931, or 1932; 825 subscribers have paid up to 1928 or 1929; 709 subscribers have paid up to 1927, and back; 117 names on the mailing list are exchanges. The Board deplores the fact that *The Sun* is not receiving a wider circulation, and urges that every agency of the Church aid in increasing the subscription list. *The Sun* is the only agency of the Convention through which all departments can be presented to the constituency; therefore, department representatives, as well as individual members, should do their very best to increase our circulation.

We recommend:

1. That the *Southern Congregationalist* be merged with *The Christian Sun* in the following manner: The name *Christian Sun* be retained, but that the phrase, "Official Organ of the Southern Christian Convention," be changed to read: "Representing the Southern Christian Convention and the Congregational Churches of the Southeast."

2. That the columns of *The Christian Sun* be open to the Congregational contingent of the united group for articles and news items at any time, but that at least two pages per issue be reserved for them if they so desire.

3. That *The Sun* remain on the present subscription basis, but that an introductory three months' subscription be offered for fifty cents (50c), and that we endeavor to secure as many subscribers as possible from the list of subscribers to the *Southern Congregationalist,* which was recently discontinued.

4. That Dr. Edwin C. Gillette, Conference superintendent of Florida, be added as associate editor to the list which was recommended by the Nominating Committee and adopted by the Convention.

5. That Rev. Milo J. Sweet, pastor-at-large for the Southeast, be added to the Board of Publications, in addition to the names submitted by the Nominating Committee and adopted by the Convention.

6. That the Secretary of the Convention serve as editor of THE CHRISTIAN ANNUAL, and that the Board of Publications be charged with the supervision of printing THE ANNUAL, and that the Board be authorized to make contract with the printer of THE ANNUAL, to-wit: that the copy of each Conference proceedings shall be delivered to the printer within one month after adjournment of said Conference, and that the printer shall have ANNUAL ready for distribution within two months after adjournment of the Conference which is last to be held.

We recommend further that the Convention make a contract with the Central Publishing Co., Richmond, Va., essentially the same as that, approved by the Convention in May, 1928, and recorded in the 1928 ANNUAL on page 50, being a part of the report of the Board of Publications; the contract to be modified, however, to suit the conditions imposed should the *Southern Congregationalist* and *The Christian Sun* be printed in a combined form, as recommended previously.

L. L. VAUGHAN, *Ch'n,*
N. G. NEWMAN,
P. H. FLEMING,
E. L. MOFFETT,
Board of Publication.

The report of the Managing Editor of *The Christian Sun* was read and adopted, as follows:

REPORT OF MANAGING EDITOR OF "THE CHRISTIAN SUN."

A population of 210,000 supports, by subscription and advertising, two daily papers, with uniform average of 70,000 each. For our purpose of illustration, we will use one of these papers.

The morning paper, Sunday edition 73,000, gives a paper to every family of three persons, with 3,000 to go out of the city. Remember that that paper is issued daily, and that the evening paper, with 70,000, is extra six times a week.

Counting three members to the Church family, we should have 10,000 families, as our statistics show we number more than 30,000 members. Congregationalists estimated 15,000, in the same ratio, would add 5,000 more families, a total of 15,000 families. One Conference, by actual count, gives two and a half persons to the Church family. One Church paper to each Church family would be a wonder, but one secular paper to each secular family is a common occurrence.

We are wont to say, does a thing pay? Does missions pay? Does the Orphanage pay? Does the college pay? Does evangelism pay? We give to them whether they pay or do not pay. They are institutions of civilization and of the kingdom of God. The Church paper advocates, fosters, and supports these things. Why not' the Church paper take its proper place in the thinking as the strong right arm and support of the institutions of the Church?

We are not aware what arrangements will be made as to the probable combination of *The Christian* Sun and the *Southern Congregationalist,* which naturally will follow the merger of the Churches of the Southern Christian Convention and the territory covered by the Congregationalists. If the territory in mind, namely: Maryland on the north, on to the Ohio River, and south along this river to the Mississippi; thence south to the Gulf of Mexico, bounding and including the States of Maryland, District of Columbia, Kentucky, Tennessee, Virginia, West Virginia, North Carolina, South Carolina, Georgia, Alabama, Mississippi and Florida.

This would be ample territory for the operations of a great Church. In this territory are 30,000 members of the Christian Church, and, we assume, a membership of the Congregationalists of 15,000, thus making the combined membership between 45,000 and 50,000. For these, the consolidated Church paper will be needed by whom it should be liberally supported, not as an institution but as an aid to the enterprises of the Church. This field will afford ample room for expansion and growth.

The 50,000 membership, with the low average of one subscriber to every ten members, will give a circulation to the Church paper of 5,000 copies. At the present price, the charge upon the general funds of the Convention should be reduced to the minimum, or next to zero.

If this is not apparent to the most anxious, then an equitable percentage, in proportion to the amounts given to the various institutions, might be contributed to the publication expense fund. To illustrate: say, missions reports in the Church paper $40,000; 3 per cent contributed to publication expense fund would be $1,200. The Secretary of Missions probably would say the paper is worth double that to the department.

In place of emphasizing circulation, the stress has been laid upon collections. Salesmanship, as applied to publications, cannot be emphasized and collections stressed at the same time. The human nature that is in man keeps him away from what is presented as a continual obligation which is to be collected for. A collecting agency in some businesses is a necessity, but such an agency cannot be a successful salesman. For a business to be successful, customers must be held. It is easier to retain an old subscriber than to get a new one; but ability to do that is not possessed by every one.

The figures show, for the four years now ending, that the subscribers to *The Sun* have not been increased; but for the four years from 1922 to 1926, the list was increased 570—an average of 142 per year. The delinquent list, while not so large in number, is greater in extent of time, the average being about the same.

In the year 1928, April 1st, the list of subscribers was 2,764; in 1930, April 1st, it is 2,763—just one less.

The renewals vary but little in number, being 2,296 for the biennium just ending, and the new subscribers 508, which equal those discontinued.

The average number of copies printed has been 2,800 plus. It seems that it is time to take some steps to increase the circulation. The publication office or managing editor believes the time has come for increasing the circulation. It has been at a standstill the past four years. He cannot fail to restate a fact disclosed previously in reckoning with the statistics. The best compilation of figures possible to make do not change the results arrived at. That one-tenth of our people read *The Christian Sun,* and this one-tenth contribute nine-tenths of the benevolences for missions, Orphanage, education, evangelism, etc.; and that one-tenth of the funds come from the remaining nine-tenths who do not read *The Christian Sun.*

This is an age of statistics and the handling of figures. If these do not tell the truth, then it is up to some one to show what they do tell, so far as the Southern Christian Convention is concerned. This is given out as a challenge to the one who can show the contrary or the real facts.

P. J. Kernodle,
Managing Editor.

Dr. Edwin C. Gillette was presented to the Convention and spoke briefly.

The circulation manager of *The Christian Sun* made report.

REPORT OF CIRCULATION MANAGER OF "THE CHRISTIAN SUN."

When we took charge of *The Christian Sun*, as Circulation Manager, July 1, 1928, we had about 2,800 names on the mailing list, including exchanges, etc., which was turned over to me. Many on the list were far in arrears in their payments. We have marked off quite a number who had passed away and in compliance with requests to discontinue, and have also added quite a few new subscribers.

On April 1, 1929, the list stood as follows: 1,118 subscribers who had paid up to 1930-'31-'32; 825 subscribers who had paid up to 1928-'29; 709 subscribers who are from 1927 and back; 117 on exchanges and some not marked, making a total of 2,769 on the mailing list April 1, 1930.

During our period of activities as Circulation Manager, we have collected $5,721.64 and have mailed Dr. L. E. Smith checks for same.

While we have not been able to increase the list of subscribers over the number we had on the list turned over to us, because of the fact of marking off so many during this period, we know we have the list in far better shape as to paid-up subscriptions, and a more dependable list.

The Christian Sun should be in every home in our Church, and while it may not be possible to get it in every home, it could be placed in many more homes if some one in each Church would assist the Circulation Manager in selling it to our people.

Chas. D. Johnston,
Circulation Manager.

Moved and carried that the report of the circulating manager be adopted.

Moved and carried that the Convention request the Board of Publications to allot to each Church within the Convention a quota of paid-up subscribers to *The Christian Sun* which will be necessary to bring the subscription list to 3,600.

The editor of *The Christian Sun* reported as follows:

REPORT OF EDITOR OF "THE CHRISTIAN SUN."

For the past two years, *The Christian Sun* has been edited by a Board of Editors, consisting of J. O. Atkinson, Elon College, N. C., Editor; Dr. W. W. Staley, Suffolk, Va.; Dr. W. A. Harper, Elon Colege, N. C.; Rev. Stanley C. Harrell, Durham, N. C., Associate Editors; Managing Editor, Dr. P. J. Kernodle, Richmond, Va. In addition to their editorial duties, Dr. W. W. Staley has contributed weekly the "Suffolk Letter," and Dr. W. A. Harper the "Elon College Letter," and Rev. Stanley C. Harrell "The Sun's Observatory," page one.

In addition to this Board, *The Christian Sun* has been served by the following regular contributors: "The Sunday School Lesson," Rev. H. S. Hardcastle,

Suffolk, Va.; "The Family Altar," Chaplain H. E. Rountree, U. S. N.; "The Christian Orphanage," Superintendent Chas. D. Johnston; and, for a part of the time, "Christian Endeavor," by Miss Jewel Truitt, and "The Christian Sun Pulpit," Rev. J. W. Fix. Each of these editors and regular contributors serve *The Sun* without cost. After six years of trial, this arrangement appears to be satisfactory. In addition to these who have contributed, others at various times have rendered assistance. Beginning with the last Convention, Superintendent Chas. D. Johnston became Circulation Manager, and he will make his report as such.

J. O. ATKINSON, Editor.

PRINCIPLES AND GOVERNMENT.

Since the last session of this Convention I have sold twenty-nine copies of "Principles and Government." Of these, three copies remain unpaid for. The total cash income from the copies sold is $13.85; also one copy of "Wellons' Family Devotions," 10 cents—total cash from these sources, $13.95. Check to cover same is attached to this report. There are on hand and unsold in the stock-room of Elon College Library forty-seven copies of "Principles and Government."

Respectfully submitted,
J. O. ATKINSON, Agent.

Motion to adopt report.

Rev. Lucy Y. Ayres, of the Congregational Church, was introduced to the Convention.

Rev. F. C. Lester reported on the success of the young people's banquet last evening, at which 150 were present.

The following resolution was presented to the Convention relative to a Promotional Agent of the Convention:

RESOLUTION.

In order to assure our Church of a well-rounded and progressive program; be it

Resolved, That it is the sense of this Convention that the Executive Committee should employ, as soon as financial arrangements can be made, a suitable person to act as "Promotional Agent," or "General Secretary," whose business it shall be to promote in every legitimate way the entire program of the Christian Church in the Southern Christian Convention.

The resolution was adopted by a rising vote.

The report of the Committee on Superannuation, which was referred back to the committee, was presented, and, on motion, was adopted, as follows:

REPORT OF BOARD OF SUPERANNUATION.

On June 28, 1928, the Board of Superannuation had a called meeting to consider the action of the Convention concerning the establishment of an endowment fund for our retired ministers and their widows. It was voted that the matter be presented to the several Conferences in their annual sessions and that we adopt the plan suggested by the Convention of seeking to secure $5.00 from each minister in the Convention, $5.00 from a layman in each Church, and $5.00 from each Church in the Convention annually. Promising as the movement seemed at our last Convention, only $51.00 has been recieved for this fund up to date.

On July 16, 1928, we were grieved by the death of the treasurer of our Board, W. K. Holt, of Burlington, N. C., a member of the Board from its beginning and a man who has rendered much valuable service to the Board by his wise counsel and sound business methods. The Executive Committee of the Convention elected J. M. Fix, of Burlington, N. C., to fill the vacancy on the Board, and the Board elected, by correspondence, Mr. Fix as treasurer of the Board. Prof. Ralph Towers, of Elon College, was appointed by the chairman of the Board to audit the books of the deceased treasurer. These were found to be correct and the chairman gave his receipt to Mrs. W. K. Holt, executrix, and turned the books over to the newly elected treasurer, J. M. Fix. Said books showed a note for endowment fund of $2,550, and the current fund overdrawn to the amount of $2.10. However a check for $50.00 in favor of Dr. J. W. Wellons, deceased, had never been cashed, and it was voted that the treasurer's account be credited with this amount, making a balance of $47.90. It was voted that the $46.00 on endowment (which was later increased to $51.00) be placed with the $2,550, making a total of $2,601 endowment fund on hand to date.

At the June, 1928, called meeting, it was voted that the treasurer of the Board should be bonded for $5,000, and at the December, 1928, Board meeting it was ordered that Mr. Fix be bonded for a like amount. This bond is in the possession of the chairman of the Board.

At our Board meeting in December, 1928, a communication from Dr. Smith, President of the Convention, was read regarding the group plan of insurance for our ministers, and the Board voted to co-operate to the extent of paying one-third of the cost of insuring our ministers up to $2,000 per person, if such insurance could be arranged for.

In December, 1928, we received $2,000 from the Convention and made appropriations to be paid one-half in December, 1928, and one-half in July, 1929, as follows:

Mrs. Ebbie Moffitt	$ 100.00
Rev. P. T. Klapp	100.00
Mrs. Geo. B. Estes	150.00
Mrs. C. C. Peele	150.00
Mrs. Mary Virginia Long	150.00
Mrs. L. I. Cox	150.00
Mrs. J. P. Barrett	150.00
Rev. G. R. Underwood	100.00
Mrs. C. M. Dollar	100.00
Mrs. B. F. Young	150.00
Mrs. Emma Fogleman	100.00
Rev. W. D. Harward	250.00
Rev. H. W. Elder	250.00
Rev. W. N. Hayes	50.00
Mrs. J. I. Jones	50.00
Mrs. J. W. Elder	50.00
Total	$2,050.00

Of these beneficiaries, we record, with regret, the death of Mrs. J. I. Jones.

The Board met in annual session at Elon College, N. C., on December 19, 1929. The treasurer reported $1,800 received from the Convention, with the possibility of something additional. Appropriations were made as follows, payable one-half in December, 1929, and one-half in July, 1930:

Rev. P. T. Klapp	$ 200.00
Rev. W. D. Harward	250.00
Rev. H. W. Elder	250.00
Mrs. Geo. B. Estes	150.00
Mrs. L. I. Cox	150.00
Mrs. Mary Virginia Long	150.00

Mrs. J. P. Barrett	150.00
Mrs. C. C. Peele	150.00
Mrs. B. F. Young	150.00
Mrs. C. M. Dollar	100.00
Mrs. Emma Fogleman	100.00
Mrs. Ebbie Moffitt	100.00
Rev. G. R. Underwood	150.00
Rev. W. N. Hayes	50.00
Mrs. J. W. Elder	50.00

Total $2,150.00

We greatly desire to have as much as $3,000 per annum from the Convention, to be able to supply the needs of our beneficiaries and to add something to our permanent fund.

J. O. ATKINSON, *Chairman.*
MRS. C. H. ROWLAND, *Sec'y.*
J. M. FIX, *Treasurer.*

The Board of Finance made supplementary report, as follows:

SUPPLEMENTARY REPORT OF BOARD OF FINANCE.

We recommend that the apportionments for publications, superannuation, and the Convention be paid first out of the funds sent to the Convention, and that the remaining funds be prorated among the other causes.

We recommend that the Conferences apportion to their Churches the total amount allotted them by the Convention, and that after discharging their current expenses, they consider the Convention call as having prior claim on their funds.

We recommend the following annual distribution of the funds for the next biennium:

Superannuation	$ 3,000.00
Publications	4,000.00
Convention	2,000.00
Convention obligations	12,750.00
Piedmont Junior College	2,000.00
Board of Christian Education	1,250.00

Total $25,000.00

L. E. SMITH.

On motion, the supplementary report was adopted.

The Committee on Resolutions reported as follows:

REPORT OF COMMITTEE ON RESOLUTIONS.

We, your Committee on Resolutions, offer the following:

1. By a rising vote of thanks, the Southern Christian Convention, in its twenty-ninth biennial session, at Raleigh, N. C., express its grateful appreciation to the United Church, its efficient pastor, excellent choir, and other people of the city for their cordial hospitality, Christian service, splendid music and delightful banquet meals, in making this session of the Convention a success.

2. Be it resolved, That we express our hearty appreciation to Prof. Clair Velie, the music faculty, and the glee club of Elon College for their delightful program rendered at the Thursday evening session.

3. Resolved, That we go on record approving the change made by the State of North Carolina in the number of trustees of the Elon Christian Orphanage from twelve to fifteen.

4. That we record high appreciation for the presence and fine Christian fellowship of the distinguished speakers and visitors in this Convention who

have contributed largely to the fine Christian spirit of the Convention; in particular, would we mention the outstanding representatives of the Congregational Church.

5. That our gratitude be shown the Committee on Publicity, and especially Mr. C. M. Cannon, the chairman, for the excellent daily reports to the press.

6. That we express to Dr. L. E. Smith, our esteemed President, and his Executive Committee, our appreciation of their untiring efforts in behalf of the work of the Convention.

7. That, in view of the union of the Congregational and Christian Churches in the South and in the nation, that we recommend to the officials of the Afro-Christian Convention, and the officials of the Colored Conferences of the Congregational Churches, that every effort be exercised to promote acquaintance and take such steps as seem advisable to them in the furtherance of Christian Union.

J. W. FIX,
J. W. MANNING,
B. J. EARP,
Committee.

On motion, the report on Resolutions was adopted by a rising vote.

The Board of Education resubmitted the items of its report, which were referred to the Finance Committee.

By motion, the items conforming to supplemental report of Finance Committee were adopted.

The Committee on Memoirs reported as follows:

Permission is requested to make written report concerning the life and labors of Bro. W. K. Holt, Dr. G. S. Watson, and Judge Jesse F. West to the Secretary of Convention, and that Convention stand in silent tribute to the life and labors of these brethren.

Motion carried to adopt the report. Convention stood in silent tribute, and was led in prayer by Dr. G. O. Lankford.

The Committee on Nominations presented additional report, nominating trustees for Elon College from Congregational fellowship as follows. (See report of Nominating Committee.)

The following is the report of the Committee on Memoirs:

REPORT OF COMMITTEE ON MEMOIRS.

HOLT.

William Kirkpatrick Holt was born in Alamance County, N. C., April 22, 1866, and passed away at the Christian Orphanage, at Elon College, on July 30, 1928. His funeral was conducted by his pastor, Rev. G. O. Lankford, and Drs. J. O. Atkinson and P. H. Fleming, in the First Christian Church, Burlington, N. C., on Tuesday following his death. Interment was in Pine Hill Cemetery of the same city.

Mr. Holt came to Burlington as a young man and entered upon a business career that led him during the busy, active years of his useful life into many lines of endeavor and into many places of trust and responsibility. He possessed a keen, analytical, constructive mind. A man of great energy, unusual determination, sound judgment, he became remarkably successful. His business insight and ability carried over into many community projects and enterprises, particularly into the field of education as a prominent and valuable member of the school board of his chosen city for many years.

In young manhood, Mr. Holt became a Christian and identified himself with the First Christian Church of the community, and through the succeeding years he was faithful and active in his Church. He was called upon during these years to serve in a number of official capacities, among which offices was that of Church secretary, chairman finance committee, member of the board of trustees, and chairman of the building committee during the erection of the present Church structure. He was a most valuable counselor in the affairs of the Church.

Probably the most outstanding service Mr. Holt rendered was as chairman of the board of trustees of the Christian Orphanage, which office he had filled for a number of years prior to his death, and which he held at the time of his going. This institution, next to his own family and home, lay closest to his heart, and it was in the service of the same that he was stricken as he presided over the dedicatory exercises of Johnston Hall, in which building the end came a few hours later. Since his departure had to be, it seems quite fitting that the end came in the midst of surroundings that stand today as a monument due largely to his able and untiring leadership of this institution that he so deeply and devotedly loved.

WEST.

Judge Jesse Felix West, son of Henry Thomas and Susan Thomas West, was born in Sussex County, Va., July 16, 1862, and died October 25, 1929, at his home in Waverly, Va.

Judge West attended Suffolk Collegiate Institute in the early eighties; graduated with Ph.D. from the University of North Carolina in 1885; completed a two-year course in law in one year at the University of Virginia, under John B. Minor; was admitted to the bar and began the practice of law in Waverly, Va., in 1886.

Married Nannie Peebles Baird September 20, 1887; judge of county court of Sussex County, Va., 1892-1904; judge of Third Judicial Circuit Court 1904-1922; associate judge of Supreme Court of Appeals of Virginia, 1921-1929; member of the State and National Bar Associations.

Member of Waverly Christian Church, a deacon, and superintendent of Sunday School for thirty years; trustee of Elon College, N. C.; chairman of committee that erected memorial on site of Old Lebanon Church, in Sussex County, Va., where the name "Christian" was adopted by the Church in 1794, and the one to James O'Kelly on the Elon College campus.

In all these positions he was wise, loyal and useful. His name and the memory of his achievements will live in all the positions and institutions he served.

He is survived by his wife and three sons, Jesse F., Jr., O. H., and Baird West; also by four brothers, John W., R. T., Col. Junius E., and Caleb D. West.

His life was devoted to his family, his Church, his community, and the State; and in all these relations he made a record that will live in memory.

WATSON.

Dr. George S. Watson was born in Alamance County, N. C., on December 31, 1844, and died in his home at Elon College, N. C., on March 4, 1930. He was graduated from the Medical College of Baltimore in 1874, and practiced his profession in northern Alamance County for thirty-one years. In 1905 he removed to Elon College, where he continued to practice his profession for about fifteen years. On November 28, 1880, he was married to Miss Mary Virginia McCauley, who on May 9, 1930, passed to her reward at her home in Elon College.

Dr. Watson was not only a capable physician, but was a loyal and devoted Church member. He was deacon in Union (N. C.) Christian Church for many years. Upon his removal to Elon College, he became deacon of the Elon Church, and at the time of his death was senior deacon in this Church and also a member of the finance board of the Church.

Dr. Watson was on the committee for the location of Elon College, and also on the provisional board of trustees when the college was incorporated on March 11, 1889. He served as a member of the board of trustees from the organization of the college until his death, March 4, 1930. Dr. Watson did not miss a session of the board of trustees during all these years except the last one, which came during his last illness. For many years he served on the executive board as well as the general board.

During these forty years of service on the board of trustees, Dr. Watson not only supported the college by attending the sessions of the board, but he gave financial support also to the college in the several financial campaigns. He felt the need of Christian education and was willing to support it in every way that offered itself to him.

· In the passing of Dr. Watson, the Christian Church has lost a devoted member and Elon College one of its most sympathetic and devoted friends.

In offering sympathy and consolation to the families of these noble men, we can offer nothing better than to commend their example and to cherish their memory by faithful service.

W. W. STALEY,
G. O. LANKFORD,
W. A. HARPER,
Committee.

On motion, the nominees were elected.

The Committee to Revise Church Letter-blanks made report.

Moved and carried that the committee be continued, with instruction to complete work and make report to Executive Committee of Convention for adoption.

The Committee on Credentials submitted report. (See list of delegates in record.)

By motion, the report was admitted to record.

Moved and carried that the Convention authorize the printing of proceedings of this Convention in pamphlet form, same to be later incorporated in THE ANNUAL.

Moved and carried that the matter of appointing standing committees from Christian constituency be referred to the Committee of Twenty-four for consultation.

Moved and carried that all special elections of committees and boards appear as in regular election of officers and boards.

Minutes of yesterday's and today's sessions were read, and approved as corrected.

Moved and carried that following the worship service conducted by Dr. N. G. Newman, the Convention adjourn.

Worship service and benediction by Dr. N. G. Newman.

L. E. SMITH, *President.*
S. C. HARRELL, *Secretary Pro Tem.*
I. W. JOHNSON, *Secretary.*
MRS. MARY A. ROLLINGS, *Ass't Sec'y.*

Proceedings of Regular Session of the Woman's Missionary Convention.

MORNING SESSION.

The Southern Christian Convention Woman's Missionary Convention met in United Church, Raleigh, N. C., on Tuesday, April 29, 1930, and was called to order at 10 o'clock by the President, Mrs. J. A. Williams.

Owing to indisposition of the Recording Secretary, Miss Margaret Alston, Mrs. L. W. Stagg was asked to serve in her stead.

Devotional services were led by Mrs. Stanley Harrell.

The roll of Conferences was called, as follows:

Georgia and Alabama Conference—Mrs. C. L. Royston.

Alabama Conference—Mrs. G. L. Stevens, Mrs. V. E. Kitchen.

Virginia Valley Central Conference—Mrs. R. L. Williamson, Mrs. A. W. Andes.

North Carolina Conference—Mesdames W. R. Sellars, George Mc-Cullers, Grady Leonard, W. H. Boone, W. M. Jay, J. D. Kernodle, J. P. Foster, S. O. Spruill, Chas. Clark, C. V. Dunn, R. J. Newton, Daniel Stephenson, J. B. Montgomery, R. O. Caviness, Doyle Mac-Farland, Alfred Hayes, E. M. Carter, S. C. Harrell, W. H. Carroll, J. Lee Johnson, R. M. Rothgeb, Miss Emma Thomas, Miss Myrtle Bridgers, Miss Ruth Gunter, Miss Essie Cotton, Miss Lucille Mulholland.

Eastern Virginia Conference—Mesdames W. V. Leathers, J. W. Manning, O. M. Cockes, W. D. Harward, H. C. Caviness, B. D. Jones, O. S. Mills, J. E. Cartwright, J. W. Fix, W. H. Andrews, L. B. Norfleet, L. W. Stagg, W. K. Saunders, R. L. Odom, J. F. Morgan, C. W. King, A. M. Johnson, J. E. Corbett, Waverly Barrett, J. W. Felton, C. J. Heath, C. W. Rountree, C. C. Ryan, M. L. Bryant, E. P. Jones, H. B. Everett, E. T. Holland, W. A. Warner, M. T. Whitley, N. Y. Byrd, Frank Johnson, M. F. Allen, W. C. Moore, F. F. Jenkins, C. C. Rawls, E. L. Gray, J. M. Rabey, A. B. Greff, Miss Lillie Benton, Miss Louise Pittman.

ANNOUNCEMENT OF COMMITTEES.

Recommendations—Mesdames M. L. Bryant, C. H. Rowland, T. F. Roquemore, R. A. Larrick, V. S. Kitchen.

Nominations—Mesdames W. H. Andrews, L. B. Norfleet, G. L. Stevens, B. F. Franks, J. E. Cartwright.

Report Blanks—Mesdames W. R. Sellers, W. V. Leathers, B. D. Jones.

Banner—Mesdames H. C. Caviness, Virdie Showalters, J. W. Manning, Miss Essie Mae Cotton, Miss Ruth Gunter.

Resolutions—Mesdames E. P. Jones, I. W. Johnson, J. Lee Johnson.

Finance—Mesdames L. W. Stagg, H. S. Hardcastle, A. M. Johnson.

Program—Mesdames W. V. Leathers, R. T. Bradford, R. B. Wood.

Report of Treasurer was read by Rev. H. S. Hardcastle, and adopted, after the acceptance of report of Committee on Finance.

REPORT OF TREASURER.

RECEIPTS.

From June, 1928, to June, 1929.

Balance on hand, May 1, 1928		$ 612.75
Received on Convention floor, Richmond, Va		27.70
Mrs. D. P. Barrett, life membership		10.00
Refund on literature by Mrs. C. H. Rowland		6.00
		$ 656.45
From Alabama Conference:		
First quarter	$ 83.87	
Second quarter	21.85	
Third quarter	339.01	
		$ 444.73
From Eastern Virginia Conference:		
First quarter	$1,241.53	
Second quarter	3,611.77	
Third quarter	909.11	
Fourth quarter	1,415.58	
		7,177.99
From North Carolina Conference:		
First quarter	$1,157.97	
Second quarter	1,562.20	
Third quarter	774.56	
Fourth quarter	1,200.56	
		4,695.29
From Valley Virginia Central Conference:		
First quarter	$ 154.30	
Second quarter	148.96	
Third quarter	141.54	
Fourth quarter	64.83	
		509.63
From Georgia and Alabama Conference	34.38	
		13,518.47

From June, 1929, to May, 1930.

From Alabama Conference:		
First quarter	$ 75.00	
Second quarter	100.00	
Third quarter	126.30	
Fourth quarter	10.00	
		$ 311.30
From Eastern Virginia Conference:		
First quarter	$2,700.21	
Second quarter	2,003.78	
Third quarter	782.10	
Fourth quarter	2,021.38	
		7,507.47

From North Carolina Conference:
```
First quarter ...............................$1,235.54
Second  quarter  ............................ 1,628.53
Third quarter .............................   523.23
Fourth quarter ............................ 1,303.35
                                                        ————————
                                                        4,690.65
```

From Valley Virginia Central Conference:
```
First quarter ...............................$  256.51
Second quarter ............................    85.40
Third quarter .............................    94.29
Fourth quarter ...........................     62.67
                                                        ————————
                                                        498.87
```

From Georgia and Alabama Conference:
```
First quarter ...............................$   70.00
Fourth quarter ...........................     20.00
                                                        ————————
                                                        90.00
                                                                    ————————
                                                                    13,098.29
```

```
Total for biennium ....................................... $26,616.76
```

DISBURSEMENTS.
From May 1, 1928, to June, 1929.

```
1928.
May   6.  Telegrams sent during S. C. C. ...............$    1.38
          Mrs. McD. Howsare, expenses to S. C. C......    45.00
          W. C. Wicker, Treas., Porto Rico auto fund...   250.00
     17.  Christian Publishing Association ...........     3.40
          Eugene L. Graves, printer...................    24.25
          Artcraft Corporation, printer ...............   10.00
June 20.  Expenses Board meeting, Franklin, Va........    80.58
July 23.  W. C. Wicker, Treas., home missions......... 1,315.18
          W. C. Wicker, Treas., foreign missions....... 1,117.19
Oct. 17.  W. C. Wicker, Treas., Porto Rico relief fund..   65.65
Nov. 11.  W. C. Wicker, home missions................ 2,401.88
          W. C. Wicker, foreign missions.............. 2,819.28
          Artcraft Corporation, W. M. B. report blanks..   93.83
          Literature Dept., W. M. B., Dayton..........    3.63
          Christian Publishing Association ............    1.60
     31.  Christian Publishing Association ............    1.25
          Mrs. J. A. Williams, travel, postal, tel. exp....   20.03
1929.
Jan. 10.  A. D. Pate Co., printers ...................    10.00
          A. D. Pate Co., printers ...................    12.50
          Dr. J. O. Atkinson ........................     1.50
     24.  W. C. Wicker, Treas., home missions.........   731.66
          W. C. Wicker, Treas., foreign missions........ 1,422.56
Feb.  9.  Mrs. W. R. Sellars, expense N. C. Board......   130.00
          Mrs. H. S. Hardcastle, Treas., postage.........    3.00
Mar. 13.  West & Withers, bonding of Treas............    12.50
          Atlantic Coast Printing Co..................    12.00
Apr. 20.  W. C. Wicker, Treas., home missions......... 1,220.48
          W. C. Wicker, Treas., foreign missions........ 1,430.49
                                                                    ————————
                                                                    $13,240.82
```

From June, 1929, to May, 1930.
```
1929.
June 26.  Expenses of Board meeting, Franklin, Va.....$ 129.17
July 21.  W. C. Wicker, Treas., home missions......... 1,873.81
```

		W. C. Wicker, Treas., foreign missions.......	2,236.48	
	22.	Mrs. H. S. Hardcastle, Treas. (savings acct.)..	220.00	
Sep.	18.	W. C. Wicker, Treas., home missions..........	1,404.91	
		W. C. Wicker, Treas., foreign missions........	1,695.09	
Oct.	7.	Mrs. J. A. Williams, expenses...............	10.67	
		Mrs. Emma S. Powers, literature............	4.20	
Nov.	14.	Mrs. H. S. Hardcastle, Treas. (savings acct.)..	230.00	
1930.				
Jan.	21.	W. C. Wicker, Treas., home missions.........	360.59	
		W. C. Wicker, Treas., foreign missions........	1,156.96	
		Mrs. H. S. Hardcastle, Treas. (savings acct.)..	20.00	
Mar.	3.	West & Withers, bonding of Treas...........	12.50	
	27.	Ocean View Church	50.00	
		Mrs. J. A. Williams	19.37	
Apr.	8.	Missionary Review Publishing Co., Inc.......	2.50	
	15.	Mrs. E. L. Beale, expense of Board, Raleigh...	16.00	
	18.	W. C. Wicker, Treas., home missions........	989.80	
		W. C. Wicker, Treas., foreign missions........	1,754.70	
		Mrs. H. S. Hardcastle, Treas. (savings acct.)..	20.00	
		Mrs. J. A. Williams, printing...............	1.50	
				12,208.25

Total for biennium $25,449.07
Total receipts for biennium $26,616.76
Total disbursements for biennium 25,449.07

Balance on hand ....$ 1,167.69

Respectfully submitted,

Mrs. H. S. Hardcastle, *Treasurer*

I have audited the books and accounts of Mrs. H. S. Hardcastle, Treasurer of the Woman's Board of Missions, S. C. C., for the period from April 25, 1928, to April 26, 1930, and

I certify that the preceding statements of income and disbursements agree with the books, with the addition of $494.40 which is deposited as a savings account in the Farmers Bank of Nansemond; and, in my opinion, correctly set forth the true condition of the Woman's Board of Missions, S. C. C., as of April 26, 1930.

Herbert C. January,

Suffolk, Va., April 26, 1930. *Certified Public Accountant.*

Report of Finance Committee was adopted, as follows:

REPORT OF COMMITTEE ON FINANCE.

Your Committee on Finance begs to report that the books of Mrs. H. S. Hardcastle, Treasurer, have been audited by Herbert C. January, certified public accountant, of Suffolk, Va., on April 26, 1930, and found correct.

We would recommend:

First, that the goal for the next biennium be $27,000, to be apportioned among the Conferences as follows:

Eastern Virginia Conference $14,250.00
North Carolina Conference 10,500.00
Virginia Valley Central Conference.............. 1,150.00
Alabama Conference 800.00
Georgia and Alabama Conference................ 300.00

Total $27,000.00

Second, that the Willing Workers be released from the contingent and literature funds, and that 10 cents per member be stressed for the women and young people.

MRS. L. W. STAGG.
MRS. A. M. JOHNSON.

Report of Executive Committee was read by Mrs. J. A. Williams and adopted, as follows:

REPORT OF EXECUTIVE BOARD.

Your Executive Board submits the following report:

Since the Woman's Missionary Convention met, May 2, 1928, at Richmond, Va., your Board has met twice in Franklin, Va., June 7, 1928, and June 26, 1929.

At the last meeting, it was voted to comply with the request of the Mission Board, that the Woman's Board appropriate $2,500 annually to the Raleigh Church for a period of five years; provided the conditions of the request are met, as follows: That the entire indebtedness of the Raleigh Church be paid, as per statement to and agreement with the Mission Board of the Southern Christian Convention by pastor and officials of the Raleigh Church. Also the request of the Mission Board that the Woman's Board sponsor the Ocean View Church, provided a satisfactory pastor is secured. No other changes of funds have occurred.

We often listen to the discussion of the indebtedness of different boards— Mission Boards, etc. We can proudly say the Woman's Mission Board is not in debt; we are not a Board to make debts, but to pull the other mission boards out of debt; we do not go in debt, we pay no salary, not one penny of overhead expense; our Conference never has any overhead expense. We ask women to give their time and talent to the Lord's work. When the Board members come to a Board meeting, their traveling expenses are paid and furnish them lunch the day the Board is in session; therefore, you see, the position of officers are only honorary, with plenty of hard work but great pleasure in serving the Lord and mankind. The Woman's Missionary work is touching many lives, teaching missions and increasing missionary interest. We must look forward to the great unfinished task before us. The future is "as bright as the promise of God." The home base must be cultivated, and not neglected.

There are two things that bear upon my heart today and to which I seek to direct particular attention:

First: We must somehow interest our young people in missions. They are our hope. They have imagination and enthusiasm. There's a challenge in the missionary task, and charm also.

Second: Item of deepest interest, and that upon which we must put emphasis, is that of furthering the cause in our own ranks. None of our societies are yet measuring up to the high privilege, and there are many scores of our Churches in which there are yet no missionary organization. The unorganized Churches are needed in order that the mission work of our Church might go on into larger service.

Respectfully submitted,
MRS. J. A. WILLIAMS, *Chairman.*

REPORT OF NORTH CAROLINA CONFERENCE.

The North Carolina Woman's Missionary Conference covers a good part of central Carolina. In this territory there are about 115 Churches. The greater part of these Churches are rural. In this Conference there are seven districts; in each was held the annual spring missionary rally. The superintendents have done splendid work, and the outlook for another year is splendid. The number of Women's Societies 42, members 893; Young People's Societies 16, members 210; Willing Workers 6, members 124; Cradle Rolls 11, members 223; organizations 75, members 1,450.

There are five Churches—Greensboro, Elon College, Burlington, Durham and Raleigh—that have all four organizations.

The financial goal was $10,000; amount raised, $9,385.94.

Our annual Conference will meet with the Liberty Vance Church.

MRS. C. H. ROWLAND, *President.*

The report of the Georgia and Alabama Conference was given by the Acting Secretary, in the absence of the President, Mrs. T. F. Roquemore, and adopted, as follows:

REPORT OF GEORGIA AND ALABAMA CONFERENCE.

Work newly organized: Organizations, 3; apportionment, $250; amount raised, $124.38.

Report of Virginia Valley Central Conference was read by the Secretary, in the absence of Mrs. B. F. Frank, and adopted, as follows:

REPORT OF VIRGINIA VALLEY CONFERENCE.

Women's societies 7, members 163; Young People's Societies 4, members 64; Willing Workers 2, members 20; Cradle Roll 6, members 116; total membership, 363; apportionment, $1,000; amount raised, $1,008.50.

Report of Alabama Conference was read by Mrs. V. S. Kitchen, and adopted, as follows:

REPORT OF ALABAMA CONFERENCE.

Organizations, 7; three Churches on honor roll; apportionment, $750.00; amount raised, $756.03.

Report of Eastern Virginia Conference was given by Mrs. M. L. Bryant, and adopted, as follows:

REPORT OF EASTERN VIRGINIA CONFERENCE.

In each of the four districts we have the annual spring rally. These meetings have become a real part of the Conference. The programs are planned well in advance, and are educational as well as inspirational.

For the past two years, the attendance at our annual Conference has been more than five hundred.

We have held two meetings for the Young People's Department during the past two years. The attendance was splendid, filling the large auditorium of the Suffolk Christian Church. At the last meeting, officers were elected, as follows: president, Miss Mary Lee Williams; vice-president, Miss Carolyn Gort; secretary, Miss Sarah Norfleet Daughtery.

Much of our success has been due to the splendid co-operation of our ministers always standing back of the work.

We have 27 Women's Societies, 26 Young People's Societies, 20 Willing Workers' Societies, and 21 Cradle Rolls. Total membership, 2,282. Goal for biennium, $13,000; amount raised, $14,685.46.

New societies, 20; new members, 522; biennium per capita, $6.43.

Address: "Japan of Today," Mrs. O. P. Garmon, our missionary, on furlough from Japan.

Dr. L. E. Smith, President of the Southern Christian Convention; Dr. J. O. Atkinson, Secretary of Missions, and Dr. A. W. Sparks, Executive Secretary of Home Mission Board of the General Convention, were introduced.

Vocal solo by Mrs. Ethel Clements Huff.

Address: "The Call for the Intensive," Mrs. John Ferguson, chairman, National Commission Protestant Church Women.

Offering, $16.54.

Convention adjourned, with prayer by Dr. W. W. Staley.

AFTERNOON SESSION.

Called to order at 2 o'clock.

Devotional service by Mrs. W. A. Harper.

In the absence of Dr. W. P. Minton, Foreign Mission Secretary, Dr. A. W. Sparks on "Missions Today and Tomorrow."

On motion, it was voted to telegraph greeting and sympathy to Dr. Minton, who was recently injured in an automobile accident.

The following reports were made and adopted:

RECOMMENDATIONS.

We recommend that wherever it seems not advisable to launch a new Young People's organization, that the missionary program among the young people be promoted through the Sunday School departments and classes, thus reaching the boys as well as the girls.

Mrs. C. H. Rowland.
Mrs. V. E. Kitchen.

Adopted.

(This committee was appointed to meet with a committee of three from the Southern Christian Convention to decide upon the time this Convention shall meet.)

REPORT OF CRADLE ROLL.

Churches, 208; Cradle Rolls, 40; babies enrolled, 746; amount of money raised, $461.10.

Mrs. I. W. Johnson, Supt.

REPORT OF LITERATURE AND MITE BOXES.

We have sent leaflets on our work to the societies throughout the Convention. In the future, information on this department will be kept before our people through *The Christian Sun*.

Mrs. H. C. Caviness, Supt.

REPORT OF LIFE MEMBERSHIPS AND MEMORIALS.

Since May, 1926, the superintendent has issued 49 life memberships and memorials, as follows: Alabama, 3; North Carolina, 17; Eastern Virginia, 29—total, 49.

Mrs. Hardcastle has deposited $490 in bank, which is known as our life membership and memorials savings account.

Mrs. M. J. W. White, Supt.

Adopted.

REPORT OF SPIRITUAL LIFE.

This report has been kept before the departments of the Convention by literature being given to each local superintendent of spiritual life.

Mrs. W. H. Carroll, Supt.

Adopted.

REPORT OF CONVENTION EDITOR.

This department came into existence just before the Richmond Convention, in 1928. The present editor was the first appointee. I would suggest that the leader of each organization take the "News Bulletin," published by the General Woman's Board. It may be secured from the Literature Superintendent, Mrs. Emma Powers, C. P. A. Building, Dayton, Ohio. I would also suggest that all notices and communications referring to our woman's work be put under this head, so our women would know just where to look for material and information. Please send in your news items promptly and help make this department one of real value.

MRS. W. M. JAY,
Convention Editor.

Adopted.

Address by Miss Mary Preston, New York City, member of the Congregational Home and Foreign Mission Board.

The Report of Young People's Societies was read by Mrs. I. W. Johnson, as follows:

REPORT OF YOUNG PEOPLE'S SOCIETIES.

Reports from three of the five Conferences: Virginia Valley Central— Y. P. Societies 6, members 108, offering $241.06; North Carolina Conference— Y. P. Societies 16, members 210, Willing Workers' Societies 6, members 124, offering $1,603.19; Eastern Virginia Conference—Y. P. Societies 26, members, 608, Willing Workers' Societies 21, members 393, offering $4,492.08. Total societies, 75; members, 1,443; offering, $6,336.33; new organizations, 12.

MRS. R. T. BRADFORD, *Supt.*

Adopted.

REPORT ON REPORT BLANKS.

We recommend that the present report blanks in use be adopted for the coming biennium.

·MRS. B. D. JONES.
MRS. W. H. SELLARS.·

Adopted.

REPORT OF COMMITTEE ON RESOLUTIONS.

We submit the following:

1. That we express our thanks to the United Church of Raleigh for their gracious hospitality.

2. That we extend to the officers of the Woman's Board our appreciation for their faithful and efficient service rendered during the biennium.

3. Resolved, That we count the Convention fortunate in having Mrs. C. P. Garmon, our missionary on furlough from Japan; Mrs. John Ferguson, and Miss Mary Preston, of New York, present, and for their contribution to the Convention by their inspirational and illuminating addresses, and to all other speakers we express our thanks.

4. That we express to Mrs. Ethel Clements Huff our appreciation for her beautifully rendered solos.

MRS. E. P. JONES,
MRS. I. W. JOHNSON,
Committee.

Adopted.

REPORT OF COMMITTEE ON NOMINATIONS.

The Nominating Committee present the following names for consideration of the Convention:

For President, Mrs. J. A. Williams; Vice-President, Mrs. C. H. Rowland; Treasurer, Mrs. H. S. Hardcastle; Recording Secretary, Mrs. L. W. Stagg; Corresponding Secretray, Mrs. E. L. Beale; Superintendent of Spiritual Life, Mrs. W. H. Carroll; Superintendent Young People, Mrs. S. C. Harrell; Superintendent Cradle Roll, Mrs. I. W. Johnson; Superintendent Literature and Mite Boxes,

Mrs. H. C. Caviness; Conference Editor, Mrs. W. M. Jay; Life Membership and Memorials, Mrs. M. J. W. White.

> MRS. W. H. ANDREWS,
> MRS. L. B. NORFLEET,
> MRS. J. E. CARTWRIGHT,
> MRS. R. L. WILLIAMSON,
> *Committee.*

Adopted.

The Convention stood in recognition of the splendid service rendered by Mrs. R. C. Bradford, retired Superintendent of Young People, and Miss Margaret Alston, retiring Recording Secretary.

It was announced that there would be a called meeting of the Southern Christian Convention's Woman's Mission Board in the lecture-room of the Church immediately before the morning session of the Southern Christian Convention on Wednesday, to determine the distribution of our home special funds.

The Committee on Awarding Banner asked for more time to prepare its report. The President announced that the banner would be presented before the Southern Christian Convention adjourned, on Friday.

Reading of minutes.

The Convention adjourned, to meet on Tuesday of the week of the Southern Christian Convention in 1932.

Benediction by Dr. W. H. Denison.

> MRS. J. A. WILLIAMS, *President.*
> MRS. L. W. STAGG, *Secretary.*

Proceedings of Eighty-second Annual Session of the Virginia Valley Central Christian Conference

NEWPORT CHRISTIAN CHURCH, AUGUST 6, 1930.

FIRST DAY—MORNING SESSION.

The Eighty-second Session of the Virginia Valley Central Christian Conference met and was called to order at 10 A. M. by the President, Rev. B. J. Earp.

Devotional services were conducted by Rev. B. J. Earp.

ENROLLMENT.

Ordained Ministers—A. W. Andes, B. J. Earp, W. B. Fuller, Joe French, R. L. Williamson, W. T. Walters.

Licentiate—John W. Henderson.

Chairmen of Standing Committees—A. W. Andes, Verdie Showalter, Mrs. A. W. Andes, W. C. Wampler, Joe French, Mrs. B. F. Frank, B. J. Earp.

Conference Officers—B. J. Earp, W. C. Wampler, A. W. Andes, Joe French, Samuel Earman, R. O. Rothgeb, Mrs. J. J. Lincoln.

Churches and Delegates.

Antioch—Verdie Showalter, E. F. Showalter.

Bethel—W. H. Alger, Alfred Dofflemyre.

Bethlehem—Ella Pickering, D. H. Welch, H. G. Brown.

Beulah—Not represented.

Christian Chapel—H. R. Osbourn, Mrs. H. R. Osbourn.

Concord—Mrs. J. C. Huffman, Mollie Huffman.

Dry Run—Elma Rinker.

East Liberty—J. W. Henderson, Effie May, Sudie Davis.

High Point—Sigourney Crawford, W. A. Crawford.

Island Ford—Not represented.

Joppa—Not represented.

Leaksville—B. F. McDaniel, Eula Huffman, R. O. Rothgeb, K. T. Rothgeb.

Linville—R. Roy Hosaflook, Mrs. Samuel Earman, J. A. Taylor, Ora Scott.

Mayland—Minnie Showalter, J. M. Lohr, Delia Spitzer.

Mt. Lebanon—Ruth Comer.

Mt. Olivet (G)—Herbert Morris, B. G. Snow, Bluie Shiflett, Winona Morris, Thelma Morris, Norman Morris.

Mt. Olivet (R)—A. S. Turner, Harold Lilly, Reuben Fultz, Mrs. Reuben Fultz.

New Hope—E. M. Spitzer, Hubert E. Liskey.
Newport—C. W. Louderback, C. H. Louderback.
Palmyra—Mahlon Clem, Retta Clinedinst.
St. Peter's—Rita Snyder, C. W. McCoy.
Timber Mountain—Not represented.
Timber Ridge—A. A. Fletcher, N. L. Morris, Henry Seldon, Loy H. Hook.
Washington—Not represented.
Whistler's Chapel—John Dean, R. L. Ettel.
Winchester—Mrs. Boyd Richards, Mrs. R. A. Larrick, Mrs. R. L. Williamson, E. W. Cather, J. A. Spaid.
Woods' Chapel—J. A. Kagey, Ray Stroop.

Welcome address by Rev. A. W. Andes. Response by Hermon Eldredge.

REPORT OF PROGRAM COMMITTEE.

We, your Program Committee, have arranged the program now in your hands and have had 250 copies printed, at a cost of $4.00.

> A. W. ANDES,
> B. J. EARP,
> JOE FRENCH,
> *Committee.*

Report adopted.

REPORT OF EXECUTIVE COMMITTEE.

We, your Executive Committee, report that we met in joint session with the Home Mission Committee on December 2, 1929. The following paper was adopted:

"That we, the Home Mission and Executive Committees of the Virginia Valley Central Christian Conference, request our Churches, especially those helped from Conference, not to put outside speakers and ministers into their pulpits unless such speakers are invited or approved by the pastor or trustees of the local Church."

A motion passed that A. W. Andes be paid $5.25 for having Conference Constitutions printed.

The following appropriations were made from the Home Mission Fund: Beulah, $60; Bethel, $59; Joppa, $35; Timber Mountain, $35; Mt. Lebanon, $35; St. Peter's, $35; East Liberty, $35; Woods' Chapel, $60; Whistler's Chapel, $60; Palmyra, $60; Christian Chapel, $35; High Point, $35; Island Ford, $35; Sandy Bottom, $35; Gentry's, $35—the larger appropriations being made where two services per month are given; these appropriations to be paid in quarterly installments.

> A. W. ANDES,
> B. J. EARP,
> JOE FRENCH,
> *Committee.*

Report adopted.

The President asked the Apportionment Committee to act as Finance Committee. Other special committees were appointed, as follows:

Nominations—Joe French, J. C. Bradford.
Press—Hermon Eldredge, Joe French, C. D. Johnston.

Resolutions—R. R. Hosaflook, Mrs. Boyd Richards, A. S. Turner.
Place—C. W. Louderback, J. E. Foster, Norman Morris.

Three additional members of the Nominating Committee were elected, as follows: Loy H. Hook, R. Roy Hosaflook and J. E. Foster.

Church and ministerial reports were read.

The following were invited to seats as deliberative members at some time during the Conference: Hermon Eldredge, Rev. E. B. White, Rev. W. C. Hook, Dr. W. A. Harper, Prof. A. L. Hook, C. D. Johnston, Miss Jewel Truitt, Rev. H. George Robertson, Rev. and Mrs. F. D. Ballard.

REPORT OF COMMITTEE ON GROUPING CHURCHES.

The Committee on Grouping Churches in the Virginia Valley Central Christian Conference met in New Market, Va., Wednesday, May 7, 1930. Rev. B. J. Earp and R. O. Rothgeb were invited to deliberate with the committee. R. A. Larrick was elected secretary.

The following grouping of the Churches was recommended by the committee:

Timber Ridge	Bethlehem	Antioch	Leaksville
Timber Mountain	Concord	Linville	Newport
Dry Run	Mayland	Mt. Olivet (R)	Mt. Lebanon
Joppa	Mt. Olivet (G)	New Hope	East Liberty
Palmyra	High Point	Beulah	St. Peter's.
Whistler's Chapel	Island Ford		Bethel
Woods' Chapel	Christian Chapel		

A vote of thanks was given Mr. and Mrs. Henkel for the use of their room for the meeting, and for the refreshments they served to those present.

The meeting of the committee was closed by prayer, offered by Rev. B. J. Earp.

SAMUEL EARMAN,
J. C. BRADFORD,
R. A. LARRICK,
J. E. FOSTER,
J. A. KAGEY,
Committee.

On motion, consideration of the report was postponed until 2 o'clock this afternoon.

Address by Hermon Eldredge; subject, "The Outlook for Our Church Publications."

Adjourned for dinner.

FIRST DAY—AFTERNOON SESSION.

Conference called to order at 1:45 by the President. Devotional services conducted by Hermon Eldredge.

The report of the Committee on Grouping the Churches was taken from the table and discussed. A motion was passed, limiting the speeches to five minutes each.

Report adopted.

REPORT OF COMMITTEE ON RELIGIOUS LITERATURE.

We, your Committee on Religious Literature, wonder if the Christian people of today realize the importance of religious literature in the homes, Sunday Schools, Churches, and other organizations throughout our land and nation. We feel there are many who do, but so many who do not; therefore, we earnestly urge upon you, Christian friends, to search through the abundance of literature coming from the publishing houses daily and secure the vital truths contained therein, as the literature we read has much to do with our lives and conduct.

But, first of all, we recommend that the great and perfect Book, the Bible, be read more carefully and prayerfully.

Secondly, that the Church papers, namely: *The Christian Sun* and the *Congregationalist and Herald of Gospel Liberty*, be read in the homes of our Conference. We commend these two, as through them we learn of the work of our Churches and Sunday Schools, besides other Church interests that are made known to the people.

Thirdly, we urge our constituency to support and patronize our own publishing houses in the way of Sunday School and Church literature.

MARVIN SELDON,
A. S. TURNER,
MRS. J. J. LINCOLN,
Committee.

An address on "The Outlook of Our Publications," by C. D. Johnston.

Report adopted.

Annual address by Prof. A. L. Hook.

An address on "Our Orphanage," by C. D. Johnston.

REPORT OF DIRECTOR OF RELIGIOUS EDUCATION.

It is recommended that our Sunday School and Church workers use every means possible to attend schools of religious education and to try to improve their work as much as possible by reading good books and religious periodicals, and, above all, to read the Holy Bible.

Every Church worker should be present at some Church service each Sunday unless hindered by some cause which they can conscientiously give to their Lord and Saviour Jesus Christ.

As workers for our Lord, let us strive to do more and better work for Him this coming year than we have done in the past.

ROY A. LARRICK,
Director of Religious Education.

Report adopted.

REPORT OF COMMITTEE ON EVANGELISM.

The first work of the Church is to carry out the work and mission of the divine Redeemer—giving the gospel to the world. Then it is the primary duty of the individual Christian to have in his heart as the one main object, to help evangelize the world. Evangelism brought the Church into existence. Without evangelism, the Church may become a society for religious culture, a school, a social club, but not a Church of Jesus Christ. We must emphasize evangelism, because Christ declared the reason for His coming into the world was that the world might be saved through Him. The ordinary convert confesses Christ, joins the Church, helps in a very mild way, just enough to enable him to escape torment. This accounts for the fact that it takes an average of twenty Church members in the Southern Christian Convention to win one soul to Christ. Some soul-winning plan different from that usually followed needs to be adopted by us. The one recommendation of your committee is that each Church member make a list of the unsaved friends in whom he is interested, and make them a matter of special prayer, day after day, and year after year, or until they are converted. An all-the-year-'round plan of evangelism is the only reasonable and successful plan.

Mrs. A. W. ANDES,
SIGOURNEY CRAWFORD,
L. H. HOOK,
ORA SCOTT,
Committee.

Report adopted.

REPORT OF COMMITTEE ON SOCIAL SERVICE.

A gospel or a religion that does not make men and women better is worthless. A gospel that does not make men and women live together in love is worthless. A gospel that does not improve men and women socially, mentally and spiritually is worthless.

We, your committee, advise:

1. The reading of "The Social Teachings of Christ Jesus," by W. B. Jennings, and other similar books on the social gospel.

2. Co-operation with the Red Cross and social service workers and boards of health.

3. The preaching and the practice of the social teachings of Jesus.

JOE FRENCH,
MRS. BOYD RICHARDS,
R. ROY HOSAFLOOK,
Committee.

Report adopted.
Adjourned.

FIRST DAY—EVENING SESSION.

A program was rendered by and for the young people, the service being in charge of Rev. Joe French.

Addresses were made by Leonora Welch, Kenneth Hook, Alfred Dofflemyre, Miss Jewel Truitt, and Hermon Eldredge.

The theme of the service was "Adventures in the Christian Quest."

SECOND DAY—MORNING SESSION.

Conference was called to order at 9:30 by the President. Devotional services were conducted by Rev. R. L. Williamson. Roll called. Minutes of yesterday read and approved.

REPORT OF COMMITTEE ON EDUCATION.

We, your Committee on Education, offer the following report:

We believe in education of the heart as well as the head. The education of our youth should include a bountiful supply of religious training, and the whole school career should, as far as possible, pass through the safest of moral and religious atmosphere. This is especially true in these days when so much is being taught in many schools to undermine the faith once delivered to the saints. For this reason, among many others, we recommend our own Elon College to our people as a safe educational institution.

We also recommend that our Sunday Schools take the fifth Sunday's offerings for Elon College, as requested by the Southern Christian Convention, and thus keep the college prominently before our young people, and at the same time lend financial assistance to this worthy institution.

We urge our people also to be loyal to the college in the million-dollar campaign soon to be launched by the college.

Bro. Alfred A. Dofflemyre desires to be continued as a candidate for the ministry, and we recommend his continuance.

Bro. W. T. Walters has applied to this committee for reinstatement. After having made such investigation as we have had opportunity to make, we find no charges sustained against him during the past two years, and, in accordance with the recommendation made by the committee of twelve ministers two years ago, we recommend that his full ordination credentials be restored to him.

Bro. Walters also asks for a letter of transfer to the Ray's Hill and Southern Pennsylvania Conference. We recommend that this request be granted.

We have received a request from Bro. H. R. Osbourne to be admitted as a candidate for the ministry. In view of the fact that our acquaintance with Bro. Osbourne is very limited, and that he comes without the necessary recommendation, we think best to defer action on his request for one year, and in the meantime bid him godspeed in any work he may do for the kingdom wherever his services may be desired, requesting, however, that in doing such work he be careful not in any way to interfere with the work of the pastor in charge, nor to violate the request of the Executive and Home Mission Committees made in their session of December 2, 1929, which request appears in the report of the Executive Committee made yesterday.

A. W. ANDES,
B. J. EARP,
R. L. WILLIAMSON,
JOE FRENCH,
Committee.

Address on "Education," by Dr. W. A. Harper.
Report of Committee on Education adopted.

REPORT OF STEWARDSHIP SECRETARY.

Primarily, Christian stewardship is a business. It pertains first to work—constructive Christian work. As is true of us denominationally, this Conference, more than eighty years old, indicates that stewardship's initial component has been poorly developed. As to present stewardship status, three notes should be sounded. If possible, it were better to smite with might on all the chords of life—life as an all-in-all stewardship.

It does not deprecate youth's contribution to Church work to say that too much is being left to youth. Nor is youth's enthusiasm license for maturity's apathy; rather, it is cause for wholesome example. Lack of an aroused, mature leadership, resulting from a deep-set indifference to the use of opportunities for Christian information, is the deterring note.

The discomfiting note is the incongruity between the number of tithers and the weakness of the Conference regime. Tithing in good faith may err. Stewardship's peril is in supposing that paying the required tenth fulfills responsibility. It must be remembered that effective tithing is a consequence. One hundred and fifty members tithing understandingly should provoke attitudes and activities which are unapparent.

The note of promise is that every incumbent pastor stands committed to the undertaking, and even now is leading and helping his Churches each to find its point of entry into the verities of Christian stewardship. Some pure leaven, not inactive because unseen, is hidden away.

To know, to do, to be. With the full purpose and ability of each aspirant turned first into the Church, these pursuits, as outlined on the placard before us, become inclusive of the stewardship of all of life.

MRS. J. J. LINCOLN,
Stewardship Secretary.

An address on "Stewardship" was given by Mrs. J. J. Lincoln.

An address on "Stewardship" was given by Hermon Eldredge.

Adjourned for dinner.

SECOND DAY—AFTERNOON SESSION.

Conference called to order at 1:45 by the President. Devotional services conducted by Rev. H. George Robertson.

* * * * *

CONFERENCE MISSIONARY ASSOCIATION.

In the absence of the President, Roy A. Larrick, the Association was called to order by the Secretary-Treasurer, A. W. Andes. Rev. R. L. Williamson was elected temporary Chairman. The roll was called by the Secretary.

REPORT OF TREASURER.

The following membership fees have been received: Ladies' Bible Class, Linville, $2.50; S. S. & C. E. Convention, $10; Olive E. Showalter, $2.50; Verdie C. Showalter, $2.50; Barbara Andes, $2.50; Mrs. J. J. Lincoln, $5; Minnie Showalter, $2.50; Alice A. Lincoln, $2.50; Antioch, $5; J. O. Atkinson, $5; Mrs. Boyd Richards, $2.50; A. W. Andes, $5; Mrs. A. W. Andes, $2.50; Mrs. R. A. Henton, $2.50; Sophia Byrd, $2.50; Owen W. Andes, $5; Roy A. Larrick, $5; Ladies' Bible Class, Timber Ridge, $2.50; Mary Pickering, $5; Ever-Ready Missionary Society, Winchester, $2.50; Philathea Class, Winchester, $2.50; Palmyra, $2.50; Linville, $5; Mt. Lebanon, 50c; Win-One Bible Class, Winchester, $5; Joe French, $5; Samuel Earman, $5; Mrs. Samuel Earman, $2.50; B. J. Earp, $5; Mrs. B. J. Earp, $2.50; Mrs. R. C. Myers, $2.50; New Hope, $5; Ladies' Bible Class, New Hope, $5; R. L. Williamson, $5; Mrs. R. L. Williamson, $2.50; Bethlehem, $10; Woman's Missionary Society, Linville, $5; Adult Class, Antioch, $2.50; Roy Hosaflook, $5; Mrs. Roy Hosaflook, $2.50— total, $155.50.

A. W. ANDES,
Treasurer.

By motion, the names of the Live Wire Class, of Linville, and of Dr. and Mrs. W. T. Walters were dropped, according to their requests.

By motion, Treasurer was instructed to pay over to Conference Treasurer the amount in hand or that may be collected later.

Election of officers: Rev. R. L. Williamson was elected President; R. C. Myers, Vice-President; Rev. A. W. Andes, Secretary-Treasurer.

By motion, the Association adjourned.

* * * * *

CONFERENCE IN SESSION AGAIN.

REPORT OF COMMITTEE ON S. S. AND CHRISTIAN ENDEAVOR.

We believe that the Sunday School and Christian Endeavor are the greatest forces for the advancement of our young people and all others in living and teaching the principles of our Saviour. If we accept this statement as being correct, then we should do everything possible to help advance the work of our Sunday Schools and Christian Endeavor Societies.

We recommend that our Sunday Schools and Christian Endeavor Societies use the best equipment possible in their work, and that they put into the hands of their members good reading material.

R. A. LARRICK,
J. E. FOSTER,
J. A. KAGEY,
Committee.

Report adopted.

Address by Hermon Eldredge; subject, "Good Will to Men."

An offering was taken to defray expenses of Hermon Eldredge. Offering amounted to $21.86.

REPORT OF COMMITTEE ON NOMINATIONS.

We recommend the following nominations: President, Rev. R. L. Williamson; Vice-President, Rev. B. J. Earp; Secretary, Rev. A. W. Andes; Assistant Secretary, J. Warner Stearn; Treasurer, Samuel Earman; Director of Religious Education, Roy A. Larrick; Mission Secretary, R. O. Rothgeb; Stewardship Secretary, Mrs. J. J. Lincoln. We recommend that each of these nominations be voted on separately.

We recommend for the officers of the Woman's Mission Board (August, 1930 to October, 1931): President, Miss Ora Scott; Vice-President, Mrs. A. W. Andes; Secretary, Mrs. B. F. Frank; Treasurer, Miss Verdie C. Showalter; Superintendent of Spiritual Life, Miss Amy Louderback; Superintendent of Women's Work, Mrs. R. C. Myers; Superintendent of Young People, Mrs. A. F. Kite; Superintendent of Literature and Mite Boxes, Miss Ella Pickering; Superintendent of Cradle Roll, Mrs. E. Lena Rothgeb.

JOE FRENCH,
J. C. BRADFORD,
L. H. HOOK,
J. E. FOSTER,
R. ROY HOSAFLOOK,
Committee.

Report adopted.

Adjourned.

SECOND DAY—EVENING SESSION.

Conference called to order at 8 P. M. Prayer by Rev. A. W. Andes.

REPORT OF COMMITTEE ON FOREIGN MISSIONS.

During the past year our Church has taken a great step forward by uniting with the Congregationalists, and we are at last beginning to go into all the world and preach the gospel. By this union, the doors to many new fields have been thrown open to us, challenging us to a greater and more effective service. While the Congregationalists are helping to share our work in Japan, we have joined hands with them in China, Greece, Africa and Turkey to help them lead the many lost souls of these fields into a saving knowledge of our Lord and Saviour.

May the Lord help each member of this Conference to look out upon this enlarged task with a new vision and a greater determination to do more in the coming year than we did in the past to make Christ known in the foreign field.

Feeling that it is the desire of each member of the Church to do his best, we recommend:

That our people support and read the *Missionary Herald* and keep themselves informed of the work being done by the united Church.

Also that our mission workers keep the work and its needs before our people until this "great task" shall fade away and become a glorious opportunity to serve our Lord and Master, and that we may prove our love to him by being ever ready and willing to say, "Here am I; send me."

VERDIE SHOWALTER,
N. L. MORRIS,
R. O. ROTHGEB,
Committee.

The service was then turned over to the Woman's Mission Board. Scripture lesson was read by Mrs. Irene Kite, which was followed by a number of sentence prayers.

The following report of the women's work was read:

REPORT OF WOMAN'S BOARD.

The Woman's Board held a midyear business meeting in February and planned the district rallies. Several members of the Board were appointed to visit two of the Churches where no missionary organizations exist and try to interest them in the work.

The five district rallies were held in June, as follows: Northern, at Winchester, Green County, at Mt. Olivet (G); Rockingham, at Mayland; Shenandoah, at Woods' Chapel, and Page Valley at Bethel. All the rallies were well attended, and good addresses were enjoyed at each one. The pastors of the Conference were very kind to help out in this respect.

The Woman's Missionary Conference was held August 1st at Antioch, presided over by Mrs. R. A. Larrick, who has proven her ability to handle a session of this kind. At the Conference, ten Churches were represented by delegates and four others by reports. Reports showed seven women's societies with 192 members, five young people's societies with 88 members, five cradle rolls with 57 members, and one Church helping through their Ladies' Aid and Christian Endeavor Societies.

The Treasurer, Miss Verdie Showalter, made her report as follows:

RECEIPTS.

Women's Societies.

Bethel	$ 1.70	Linville	81.10
Bethlehem	30.00	Mt. Olivet (R)	12.40
Dry Run	11.54	New Hope	14.85
Leaksville	42.70	Winchester	86.53
		Total	$280.82

Young People's Societies.

Antioch	$ 24.31	Mt. Olivet (R)	5.00
Bethel	3.00	Timber Ridge	10.60
Bethlehem	3.00	Winchester	54.27
		Total	$100.18

Cradle Rolls.

Antioch	$ .60	Linville	8.30
Bethlehem	2.61	Winchester	2.50
		Total	$ 14.01

Rally Offerings.

Bethel	$ 5.06	Winchester	2.50
Mayland	3.75	Woods' Chapel	4.57
Mt. Olivet (G)	10.50		

Total .... $ 26.38

Amount in treasury for the Conference's own use.................... $ 8.30
Amount carried from last year..................................... 9.88

$ 18.18

Women's Societies $280.82
Young People's Societies 100.18
Cradle Rolls 14.01
Rally offerings 26.38
Offering at Leaksville Woman's Conference.................. 12.51
Offering at Conference "Women's Night".................... 20.26

454.16

Grand total $472.34

DISBURSEMENTS.

1929.
Aug. 1. To Mrs. B. F. Frank, postage ....$ 2.29
Sep.   9. To Mrs. Hardcastle 85.40

1930.
Jan. 6. To Burke & Price, for bond...................... 2.50
       13. To Mrs. Hardcastle 94.29
Apr. 15. To Mrs. Hardcastle 62.67
July 16. To Mrs. Hardcastle 218.78

465.93

Balance in treasury for own use.................................. $ 6.41

Received after closing book:
Leaksville Woman's Society ....$ 1.50
Leaksville Cradle Roll 5.75

7.25

Total on hand .... $ 13.66

We submit for your approval the following officers for the year 1930-'31: President, Miss Ora Scott; Vice-President, Mrs. A. W. Andes; Secretary, Mrs. B. F. Frank; Treasurer, Miss Verdie Showalter; Superintendent of Spiritual Life, Miss Amy Louderback; Superintendent of Women's Societies, Mrs. R. C. Myers; Superintendent of Young People's Societies, Mrs. A. F. Kite; Superintendent of Literature and Mite Boxes, Miss Ella Pickering; Superintendent of Cradle Roll, Mrs. E. Lena Rothgeb.

MRS. B. F. FRANK,
MRS. SAMUEL EARMAN,
R. L. WILLIAMSON,
ELLA PICKERING,
Committee on Woman's Board.

An address was given by Hermon Eldredge.

Report of Committee on Foreign Missions was adopted.

THIRD DAY—MORNING SESSION.

Conference called to order at 9:30 by the President. Devotional service conducted by A. W. Andes. Roll called. Minutes of yesterday read and approved.

REPORT OF COMMITTEE ON CHRISTIAN UNION.

Through all our history as a Church we have preached Christian union, though our practices may sometimes have been at variance with our preaching. However, we are coming more and more to preach and practice the teaching of our Lord in this important matter.

And in this we are not alone. Other denominations are catching the spirit of union and brotherly love and manifesting the same in their attitude towards one another. This is cause for gratitude.

Our own Church and the Congregationalist Church have set a new pace in Church history by the splendid way in which they have come together and joined forces for mutual helpfulness and world conquest for Christ. To the end that this union may be a great blessing, and that other denominations may follow this good example may we give our prayers and our co-operation.

We endorse the action of the General Convention, and of the Southern Christian Convention in the matter of the union.

A. W. ANDES,
R. L. WILLIAMSON,
B. F. McDANIEL,
Committee.

Address by Hermon Eldredge; subject, "Where We Are, and What Is Before Us in the Congregational-Christian Merger."

Report adopted.

REPORT OF CONFERENCE MISSION SECRETARY.

As we come to this eighty-second session of the Virginia Valley Central Christian Conference, we should come with rejoicing, not because of any great accomplishments of our own, but because God has seen fit to entrust to us greater responsibilities.

With the merging of the Congregational and Christian Churches, our horizon has indeed been widened, and today we look out upon new fields of service which challenge our best for Him who said, "Go ye into all the world and preach my gospel to every creature."

We feel that, in part at least, the things the Christian Church has stood for through the years has been realized, and that we, the Congregational-Christian Church, should now labor together as one in advancing His kingdom on earth. Let us accept the challenge that comes to us through the eight or nine new mission fields. Let us continually keep before the children of our Sunday Schools the great mission of the Church. Let us try to acquaint ourselves with our missionaries and their work, and thus increase our interest in them. Let us say more, pay more, and pray more for them. Let us not grow weary in well doing, for in due season we shall reap if we faint not.

R. O. ROTHGEB,
Conference Mission Secretary.

Moved and carried that we pay half the expenses of Rev. R. L. Williamson, the newly elected Conference President, to the General Convention at Seattle, Wash., next summer.

Moved and carried that we have our minutes printed in THE ANNUAL, as usual, and buy 150 copies and sell them at half price.

Dr. W. T. Walters was elected to deliver the annual address next year. T. W. Matthews was elected alternate.

By motion, the Secretary was instructed to send a telegram to Dr. J. O. Atkinson, expressing our sympathy for him in his affliction and our earnest hope that he may soon be sufficiently improved to continue his active service in the great work he has been doing. Special prayer for Dr. Atkinson was offered by Rev. R. L. Williamson.

REPORT OF COMMITTEE ON PLACE FOR NEXT MEETING.

We recommend that we accept the invitation to meet at Mt. Olivet, in Green County, Va., next year.

C. W. LOUDERBACK,
J. E. FOSTER,
NORMAN MORRIS,
Committee.

Moved and carried that an official delegation be sent to the Disciple Convention, now in session at Shenandoah. Rev. Joe French and Miss Jewel Truitt were chosen to go.

By motion, a committee was appointed to consider a change in time of meeting of Conference. R. L. Williamson, Mrs. R. A. Larrick, J. A. Kagey, Mrs. J. J. Lincoln, Joe French, and A. W. Andes were appointed.

Adjourned for dinner.

THIRD DAY—AFTERNOON SESSION.

Conference called to order at 1:15. Devotional services conducted by Rev. F. D. Ballard.

REPORT OF FINANCE COMMITTEE.

We recommend the following bills be paid: Rev. A. W. Andes, for printing programs, $4.00; Rev. B. J. Earp, for printing order blanks, $1.25; Hermon Eldredge's expenses, $35.00; half the expenses of Leona Dofflemyre and Norman Morris to go to Young People's Convention at Elon College.

We recommend that the money raised next year be left in the hands of Conference, to be apportioned by same.

J. M. LOHR,
J. C. BRADFORD,
R. ROY HOSAFLOOK,
Committee.

Report adopted.

REPORT OF TREASURER.

HOME MISSIONS.

Cash on hand	$ 649.11
Conference collections	327.84
Conference Missionary Association	155.50
Total amount received	$1,132.45

Paid B. J. Earp $355.00
Paid A. W. Andes 129.00
Paid W. B. Fuller 60.00
Paid Joe French 105.00
                                                    ———   649.00

Balance on hand .... $ 483.45

CHURCH EXTENSION.

Cash on hand .... $ 100.47
Conference collections 36.41

Total amount received .... $ 136.88

Paid A. W. Andes for Bethel Church...........................   100.00

Balance on hand .... $ 36.88

CONFERENCE FUND.

Cash on hand .... $ 107.03
Conference collections 74.82
Received on ANNUALS 32.00
Received on Conference Constitutions...........................   1.70
Collection for Hermon Eldredge 21.86

Total amount received .... $ 237.41

Paid A. W. Andes, service as Secretary...................$ 20.00
Paid Samuel Earman, service as Treasurer................   15.00
Paid for programs 4.00
Paid for Conference Constitutions 5.25
Paid Central Publishing Co. for ANNUALS.................   75.00
Paid Burke & Price for bond............................   3.75
                                                    ———   123.00

Balance on hand .... $ 114.41

SOUTHERN CHRISTIAN CONVENTION.

Cash on hand .... $ 913.66
Conference collections 801.46

Total amount received $1,715.12
Paid W. C. Wicker, Treas. S. C. C............................   913.66

Balance on hand .... $ 801.46

SAMUEL EARMAN,
Treasurer.

By motion, report was referred to the Finance Committee.

REPORT OF COMMITTEE ON HOME MISSIONS.

As your Home Mission Committee, we make the following recommendations:

1. Any pastor serving the weaker Churches and applying for help from the Southern Christian Convention shall have such application endorsed by the Executive and Home Mission Committees.

2. Churches receiving help from the Home Mission Fund of this Conference shall be urged to raise their Conference apportionments as designated by the Conference.

3. That all home mission funds be left in the hands of the Executive and Home Mission Committees for distribution.

W. C. WAMPLER,
SAMUEL EARMAN,
J. A. KAGEY,
W. A. CRAWFORD,
Committee.

Report adopted.

An address was given by Rev. F. D. Ballard; subject, "Salesmanship and Christianity."

REPORT OF COMMITTEE ON CHANGE OF TIME OF CONFERENCE.

Your committee would recommend that the time of holding this Conference remain unchanged.

In keeping with a request coming from a meeting of the Committee on Grouping the Churches, we would recommend that the ministers and representatives of the Churches hold a midyear session of one day at Bethlehem; time of such meeting to be determined by the Executive Committee of this body.

R. L. WILLIAMSON,
J. A. KAGEY,
JOE FRENCH,
MRS. ROY A. LARRICK,
MRS. J. J. LINCOLN,
A. W. ANDES,
Committee.

Report adopted.

REPORT OF COMMITTEE ON APPORTIONMENTS.

We recommend apportionments for next year as follows: Antioch, $100; Bethel, $35; Bethlehem, $120; Beulah, $18; Concord, $50; Dry Run, $50; East Liberty, $20; High Point, $20; Joppa, $20; Leaksville, $175; Linville, $125; Mayland, $70; Mt. Lebanon, $40; Mt. Olivet (G), $75; Mt. Olivet (R), $50; New Hope, $40; Newport, $100; Palmyra, $20; St. Peter's, $25; Timber Mountain, $25; Timber Ridge, $90; Whistler's Chapel, $25; Winchester, $175; Woods' Chapel, $25—total, $1,493.

J. M. LOHR,
J. C. BRADFORD,
R. ROY HOSAFLOOK,
Committee.

Report adopted.

Standing committees were announced as follows:

Education—A. W. Andes, B. J. Earp, W. B. Fuller, R. L. Williamson.

Foreign Missions—R. O. Rothgeb, Verdie Showalter, Norman Morris, Marvin Seldon.

Evangelism—Mrs. A. W. Andes, Loy Hook, N. L. Morris, H. R. Osborne.

Religious Literature—Joe French, A. S. Turner, Marvin Seldon, Mahlon Clem.

Christian Union—A. W. Andes, B. F. McDaniel, Alfred Dofflemyre, J. A. Kagey.

Home Missions—W. C. Wampler, W. A. Crawford, C. W. Louderback, Samuel Earman.

Sunday Schools and Christian Endeavor—R. A. Larrick, J. E. Foster, T. Z. Alger, D. H. Welch.

Social Service—R. Roy Hosaflook, Mrs. Boyd Richards, J. M. Lohr, John Dean.

Woman's Board—Mrs. B. F. Frank, Ora Scott, Ella Pickering, Mrs. Samuel Earman.

Executive—R. L. Williamson, A. W. Andes, B. J. Earp.

Apportionments—J. C. Bradford, J. M. Lohr, R. R. Hosaflook.

REPORT OF COMMITTEE ON RESOLUTIONS.

We, your Committee on Resolutions, submit the following:

1. That this Conference express its appreciation of the work done by its officers the past year.

2. That we express to Rev. B. J. Earp, our retiring President, our appreciation for his three years of service.

3. That we express by a rising vote our appreciation to the pastor, members, and community of Newport Church for the most cordial and efficient manner in which we, as a Conference, have been entertained.

4. That we express, by a rising vote, our appreciation to those who have been seated as deliberative members, and for the splendid addresses and help they have given during this Conference.

R. ROY HOSAFLOOK,
NORMAN W. MORRIS,
E. W. CATHER,
Committee.

Report adopted by items.

Minutes of today read and approved.

On motion, Conference adjourned, to meet in midyear session at Bethlehem at such time as may be designated by the Executive Committee.

B. J. EARP, *President.*
A. W. ANDES, *Secretary.*

BANNER CHURCHES.

The following Churches, having paid all Conference apportionments, are enrolled as "Banner Churches": Bethel, Dry Run, Leaksville, Mayland, Mt. Olivet (G), St. Peter's, Whistler's Chapel, Winchester, Woods' Chapel.

MINISTERIAL REPORTS.

A. W. Andes—Churches: Leaksville, Newport, Dry Run, Joppa, Timber Ridge, Timber Mountain, Bethel. Sermons, 237; addresses, 5; conversions, 28; baptisms, 25; members received, 32; pastoral visits, 891; marriages, 2; funerals, 27. Salary, $1,646.53.

W. M. Clem—No report.

B. J. Earp—Churches: Woods' Chapel, Whistler's Chapel, Palmyra, Mt. Olivet (G), High Point, Christian Chapel, Island Ford. Sermons, 157; addresses, 14; conversions, 51; baptisms, 28; members received, 53; pastoral visits, 522; marriages, 4; funerals, 6. Salary, $1,106.23.

Joe French—Churches: Bethlehem, Concord, East Liberty, Mayland, Mt. Lebanon, St. Peter's. Sermons, 140; addresses, 5; conversions, 12; baptisms, 12; members received, 19; pastoral visits, 480; marriage, 1; funerals, 4. Salary, $740.85.

W. B. Fuller—Churches: Antioch, Beulah, Linville, Mt. Olivet (R), New Hope. Sermons, 130; addresses, 2; conversions, 40; baptisms, 20; members received, 22; pastoral visits, 400; funerals, 12. Salary, $1,108.

J. W. Henderson—No charge. Sermons, 20; addresses, 3; conversions, 20; pastoral visits, 7; funerals, 5.

W. T. Walters—Churches: District No. 6, in Ray's Hill and Southern Pennsylvania Conference. Sermons, 165; addresses, 16; baptisms, 7; members received, 7; pastoral visits, 649; funerals, 16. Salary, $1,247.

R. L. Williamson—Church: Winchester. Sermons, 91; conversions, 14; baptisms, 9; members received, 20; pastoral visits, 505; marriages, 9; funerals, 2. Salary, $1,400.

Church Statistics—Virginia Valley Central Conference

CHURCHES	PASTORS	SECRETARIES AND ADDRESSES	Members Reported Last Year	Present Membership	Conference Apportionments	Amount Paid on Apportionments	Home and Foreign Missions	All Other Benevolences	Paid on Pastor's Salary	All Other Expenses	TOTAL	Value of Church Property
●tt	W. B. Fuller	E. A. ●, Harrisonburg, Va.	70	68	$125.00	$36.00	$95.02	$65.37	$297.00	$36.28	$529.67	$3,000
Bethel†	A. W. ●es	D. F. Dofflemyre, Elkton, Va.	107	126	32.00	32.00	10.92		127.15	144.60	314.67	6,000
Bethlehem*†	Joe French	Miss Ella Pickering, Broadway, Va.	126	132	150.00	11.70	88.33	12.53	225.00	113.12	450.68	3,000
Beulah†	W. B. Fuller	Miss Ollie Tibbins, Keezletown, Va.	26	29	25.00	20.00	10.00		100.00		130.00	500
Christian Chapel	B. J. Earp	Mrs. Harry Bruce, Boonesville, Va.		14			1.00		35.58	15.00	51.53	500
●rd	Joe French	J. C. Huffman, ●le, Va.	86	93	58.00	42.20	11.00	2.02	91.15	73.02	219.39	900
Dry Run*	A. W. Andes	W. B. Burke, Seven Fountains, Va.	86	79	68.00	68.00	53.60	15.00	164.95	35.00	336.55	5,000
East Liberty	Joe French	Mrs. Effie May, Shenandoah, Va.	122	122	25.00	7.00	3.50		41.30		51.80	500
Island Ford	B. J. Earp	Mrs. Lula Roach, Elkton, Va.		26			1.00		17.43	7.00	25.43	500
Joppa	A. W. Andes	Miss Susie Duncan, Edinburg, Va.	49	47	25.00	20.00	11.25		42.55	8.06	81.86	700
Leaksville*†	A. W. ●es	R. O. Rothgeb, Luray, Va.	160	162	180.00	180.00	111.52		407.91	45.60	745.03	3,500
Linville*†	W. B. Fuller	Miss Sallie A. Payne, Harrisonburg	134	160	125.00	120.00	116.10	7.50	400.00	56.00	699.60	4,000
Mayland	Joe French	●er A. Spitzer, Broadway, Va.	89	91	70.00	70.00	93.32	117.00	230.00	98.43	608.75	1,500
Mt. Lebanon	Joe French	Mildred ●r, Shenandoah, Va.	94	94	40.00	33.90	8.55				42.45	1,000
Mt. ●let (G)	B. J. Earp	E. S. Morris, March, Va.	154	159	90.00	90.00	57.18		300.00		447.18	2,500
Mt. Olivet (R)†	W. B. Fuller	Edna Life, Elkton, Va.	52	46	50.00		15.00		187.00	45.60	247.60	2,500
New Hope*†	W. B. Fuller	Hubert E. Liskey, Harrisonburg, Va.	172	171	80.00	36.00	31.55		126.50	13.74	207.79	3,867
Newport	A. W. Andes	C. W. Louderback, Stanley, Va.	97	102	120.00	98.00	21.15	12.75	286.15	559.83	977.88	2,500
Palmyra	B. J. Earp	Mrs. Wm. Newland, Edinburg, Va.	61	65	25.00	14.75	2.50	4.50	86.12	31.45	139.32	1,300
St. Peter's	Joe French	● L. W. ●der, Elkton, Va.	52	55	20.00	20.00			37.94	14.50	72.44	
Timber M'ntain	A. W. Andes	J. H. Park, Capon Bridge, W. Va.	201	202	25.00	15.25			52.67		67.90	
Timber Ridge*	A. W. ●es	J. E. Eaton, Gore, Va.	67	71	105.00	83.75	29.48	50.77	436.15	108.15	708.32	8,000
Whistler's Chapel*	B. J. Earp	John C. Dean, ●r, Va.	187	202	32.00	32.00	10.00	25.00	124.00	3.00	194.00	
●●●	R. L. Williamson	R. A. Larrick, Winchester, Va.			175.00	175.00	235.86	21.49	1200.00	1439.03	3,071.38	45,000
●ds' Chapel	B. J. Earp	M. J. F. Kingree, New Market, Va.	85	94	35.00	35.00	9.00	190.75	124.00		353.75	500
Totals			2435	2558	$1680.00	$1240.55	$1026.83	$524.68	$5140.55	$2847.41	$10,780.02	$96,767

*Church has Missionary Society.   †Church has C. E. Society.   ‡Church has Parsonage.

NOTE: Amount reported here for Missions includes amount paid by S. S. for Missions.

SUNDAY SCHOOL STATISTICS—VIRGINIA VALLEY CENTRAL CONFERENCE

SUNDAY SCHOOL	NAME AND ADDRESS OF SUPERINTENDENT.	No. Officers and Teachers.	No. on Cradle Roll.	No. of Scholars in School.	No. in Home Department.	Total Enrollment.	Amount Raised for Orphanage.	Total Raised During Year.
Antioch*	O. W. Andes, Harrisonburg, Va.	7	20	44	6	70	$75.84	$165.81
Bethel*	M. A. Dofflemyre, Elkton, Va.	11		79		79		101.51
Bethlehem*	D. H. Welch, Broadway, Va.	12	27	110	12	149	39.62	164.00
Beulah*	O. K. Hoskins, Keezletown, Va.	6	10	48		48		
Concord*	V. T. Huffman, Timberville, Va.	8	8	86		86		69.14
Dry Run*	W. B. Burke, Seven Fountains, Va.	8	16	50	10	70	19.00	60.00
Island Ford	Casper Harlin, Harrisonburg, Va.	8		55		74		20.00
Leaksville*	B. F. McDaniel, Luray, Va.	9	18	58	12	97	5.00	134.13
Linville*	Roy Hosaflook, Linville, Va.	15	20	135	3	173	130.06	422.78
Mayland*	Nettie Derrow, Broadway, Va.	9	10	59	11	95	58.50	125.00
Mt. Lebanon*	I. N. Comer, Shenandoah, Va.	5	9	70	8	75		48.90
Mt. Olivet (G)*	E. S. Morris, March, Va.	12	7	69		98		102.35
Mt. Olivet (R)*	A. S. Turner, Elkton, Va.	13	9	151		151		162.66
New Hope*	N. M. Hasler, Harrisonburg, Va.	7		28	5	49	29.69	90.11
Newport*	J. Z. Alger, Stanley, Va.	9	16	65	9	74	54.81	100.02
Palmyra*	J. L. Carper, Edinburg, Va.	10		35		61		50.53
St. Peter's	C. M. Dovel, Elkton, Va.	11	15	117		128	5.86	14.66
Timber Ridge*	H. F. Seldon, Gore, Va.	14		81		95	31.66	115.09
Whistler's Chapel*	R. L. Ettel, Mt. Jackson, Va.	8		40		40		68.00
Winchester*	R. A. Larrick, Winchester, Va.	25	15	134	8	182	88.96	373.77
Woods' Chapel*	J. A. Kagey, Mt. Jackson, Va.	5	5	32	2	42	11.00	41.06
Totals		212	205	1546	86	1936	$550.00	$2,429.52

*Use our denominational literature.

Proceedings of the One Hundred and Tenth Annual Session of Eastern Virginia Christian Conference

SOUTH NORFOLK CHRISTIAN CHURCH, SOUTH NORFOLK, VA.

OCTOBER 29-31, 1930.

FIRST DAY—MORNING SESSION.

The Eastern Virginia Christian Conference met in the One Hundred and Tenth Annual Session, and was called to order at 10:30 o'clock, Rev. H. S. Hardcastle presiding.

Song service conducted by Rev. J. F. Morgan. Devotional service conducted by Rev. O. D. Poythress. Scripture lesson, John 3:1-17.

The roll was called, and the following ministers and laymen were enrolled (this list includes the enrollment for the session):

ENROLLMENT.

Ministers—M. F. Allen, R. E. Brittle, H. C. Caviness, W. H. Denison, W. H. Garman, J. W. Fix, H. S. Hardcastle, W. D. Harward, I. W. Johnson, T. N. Lowe, F. C. Lester, J. F. Morgan, J. E. McCauley, O. D. Poythress, N. G. Newman, H. E. Rountree, C. C. Ryan W. W. Staley, J. N. Cutchins, L. E. Smith, L. L. Lassiter, J. M. Roberts, C. E. Gerringer, E. B. White, D. M. Spence, Charles Eldred Shelton (Congregational)—total, 26.

Churches and Delegates.

Antioch—W. E. Garrison, J. T. Godwin.

Barrett's—No report.

Berea (Nansemond)—A. S. Hargroves, Mrs. A. S. Hargroves, Mrs. H. P. Harrell, R. B. Odom.

Burton's Grove—E. W. Carroll, J. W. Pittman.

Berea (Norfolk)—Mrs. C. E. Hanbury, C. E. Hanbury.

Bethlehem—Miss Doris Eure, Mrs. C. W. King, O. D. King, C. F. Savage.

Centerville—No report.

Christian Temple—A. M. Johnson, S. M. Smith, Mrs. Dennis Tuttle, Jr., F. M. Brewer.

Cypress Chapel—R. M. Jones, Mrs. Hugh Dudley, Mrs. W. L. Harrell, Mrs. A. E. Bowden.

Damascus—Miss Margaret Corbitt, L. Corbitt, Miss Blanche Pierce, Richard Corbitt.

Dendron—No report.

Elm Avenue—Ellsworth Savage, J. W. Felton, Mrs. W. O. Daughtridge.

Eure—M. T. Felton, Z. D. Eure, W. J. Askew.

Epworth—No report.

First, Norfolk—George H. Frey, Mrs. C. A. Marwitz, Miss Annie Winborne, Mrs. George H. Frey.

First, Portsmouth—C. J. Heath, W. H. Spivey, G. W. Hamer.

First, Portsmouth (Congregational)—No report.

First, Richmond—Mrs. W. J. Stephenson, Mrs. Annie M. Brown.

Franklin—L. R. Jones, J. A. Williams, Mrs. J. A. Williams, Mrs. E. P. Jones, Mrs. Joe Bynum Gay.

Hobson—No report.

Holland—J. P. Dalton, Mrs. J. R. Darden, A. L. Jolly, E. L. Daughtrey.

Holy Neck—Mrs. J. T. Lewis, H. L. Worrel, J. O. Davidson, E. T. Holland.

Hopewell—Mrs. E. S. Ryan, L. E. Hurlburt, Mrs. Geo. A. Robertson.

Isle of Wight—J. M. Roberts, Jr., L. H. Johnson.

Ivor—No report.

Johnson's Grove—No report.

Liberty Spring—J. S. Powell, H. E. Savage, M. G. Bryant, I. T. Byrd.

Mt. Carmel—E. W. Beale, C. E. Joyner.

Mt. Zion—No report.

New Lebanon—H. O. Burges, O. J. Cockes.

Newport News—C. D. West, Mrs. W. B. Williams, Mrs. M. E. Lauderback, Mrs. J. W. Payne.

Oak Grove—W. C. Beamon.

Oakland—W. K. Wagner, Mrs. C. W. Darden, Mrs. W. K. Wagner.

Ocean View—Mrs. B. G. Harrell, Mrs. Joe Harris.

Old Zion—Walter Pearson, Mrs. W. H. Garman, Mrs. C. C. Etheredge, R. M. Givler.

Rosemont—Mrs. B. H. Gibson, Mrs. H. E. Roane, Mrs. O. S. Mills, Mrs. H. C. Hadley.

St. Luke's—No report.

Sarem—Mrs. D. S. Harrell, R. H. Smith, Mrs. R. H. Smith.

Suffolk—J. E. West, Dr. J. E. Rawls, Mrs. B. D. Crocker, Mrs. I. W. Johnson.

South Norfolk—Aubrey Todd, Albert Gatling, R. W. Spruill, A. B. Creef.

Spring Hill—G. C. White, Mrs. G. C. White.

Union (Southampton)—B. D. Drake, C. W. Burges.

Union (Surry)—No report.

Wakefield—Mrs. L. B. Faison, Mrs. J. R. Elmer.

Waverly—J. W. West, B. E. White, R. T. West, Mrs. Ella Gray.

Webster—No report.

Windsor—No report.

Total laymen, 103; total number of delegates and ministers for the session, 129.

Address of welcome by Rev. O. D. Poythress, pastor.

Response by Rev. R. E. Brittle, Cypress Chapel, Va.

The following visitors were introduced to the Conference: Dr. J. O. Atkinson, C. D. Johnston, superintendent of Orphanage; Rev. J. W. Warren, of the M. E. Church, and Rev. W. E. Fitchett.

Report of the Committee on Program was submitted, and the program was adopted, subject to change by Conference, with a provision that time be given for laying the corner-stone of Rosemont Christian Church, Friday at 3 P .M.

The President announced the following special committees for this session:

Nominations—C. C. Ryan, M. J. W. White, W. H. Garman, W. D. Harward.

Finance—J. A. Williams, E. T. Holland, I. T. Byrd.

Resolutions—H. E. Rountree, F. M. Brewer, Mrs. W. B. Williams, Mrs. I. W. Johnson.

Press—Rev. J. F. Morgan.

Place for Next Session—J. E. McCauley, Mrs. M. J. W. White, C. J. Heath.

Collectors—R. C. Norfleet, A. L. Jolly, M. W. Hollowell.

Memoirs—N. G. Newman.

Apportionments—R. B. Odom, L. R. Jones, C. D. West, B. E. White.

The report of the Committee on Home Missions was read by Col. J. E. West, chairman, and, on motion, adopted, as follows:

REPORT OF COMMITTEE ON HOME MISSIONS.

On account of obligations already assumed, and for lack of funds, we are unable to employ a Conference missionary to extend our borders, and must rely on our pastors to increase the membership of their local Churches, so that the Conference shall have a reasonable increase in membership. We regret that the increase was only 176 from 1928 to 1929.

We recommend the usual appropriation of $1,000 to the Christian Temple, which leaves a balance of $4,000 on pledge heretofore made.

We recommend the appropriation of $500 to South Norfolk Church, or so much thereof as the Home Mission Fund of this Conference will permit.

Respectfully submitted,

J. E. WEST, *Chairman.*
E. E. HOLLAND.
I. T. BYRD.
E. T. HOLLAND.

It was moved and carried that each Church be requested to include its total membership, both active and inactive, in the annual report to the Eastern Virginia Christian Conference.

Address, "Looking Westward," by Rev. F. C. Lester.

President's address, "Hard Times and the Kingdom," by Rev. H. S. Hardcastle.

It was moved and carried that the President be requested to furnish his address for publication in *The Christian Sun*.

Communion service conducted by Dr. W. W. Staley, assisted by several deacons of Churches of the Conference.

Conference adjourned for dinner. Benediction by Dr. W. W. Staley.

FIRST DAY—AFTERNOON SESSION.

Conference met and called to order at 2:15 o'clock. Devotional service conducted by Rev. D. M. Spence, Ocean View, Va. Scripture lesson, Heb. 11th chapter.

Rev. Mr. Hudgins, of the Ocean View Mission, and Dr. F. E. Jenkins, of Piedmont Junior College, were introduced to the Conference.

Digest of ministerial and Church reports by Dr. I. W. Johnson, Secretary.

Report of the Committee on Stewardship was read by Rev. J. W. Fix, chairman. It was moved and carried that the report be adopted, as follows:

REPORT OF COMMITTEE ON STEWARDSHIP.

Your Committee on Stewardship and Church Finance has endeavored to encourage the larger stewardship throughout the entire Conference during the past year, and to that end great emphasis has been placed upon the consecration of all of life instead of the stewardship of money. The committee believes with St. Paul, that in stewards, a man should be found faithful in the distribution of his time, his talents, his opportunities and his life.

We, your committee, have sought to discover what pastors and Churches have been doing toward the promotion of this vital subject among their people. The chairman of the committee has written twenty-five letters in the interest of the work of stewardship, tithing and consecrated wealth.

The following facts have been compiled from questionnaires sent to the various ministers of the Conference:

1. What books have you read during the past year on stewardship? To this question, only five ministers reported having read any books at all on stewardship, ownership, tithing or giving. Among books listed as read were such as "The Larger Stewardship," by Cooke; "The Stewardship of Life," by Crawford; "Stewardship for All of Life," Lovejoy; "A Man and His Money problems"; "Money the Acid Test"; "Studies in Christian Stewardship"; "Life as a Stewardship," Merrill.

The committee wonders why the ministry fails to read more good books on these vital questions, especially in view of the great number that are continually coming from the press and are sold at such reasonable prices.

2. Do you put special stress on the every-member canvass? To this question, ten answered "yes" and three "no," while three others did not answer the question.

3. (Deleted.)

4. Does your Church use the budget plan, and is it satisfactory? To this question, fourteen Churches reported "yes," and as a result, ten reported no deficit at end of year.

5. Has your Church had a stewardship play, pageant, pantomime or institute during the past year? Only three Churches reported having made such a presentation of the message.

6. How many sermons have you preached during the past year on the subject of "Stewardship"? To this came answers in the affirmative that all have delivered sermons on this subject. Some have preached only one sermon; others as many as fifteen.

7. Has your Church a stewardship secretary? To this came affirmative answers from Franklin, Christian Temple, Suffolk, Holy Neck, First (Norfolk).

8. To the question, Do you tithe? every minister answered "yes." Most of them reported that all members of their families tithed.

9. From reports received, there are approximately fifty tithers in Christian Temple; Elm Avenue reports 20 tithers; First, Norfolk, 12; Franklin, 45; Portsmouth, 35. Others no report; but from last year's report we find that over 200 tithers are in the Conference.

10. To the question, What per cent of your membership contribute toward local and benevolent expenses? we report: Holland, 70 per cent; Portsmouth, 85 per cent; Richmond, 50 per cent; Suffolk, 45 per cent; First Church, Norfolk, 50 per cent; Christian Temple, 60 per cent; South Norfolk, 65 per cent; Portsmouth Congregational Church, 75 per cent; Holy Neck, 75 per cent; Franklin, 80 per cent; Dendron, 60 per cent; Elm Avenue, 40 per cent; Waverly, 50 per cent.

11. Recommendations. Your committee recommends that:

(1) Every pastor read at least one good book on stewardship each quarter during the coming year.

(2) That he encourage the laymen of his Church to read books, leaflets and articles on the subject, and that attention be called to such subject-matter personally and from pulpit.

(3) That at least one month of special preparation be given to the every-member canvass.

(4) That during the stewardship period of our Church, effort be put forth to enroll and enlist tithers.

(5) That each Church have a "stewardship secretary," whose duty it will be to promote the work of finances, introduce new material on stewardship, and present pageants, plays and contests on stewardship.

(6) That a series of stewardship institutes be held throughout the Conference during the coming year.

J. W. FIX, *Chairman.*
W. C. HOOK.
W. H. DENISON.

Address on "Stewardship" by Dr. W. H. Denison, Dayton, Ohio.

Report of the Committee on Foreign Missions was read by Dr. L. E. Smith, chairman, and, on motion, adopted, as follows:

REPORT OF COMMITTEE ON FOREIGN MISSIONS.

We are in a period of transition, going from a single denomination to a United Church. Steps to unite the Congregational and Christian Churches throughout the country are about completed. Individual Churches have already merged. Conferences and State organizations in different parts of the country have united and are functioning as one. The union has already been completed in Porto Rico and Japan.

The Southern Christian Convention and the Congregational Church of the Southeast took formal action uniting the two bodies in convention assembled at Raleigh, N. C., last May. Officials of the two bodies were charged with the responsibility of completing the organization of the United Church and formulating plans for co-operation and advance.

The General Mission Boards (home and foreign) of the Congregational Church and the Christian Church have already united, and our secretaries, Drs. Sparks and Minton, are retained by the United Church. Dr. Sparks will divide his time with the Congregational and Christian wing of the Church; Dr. Minton is retained as Secretary of the Commission on Missions, with office in Dayton, Ohio, directing his attention largely to the constituency of the Christian Church. The Congregational and Christian Churches will hold a joint session in Seattle, Wash., next June, when the final actions will be taken completing the merger nationally and internationally. Naturally, members of the Southern Convention and of this Conference will be wondering what effect, if any, the merger will have on our missionary efforts locally. It will have no adverse or disintergrading effect whatsoever; but, on the other hand, will greatly widen our vision, increase our opportunities, and multiply our responsibilities. Whereas, heretofore, our efforts have been centered necessarily at home, in Porto Rico, and in Japan, now the home field is enlarged and the possibilities for foreign work are multiplied over and over again. We now have the privilege of going literally into all the world to carry the gospel. The great mission fields of the world become ours. This very fact should allay any fancied disturbance and greatly enlarge our work and giving. Therefore, be it resolved:

First: That we express our gratitude to Almighty God for these enlarged opportunities that have come to the kingdom in our day.

Second: That we approve the Southern Convention's asking for $50,000 this year for missions, and that we pledge ourselves and the Churches of our Conference to put forth every possible effort to raise this amount.

Fourth: That we accept the Mission Board's request that we, as individual Churches, accept as our quota for missions during the year one-third as much as we pay our pastor, and that we pledge ourselves and our Churches to undertake to raise this amount.

Fifth: That we urge the Churches of our Conference to adopt the plan of systematic giving to missions. That they use the duplex envelope so as to give every member the opportunity of making a contribution to benevolences every Sunday, or as often as he may meet for worship in his Church.

Sixth: That we greatly thank the Congregational Church for giving to us the "Guest Book" idea, which brings to us and to our families in a very effective way our mission fields and our missionaries engaged in their work; and that we, as a Conference, adopt this idea and urge our Churches to join heartily in the plan another year when suggested by our national organization.

Seventh: That we express to the Woman's Mission Board of our Conference our great appreciation of their splendid organization and commendable work that they are doing for our Church at home and abroad.

Eighth: That we express to our Mission Secretary, Dr. J. O. Atkinson, and his assistant, Mr. J. M. Darden, our recognition of the disadvantage under which they have been compelled to work during the past year, and our appreciation for the splendid achievements of their efforts; that we pledge to them our full co-operation in an endeavor to reach the Convention's goal during this year.

Respectfully submitted,
L. E. SMITH.
J. M. DARDEN.
M. J. W. WHITE.

Address, "The Guest Book," by Dr. Charles Eldred Shelton.

Address, "God Never Quits," by Dr. J. O. Atkinson, Mission Secretary.

It was moved and carried that a committee be appointed to confer with a committee from the Middle Atlantic Conference of Congregational Churches, concerning the union of Congregational and Christian Churches in this section, under the name of the Eastern Virginia Conference of Congregational and Christian Churches.

The minutes were read and approved.

Conference adjourned till evening session. Benediction by Dr. W. H. Denison.

FIRST DAY—EVENING SESSION.

Conference met at 7:30 o'clock. Service of worship in charge of Rev. O. D. Poythress. Devotional service conducted by Rev. M. F. Allen. Prayer by Dr. W. D. Harward.

Address, "The Christian Orphanage," by Mr. Chas. D. Johnston, superintendent.

The report of the Woman's Missionary Conference was read by Mrs. Russell T. Bradford and, on motion, adopted, as follows:

REPORT OF WOMAN'S MISSIONARY CONFERENCE.

The eighteenth annual session of the Woman's Home and Foreign Missionary Conference met at the Christian Temple Friday, October 24, 1930, with a splendid attendance. The main auditorium was filled with women from all parts of our Conference who came to enjoy the program and hear the reports for the year. Every officer and superintendent was present, except our Conference Editor, Mrs. J. W. Fix, whose place was taken on the program by her worthy husband, she being busy at home entertaining her new son, who had very recently arrived.

The Conference theme, "Shall We Be Witnesses," was carried out in the entire program. From the opening devotional service, led by Mrs. H. C. Caviness, until the benediction by Mr. Caviness, we were made to feel that we were witnesses and that we were necessary in our various phases of the work. Each district superintendent read with enthusiasm her report for the year and demonstrated by figures, numbers of meetings held, and results obtained, that the Conference had some very faithful witnesses during the year 1930. The departmental superintendent gave illuminating reviews, and one thought as one listened that, with the cultivating of our spiritual life program under the direction of Mrs. W. H. Andrews, of Suffolk, and the literature department under Mrs. J. E. Cartwright, our work would necessarily go forward. To be enriched with a deeper spiritual thinking and informed from a broader study will bring about a new zeal in our cause and add to our number many other witnesses.

Our Treasurer, Mrs. W. V. Leathers, brought her splendid report, showing charts and stars for special recognition. In spite of the financial depression so much talked of, our receipts were exactly the same as last year, $7,291, with a total membership of 2,290. This amount was made possible through the liberality of our faithful friend, Mr. J. M. Darden, of Suffolk. Because of Mr. Darden's challenge at our spring rallies, we actually added nearly $800 to our total. He gave us $500 as a gift, and we raised nearly $300 extra because of his challenge.

Mrs. Clark Tillinghast, of New York City, brought us an inspiring message, with a subject "Modern Miniatures." These modern miniatures that she presented proved to be a marvelous type of witnesses for Christ. At times her message put us to shame because of our poor efforts when compared with those she presented. Dr. L. E. Smith, using as his theme, "The Passion Play—A Witness," gave us a wonderful interpretation of that great event.

Banners were awarded to Holy Neck Woman's Missionary Society, Franklin Willing Workers, Holy Neck Cradle Roll. Honorable mention was given the Woman's Societies at Holland, the Temple, First Church (Portsmouth), and Bethlehem. The Willing Workers who received honorable mention were Holy Neck, Holland and Windsor.

Mrs. I. W. Johnson had charge of a service devoted to the memory of those of our ranks who had been called to their reward during the year.

At the Young People's Conference, held on Tuesday evening, October 21st, at Suffolk Christian Church, and presided over by Miss Mary Lee Williams, the Young People's Conference banner was awarded to the Berta Rowland Missionary Society at Holland, with honorable mention going to the Young People's Societies at Franklin, Holy Neck and Bethlehem. The attendance banner for that occasion going to Old Zion, Norfolk, and Bethlehem. The Conference attendance banner went to the Young People of Cypress Chapel and Barrett Society of Holland. Holy Neck Cradle Roll Society, having won their banner for three consecutive times, will keep it. This is the first banner to be kept by a society in the history of our Conference.

It was the regret of every one present that our field secretary, Dr. J. O. Atkinson, was not present. He had been sent as our ambassador to another meeting. We received his message and his place was taken on the program by his assistant secretary, Mr. J. M. Darden.

In closing fifteen years of work, which has been such a happy work, I want to tell you that my deepest interest will always be your growth and usefulness. I am leaving a task that has been a pleasure from the very beginning. No person has ever received more hearty and loyal support from every source possible than it has been my pleasure to experience. The splendid co-operation of the ministers has been our corner-stone.

We submit to you the following officers for the year 1930-'31:

WOMAN'S CONFERENCE.

President—Mrs. R. T. Bradford, R. F. D. 5, Suffolk, Va.
Vice-President—Mrs. O. M. Cockes, Elberon, Va,
Secretary—Mrs. L. W. Stagg, Norfolk, Va.
Treasurer—Mrs. W. V. Leathers, Suffolk, Va.
Sup't of Literature—Mrs. J. E. Cartwright, Norfolk, Va.
Sup't of Spiritual Life—Mrs. W. H. Andrews, Suffolk, Va.
Sup't of Life Membership and Memorials—Mrs. O. S. Mills, Norfolk, Va.
Sup't of Young People—Mrs. E. L. Beale, Franklin, Va.
Sup't of Cradle Roll—Mrs. F. M. Nelson, Norfolk, Va.
Conference Editor—Mrs. W. M. Jay, Holland, Va.

YOUNG PEOPLE'S CONFERENCE.

President—Miss Mary Lee Williams, Franklin, Va.
Vice-President—Miss Carolyn Gort, Portsmouth, Va.
Secretary—Miss Sarah Norfleet Daughtrey, Holland, Va.
Assistant Secretary—Miss Rachael Brinkley, Suffolk, Va.

Respectfully submitted,
MRS. J. MONROE HARRIS.

Conference sermon, "Loosed for Service," by Rev. J. F. Morgan.

Conference adjourned till 9:30 A. M. Thursday. Benediction by Dr. L. E. Smith.

SECOND DAY—MORNING SESSION.

Conference met and called to order at 9:30 o'clock. Song service conducted by Rev. J. F. Morgan. Devotional service conducted by Rev. T. N. Lowe, Portsmouth, Va.; Scripture lesson, Rom. 8:1-15.

Report of Committee on Religious Literature was read by Rev. J. E. McCauley, chairman, and, on motion, adopted, as follows:

REPORT OF COMMITTEE ON RELIGIOUS LITERATURE.

Every progressive move in religion, and every great revival of religion since the time of Christ has been fostered by a return to something. These moves of progress have been a turning back to catch up the broken chords that they might respond again. The Renaissance was a return to the ancient classics; the Reformation was a return to the biblical interpretation of Christ and God's word. It was a return to the experimental religion of the early Church. The great spiritual awakening of the Wesley brothers and eighteenth-century revival was simply a return to the new emphasis upon an old truth which is found in the great Book of books.

That such a need is prevalent in this age cannot be denied by any clear-thinking individual. The daily newspaper, the most of the magazines, and, in many instances, the so-called religious literature are not conducive to developing Christian character; nor do they promote high ideals and lofty thinking. The daily paper is filled with attacks on so much of the fundamentals of Christian character that one is almost prone to denounce the whole of the daily press. So many of the magazines, either by its literature or its advertisements, appeal to the sexual and sensual, that one hardly knows what to allow in his home. There is much in religious literature that is to be looked upon with suspicion and caution. We are not so sure that many of the changes made in our Sunday School materials and organizations mean real progress. It seems, from some of the harvest that we are reaping in our Churches, that we are to guard with care for the next few years the type of literature which we are to use. Each of these problems adds new responsibilities to the religious leaders of our denomination and Churches. It is the opinion of your committee that the only safe course is to return to something that has been lost. That loss is a devout study of the Word of God. This is needed in the home, in the pulpit and in the Sunday School.

We, therefore, urge that it be the sentiment of this Conference that more careful study be given to the Bible in the above-mentioned places. "Thy Word is a lamp unto my feet and a light unto my path" (Psa. 119:105).

We urge an attempt on the part of the ministry and Church leaders to get more subscriptions to *The Christian Sun, Congregationalist and Herald of Gospel Liberty* and *Missionary Herald.*

We, therefore, urge that increased effort be made to get homes to read more of such literature of the above-mentioned type.

> J. E. McCAULEY, *Chairman.*
> CHARLES ELDRED SHELTON.
> F. M. BREWER.
> C. E. GERRINGER.

Address, "Religious Literature," by Dr. Charles Eldred Shelton. Discussion by Dr. J. O. Atkinson, M. W. Hollowell, Dr. L. E. Smith.

Rev. Ira S. Harrell, of the Baptist Church, and Dr. W. M. Jay, Holland, Va., were introduced to the Conference.

Report of the Committee on Christian Education was read by Dr. W. W. Staley, chairman, and, on motion, adopted, as follows:

REPORT OF COMMITTEE ON EDUCATION.

Among savage nations, education rises no higher than training the body for hunting and war; if further instruction, it came through the priests of their religion. In Egypt, religion and education went hand in hand. Jews were always noted for education, and it was largely religious. In Greece, the claims of the State were supreme in religion, and prominence was given to gymnastics and music.

In early Rome, education was influenced by the home, and then followed religious schools; and down to the present, religion controls Roman schools.

Modern education in all its branches had its origin in Christianity. Jesus was the great Teacher, and wherever His gospel is taught, education takes root and all kinds of schools spring up, though many of them ignore the springs from which they came. This tendency has crept into institutions so quietly that many schools that stand for Christian education have come under the control of intellectuals who neglect the Christian values of education for the whole man, and Christian ideals drop out of the program.

The recognition of Christian character and Christian principles in human associations and service is the chief reason for a Church college; and Elon College claims as its motto, "Christian Character First and Always." If it maintains that profession, it is worthy of patronage from all families of the Southern Christian Convention and of this Conference.

The chief subject taught in Mohammedan schools is the Koran. False religions are stricter in teaching and observing their faiths than Christian schools; and this, no doubt, accounts for weak biblical teaching from pulpits, compared with former years. The schools are largely responsible for sermons based on other sources than the Word of God.

No application for ordination has been received by the committee during the year.

We recommend:

1. That Revs. D. D. Nash, J. B. Chadwick, Dennis F. Parsons, Lester Ellsworth Huber and J. T. Harrod be continued on the list of licentiates.

2. That $200 be loaned to J. Howard Smith, who will graduate from Elon College at the next commencement.

Rev. Floyd D. Ballard has paid his note in full for $150 during the present session of this Conference, and has requested a letter of transfer to the Presbyterian Church.

After considering the application of Rev. John H. Warren, of the Methodist Church, to become a member of the Eastern Virginia Christian Conference, the committee recommends that he be received and enrolled as an elder and member of this Conference upon the presentation of certificate showing good standing in the Methodist Episcopal Church.

FINANCIAL EXHIBIT.

Cash in Farmers Bank of Nansemond	$4,737.09	
Elon College bonds	6,000.00	
		$10,737.09
Notes:		
C. W. Rountree	350.00	
J. W. Barrett, Jr.	365.00	
J. C. Barrett	270.00	
Harold C. Hainer	400.00	
Fred T. Wright	500.00	
Floyd D. Ballard (paid)	150.00	
		2,065.09

Account:

J. T. Harrod 225.00
                                                        ———————
   Total $12,997.09

Respectfully submitted,

W. W. STALEY,
N. G. NEWMAN,
I. W. JOHNSON,
Committee.

Addresses by Dr. F. E. Jenkins, Mr. S. C. Heindel, Dr. L. E. Smith and Dr. W. A. Harper.

Chaplain H. E. Rountree, U. S. N., led in a devotional service.

Conference adjourned for lunch. Benediction by Chaplain H. E. Rountree.

SECOND DAY—AFTERNOON SESSION.

Conference met and called to order at 2:15 o'clock. Song service conducted by Mr. W. H. Baker. Devotional service conducted by Rev. C. E. Gerringer.

Rev. Floyd D. Ballard was granted a letter of transfer to a presbytery of the Presbyterian Church in Mississippi.

Rev. J. W. Barrett, Sr., requested that his name be dropped from the roll as an elder and member of Conference, and this request was granted.

Report of the Committee on Ministerial Ethics was read by Dr. N. G. Newman, chairman, and adopted, as follows:

REPORT OF COMMITTEE ON MINISTERIAL ETHICS.

Your committee recognizes the ministry as the highest and holiest of callings, and that it demands the highest thought, the purest life, and the most exemplary conduct possible.

We, therefore, recommend:

1. That the Conference carefully guard the portals to the ministry, that only the competent and worthy be admitted, and that it keep a jealous watch over the character and reputation of its ministers, that the worthy may be protected and the unworthy be excluded.

2. That our ministers seek to be pure in heart, chaste in speech, and prudent in social contacts; that they respect the sanctity and immunity of the pulpit, and refrain from the use therein of coarse language, improper themes, personal flings, and otherwise improper or uncalled-for remarks.

3. That our ministers recognize the moral and spiritual value of Christian brotherhood, and seek to cultivate brotherly intercourse and fellowship, that they may understand each other, have proper sympathy for, and be mutually strengthening to, each other.

4. That ministers exercise the greatest prudence in making financial obligations, and the strictest fidelity in meeting the same, and that they avoid debt for current living expenses if possible.

5. That, inasmuch as all conduct is but an expression of the spirit within, that ministers study and pray and worship until they have such an experience with God that they can bear His message and wear His character.

6. That the name of Rev. M. W. Sutcliffe be dropped from the roll of elders. (Note: This item was referred to a special committee to investigate alleged reports.—*Sec'y.*)

N. G. NEWMAN.
W. D. HARWARD.
M. W. HOLLOWELL.

Revs. N. G. Newman, W. D. Harward, and H. C. Caviness were appointed a special committee to investigate alleged reports concerning Rev. M. W. Sutcliffe and to report concerning the matter of dropping his name from the roll of elders, as recommended in item 6 of above report.

Report of W. E. McClenny, Treasurer, was read by the Treasurer, as follows, and referred to the Committee on Finance:

REPORT OF TREASURER.

1929.   CONVENTION FUND.

Nov. 6.	Balance reported	$ 23.52
12.	Deposit, Conference collections	6,802.86
		$6,826.38
	Paid Secretary's draft No. 5	6,825.00
1930.		
Oct. 29.	Balance in bank	$ 1.38

1929.   CONFERENCE FUND.

Nov. 6.	Balance reported		$ 176.05
12.	Deposit, Conference collections		400.00
			$ 576.05
Nov. 12.	Paid Secretary's draft No. 2	$ 53.48	
27.	Paid Secretary's draft No. 7	5.00	
Dec. 17.	Paid Secretary's draft No. 9	8.90	
	Paid Secretary's draft No. 8	6.15	
1930.			
Jan. 2.	Paid Secretary's draft No. 10	1.40	
Mar. 8.	Paid Secretary's draft No. 12	300.00	
			374.93
Oct. 29.	Balance in bank		$ 201.12

1929.   EDUCATIONAL FUND.

Nov. 6.	Balance reported	$3,947.09
12.	Conference collections	200.00
	By check, Rev. T. Fred Wright	100.00
1930.		
Jan. 2.	Paid by Mr. C. W. Rountree on note	50.00
June 30.	Interest on $4,000, 6 mos. in bank	80.00
Sep. 8.	By interest on $6,000 Elon College bonds	360.00
Oct. 29.	Balance in bank	$4,737.09

Active account	$ 657.09
Savings account	4,080.00
	$4,737.09

1929.   CONVENTION MISSION FUND.

Nov. 6. Balance reported .... $ 18.94
     16. Paid Secretary's draft No. 3.........................   18.94

1929.   FOREIGN MISSION FUND.

Nov. 6. Balance reported .... $ 50.25
     16. Paid Secretary's draft No. 4.........................   50.25

1929.   HOME MISSION FUND.

Nov. 6. Balance reported .... $ 34.25
     12. Conference collections 1,500.00
                                                                 $1,534.25
Nov. 15. Paid Secretary's draft No. 2...................$ 500.00
     20. Paid Secretary's draft No. 6................ ......$1,000.00
1930.   ——————— 1,500.00

Oct. 29. Balance in bank .... $ 34.25

1929.   SPECIAL COLLECTION ACCOUNT.

(Representing Conference assessments paid in before Conference.)

Nov. 6. Balance reported $3,800.00
1930.
Jan. 9. Deposit, Suffolk Christian Church 500.00
Apr. 10. Deposit, Suffolk Christian Church 500.00
July 10. Deposit, Suffolk Christian Church 500.00
Oct. 7. Deposit, Suffolk Christian Church 500.00
     22. Deposit, Liberty Spring Church 295.00

1929. $6,095.00
Nov. 12. Paid Secretary's draft No. 1......................... 3,800.00
1930.
Oct. 29. Balance in bank $2,295.00

RECAPITULATION.

Funds.	Bal. 1929.	Receipts.	Disbursed.	Bal. 1930.
Convention Missions ....$ 18.94		......	$ 18.94	......
Convention Fund	23.52	$6,802.86	6,825.00	$ 1.38
Conference Fund	176.05	400.00	374.93	201.12
Educational Fund	3,947.09	790.00	......	4,737.09
Foreign Mission Fund	50.25	......	50.25	......
Home Mission Fund	34.25	1,500.00	1,500.00	34.25
Special Collection Account....	3,800.00	2,295.00	3,800.00	2,295.00
Totals $8,050.10		$11,787.86	$12,569.12	$7,268.84

Proof.

Balance November 6, 1929.............................$ 8,050.10
Total receipts 11,787.86
                                                       ——————— $19,837.96
Disbursed $12,569.12
Balances October 29, 1930........................... 7,268.84
                                                       ——————— $19,837.96

Schedule of Bonds and Bills Receivable.

Six Elon College bonds, $1,000 each............................	$6,000.00
C. W. Rountree's note, balance	350.00
J. W. Barrett, Jr., note	365.00
J. Cleveland Barrett's note	270.00
H. C. Hainer's note	400.00
T. Fred Wright's note	500.00
F. D. Ballard's note	150.00
Total bonds and individual notes	$8,035.00

The passbook, vouchers and above securities have been exhibited to the Secretary of the Conference, and are held in the vault of the Farmers Bank of Nansemond, Suffolk, Va., subject to the order of the Conference. The bond of the Treasurer of the Conference is in the hands of the President.

Respectfully submitted,

W. E. MacClenny, *Treasurer.*

Suffolk, Va., October 29, 1930.

At the request of Mr. W. E. MacClenny, Treasurer, Eastern Virginia Christian Conference, I beg to hereby certify that he has on deposit in the Farmers Bank of Nansemond, Suffolk, Va., the balances as shown by this report to the credit of the several funds—total, $7,268.84. He has also exhibited to me $6,000 in Elon College coupon bonds.

(Signed in duplicate.) H. M. Holland, *Cashier.*

The report of the Committee on Moral Reform was read by Dr. C. C. Ryan, chairman. A supplemental report was read by Mr. S. M. Smith. It was moved and carried that both reports be referred back to the Committee on Moral Reform.

The report of Mr. W. E. MacClenny, Historian, was read and adopted, as follows:

REPORT OF HISTORIAN.

During the year just closed, nothing new has been discovered concerning the history of this Conference.

We regret that the marker to the memory of James O'Kelly, our early leader in the South, which has been erected on the campus at Elon College, is not fully paid for. This should be provided for in some way.

Many of our local Churches are now growing old, and have much history connected with them, and we would advise that each Church that is fifty or more years old hold an historical service on some anniversary date, having papers prepared by the best local talent available on its history for the occasion. By doing this, much of our history that is so fast slipping away from us will be preserved for the use of the coming generations, especially if it is published in *The Christian Sun.*

All of which is respectfully submitted.

W. E. MacClenny, *Historian.*

It was moved and carried that $100 be paid to Dr. J. O. Atkinson, treasurer of the O'Kelly Memorial Fund, and the Secretary was authorized to draw a draft for this money from the Conference fund, to assist in paying off the debt on O'Kelly Monument, erected on the campus at Elon College.

The claims of the Christian Missionary Association were presented by Rev. J. W. Fix and H. C. Caviness, president of the C. M. A.

It was moved and carried that the report of the Committee on Evangelism be carried over until tomorrow.

The report of the Committee on Christian Education was read by Rev. R. E. Brittle, chairman, and adopted, as follows:

REPORT OF COMMITTEE ON CHRISTIAN EDUCATION.

Your committee believes there is a great need for Christian education throughout the bounds of this Conference, and the Conference, through its committee, should put a great deal of emphasis upon this work.

The Board of Christian Education of the Southern Christian Convention is in a position, to a large extent, to supply a great need, if the Churches of the Conference, through the committee, will take advantage of the services of the Board. Your committee therefore recommends:

1. That the Conference pledge its support and co-operation to the Board of Christian Education of the Southern Christian Convention, and seek to raise its proportional share of funds through the Sunday Schools and Christian Endeavor Societies, and the Sunday School and Christian Endeavor Convention.

2. That a sufficient number of courses in leadership training be held at various and convenient Churches in order that all Churches throughout the Conference may have advantage of these courses.

3. That Churches be urged, through the committee, to use the field secretary of the Board of Christian Education of the Southern Christian Convention.

4. That all Churches be urged to patronize the Summer School of Methods at Elon College.

5. That the Conference, through its committee, co-operate with and assist the Youth's Congress of Eastern Virginia.

R. E. BRITTLE.
F. C. LESTER.
J. E. McCAULEY.
W. H. BAKER.

Rev. H. E. Rountree and Mr. F. M. Brewer were added to the Committee on Resolutions.

The Committee on Nominations submitted the following report:

REPORT OF COMMITTEE ON NOMINATIONS.

The Committee on Nominations submits its report as follows:

President—Rev. H. S. Hardcastle, Suffolk, Va.
Vice-President—Dr. J. W. Manning, Norfolk, Va.
Secretary—Dr. I. W. Johnson, Suffolk, Va.
Assistant Secretary—Rev. J. F. Morgan, Norfolk, Va.
Treasurer—W. E. MacClenny, Suffolk, Va.

Respectfully submitted,
C. C. RYAN,
MRS. O. D. KING,
W. D. HARWARD,
W. H. GARMAN,
M. J. W. WHITE,
Committee.

On motion, Conference adjourned till evening session. Benediction by Rev. D. M. Spence.

SECOND DAY—EVENING SESSION.

Conference met at 7:30 o'clock. Song service conducted by Rev. O. D. Poythress. An illustrated lecture on "The Passion Play" was given by Dr. L. E. Smith.

Benediction by Dr. L. E. Smith.

THIRD DAY— MORNING SESSION.

Conference met and called to order at 9:30 o'clock. Song service conducted by Rev. J. F. Morgan. Devotional service led by Rev. W. D. Harward, D. D. Scripture lesson, 96th Psalm.

Report of Committee on Apportionments was read by Mr. C. D. West and adopted, as follows:

REPORT OF COMMITTEE ON APPORTIONMENTS.

We, your Committee on Apportionments, submit the following report for the year 1930-'31:

Antioch	$ 150.00	Johnson's Grove	100.00
Barrett's	140.00	Liberty Spring	295.00
Berea (Nansemond)	200.00	Mt. Carmel	150.00
Berea (Norfolk)	150.00	Mt. Zion	40.00
Bethlehem	280.00	Newport News	300.00
Burton's Grove	75.00	New Lebanon	65.00
Centerville	45.00	Ocean View	25.00
Christian Temple	1,250.00	Old Zion	300.00
Cypress Chapel	150.00	Oak Grove	50.00
Damascus	155.00	Oakland	225.00
Dendron	65.00	Rosemont	250.00
Eure	150.00	Suffolk	2,000.00
Elm Avenue	75.00	South Norfolk	500.00
First, Norfolk	450.00	Spring Hill	50.00
First, Portsmouth	175.00	St. Luke's	10.00
First, Richmond	200.00	St. Paul's	10.00
Franklin	400.00	Sarem	35.00
Holland	450.00	Union (Southampton)	95.00
Hobson	10.00	Union (Surry)	50.00
Holy Neck	300.00	Wakefield	85.00
Hopewell	25.00	Waverly	325.00
Isle of Wight	40.00	Windsor	125.00
Ivor	40.00	Webster	50.00
Epworth	10.00		
		Total	$10,030.00

Respectfully submitted,

C. D. WEST,
R. B. ODOM,
B. E. WHITE,
L. R. JONES,
Committee.

Report of the Committee on Memoirs was read by Dr. N. G. Newman and adopted, as follows:

REPORT OF COMMITTEE ON MEMOIRS.

Your Committee on Memoirs is grateful to report that there have been no deaths during the year among our ministers or official members.

N. G. NEWMAN.

Profs. S. A. Bennet and O. W. Johnson, of Elon College, were introduced to the Conference.

Report of Committee on Place for Next Session was submitted, and it was moved and carried that the Conference accept the invitation of Cypress Chapel as a place for holding the next session of Conference.

The report of the Collectors was read by Mr. R. C. Norfleet, chairman, and adopted, as follows:

REPORT OF COLLECTORS.

We, your Collectors, beg to report that the amount collected from Churches for this session is $8,318, with the following eight Churches not reporting any amount: Dendron, Hobson, Ocean View, Hopewell, Oak Grove, St. Luke's, St. Paul's and Webster; Newport News agrees to send the balance of $225. (For amount paid by each Church, see "Statistical Table," under head "Paid of Conference Apportionments."—Sec'y.)

R. C. NORFLEET,
M. W. HOLLOWELL,
Collectors.

The following supplemental report of the Committee on Education was offered and, on motion, adopted:

SUPPLEMENTAL REPORT, COMMITTEE ON EDUCATION.

1. We recommend that Rev. W. M. Jay, D. D., a member of the N. C. and Va. Christian Conference, who has accepted the pastorate of the Holland Christian Church, be received and enrolled as a member of the Eastern Virginia Christian Conference, upon a letter of transfer to this Conference, deposited with the Secretary of Conference.

2. We recommend the licensure of J. Howard Smith, a senior in Elon College, and a candidate for the ministry, and request that Rev. W. C. Wicker, D. D., President of the Eastern North Carolina Christian Conference, license him at the approaching session of said Conference. A certificate of licensure will be furnished President Wicker by the President and Secretary of this Conference.

W. W. STALEY,
N. G. NEWMAN,
I. W. JOHNSON,
Committee.

Rev. John H. Warren was introduced to the Conference.

The report of the Committee on Moral Reform was again submitted by Dr. C. C. Ryan, chairman. After considerable discussion, the report was adopted, as follows:

REPORT OF COMMITTEE ON MORAL REFORM.

Morals mean custom, habit, way of life, conduct, springing from or pertaining to man's natural sense of what is right or proper. It means conforming to or embodying righteous or just conduct.

Knowing the rightness of God's laws, and knowing, too, that conduct in harmony with His laws need no reformation, the very expression of "moral reform" brings the overwhelming consciousness that somebody is living under the thraldom of laws and influences not in accord with His kingdom.

There are two main thoughts relative to the word reform. First, "to bring back as to a previous state; to reform." Second, "to put or change into a new or improved form or condition, and thus by an improved condition induce men and women to abandon evil ways and adhere to that which will bring the kingdom of God among men. We need not go far or search long to find the way of our Master.

The laws of God, as revealed in the Ten Commandments, and the laws of Moses may not be all-inclusive as to the proper life of men and women in home and public life actions in this twentieth century, but when Jesus Christ, bearing the significance of God, sums it all up, then He says: "Thou shalt love the Lord thy God with all thy heart, and thy neighbor as thyself."

Hence, the law that needs no amendment and the life and conduct that needs no reformation are those which harmonize with His mandate of love.

Because of all this we, as representatives of His kingdom, call upon the ministers and Church-folk of Conference to take no backward step, but to call upon (by example and preaching) the people to look the better to the conduct and lives of the ones in our homes, to teach our children the worth of clean bodies, and clean minds, and that proper living in the marriage relation is one of the essential things of this time. Therefore, we deplore the rapid increase of the divorce evil; that we enter our plea for more stringent divorce laws. That the Church should encourage that which is pure and clean and discourage all influences that are hurtful to morals and hinder the development of Christian character.

We believe that the kingdom of God is hindered and a clear conception of our religious duty is befogged by the modern social life. Too many bars let down, and too much time wasted by the so-called social life, both in and out of the Church.

·Recognizing the vital importance of the Lord's Day, the basis of all our religious work, and clearly seeing the dangers which threaten its meaning and purpose, especially through a commercialization of the day by persistent invasions of amusements and sport societies, and in view of the urgent need of a better observance of the Lord's Day and for its proper protection, we ask you to endorse the following resolutions:

First: Be it resolved, That this Eastern Virginia Christian Conference commend the Lord's Day Alliance of the State of Virginia, which is our representative in this department of Christian and civic activity.

Second: Be it further resolved, That we elect two members, one layman and one minister, for membership on the board of managers of the Alliance, and that we call upon our people of the Churches to give their support to the work of the organization of which the Rev. J. W. Morgan, of Richmond, Va., is the State secretary.

Third: That we request our preachers to preach at least one sermon annually on the subject of the Lord's Day, and request that teachers and parents give more faithful instruction in the proper observance of the Lord's Day.

Fourth: That we commend the movement for the enactment of a Sunday rest law for the District of Columbia, and that we commend the President of the United States in his faithful observance of the Sabbath and earnestly hope that he will use his influence for the attainment of a better Sabbath observance throughout the nation.

Again, we want to register our protest to any weakening or annulment of the prohibition law.

We know that today there is a mobilization of all the "wet" forces in America in one final effort to break down the morals of the Christian forces which have been the enemy of the liquor traffic. The "wet" organizations are being financed by a group of very rich men, and with the aid of the subsidized newspapers, they are flinging a challenge into the hosts of the Man of Galilee, and in His name we accept it, and in His name hurl back the defiance, "America shall not go back!"

Quoting from the Congressional Record the words of Evangeline Booth, we say, "My God, Thou knowest it. Shall America go back?"

Drink has drained more blood, hung more crepe, sold more homes, plunged more people into bankruptcy, armed more villians, slain more children, snapped more wedding rings, defiled more innocence, blinded more eyes, twisted more limbs, dethroned more reason, wrecked more manhood, dishonored more lives, driven more to suicide, and dug more graves than any other poisoned scourge that ever swept its death-dealing waves across the world.

. Can it be that men and women are so bewildered by selfishness and beset by appetite, that they will take again into their national life, into the bosom of their homes, this baneful, loathsome, reeking, wrecking abomination? Shall America go back? ·

In view of the present conditions, we ask for the adoption:

First: Be it resolved, That we, as ministers, delegates, and Church folks of the Eastern Virginia Christian Conference, deplore the present "hysteria" of "wet" propaganda, and declare that we believe it to be "all bunk"; that it is absolutely false.

Second: We, your committee, believe that the Church should present a solid front against the organized forces of evil, so we plead with every voter of our constituency to exercise his or her full power of selecting for public office men and women of character and ability who are willing to support the Constitution of the United States, including the eighteenth amendment.

Third: That we acknowledge the worth of the Anti-Saloon League as a forceful and righteous agency in the great fight for God, home and humanity against the demon liquor, and that we pledge to it our whole-hearted support, and that we acknowledge the faithful servants of the Most High in the faithful defense of the home and nation, namely: the W. C. T. U.

Fourth: We recommend that each minister in this Conference preach a sermon between now and January 1st, if possible, on "Making Prohibition Permanent and Effective," or some similar subject; that the "Committee on Moral Reform" in this Conference be hereafter known as the "Committee on Temperance and Moral Reform," and that the President of the Southern Christian Convention be requested to appoint, if within his province, in the interim, a board of that body to be known as the "Board on Temperance and Moral Reform." We recommend further that the Committee on Temperance and Moral Reform, which the President of this Conference will appoint, be requested to give its effort during the coming year to the organization of temperance societies and the holding of temperance meetings, as far as possible, in all the Churches.

C. C. RYAN, D. D.
E. B. WHITE.
F. M. ALLEN.

The report of the Committee on Evangelism was read by Rev. H. C. Caviness, chairman, and, on motion, adopted, as follows:

REPORT OF COMMITTEE ON EVANGELISM.

We, your Committee on Evangelism, beg leave to submit the following report:

We find that the spirit of evangelism continues to grow within the bounds of this Conference; that the year just passed has witnessed many splendid achievements in this, the greatest avenue of Church activities. However, in the assurance that the future growth of the Church of Christ depends upon the evangelistic fervor and vision and spirit of its membership, we urge a committal of every Church to this program, and to that end we do hereby recommend:

1. That the basis of all real evangelism being the Word of God, we, therefore, urge a revival of Bible study and Bible application in the individual lives of our people.

2. We recommend that every Church in our Conference, so far as may be possible, conduct an evangelistic campaign at least once every year; that the campaign be directed not only toward mass, but also personal evangelism.

3. We urge personal visitation among members of the Church, those who live in the territory such Church serves, on the part of pastor and people, with a view of winning such as may be lost in these homes to the saving knowledge of Jesus Christ through the Word of God and the efficacy of His shed blood upon the cross of Calvary.

4. We urge each Church in the Conference to establish, if not already established, a weekly prayer meeting, or the meeting in groups in various homes of the community, for cottage prayer meetings, the establishment of family altars in each home of our people, praying for that revival this year that shall glorify our Lord Jesus Christ.

5. We urge the adoption of such form of evangelism in each Church as will attempt a spiritual reclamation, through love and prayerful approach, of those who are no longer active in our Church council, or those who, while possessing Church membership, have never given themselves to the surrendered service required of a disciple of Christ; those who constitute a liability to the growth of our Church programs under God, and who might become great powers under Him.

6. Toward the accomplishment of the above ends, we call upon the Church as a whole for that high and holy dedication of all things unto our Lord Jesus Christ, and for that submissive surrender of ourselves under the leadership of the Holy Spirit moved by the great challenging commission of Lord Jesus Christ when He said: "Go ye into all the world and preach the gospel to every creature" (Mark 16:15).

> H. C. CAVINESS.
> W. H. GARMAN.
> J. F. MORGAN.
> O. D. POYTHRESS.

Solo: "I Would Be Like Jesus," by Rev. O. D. Poythress.

Address: "Evangelism," Rev. C. E. Gerringer. General discussion.

Report of Committee on Superannuation was read by Dr. L. E. Smith, chairman, and adopted, as follows:

REPORT OF COMMITTEE ON SUPERANNUATION.

No case of need has been presented to your committee during the year. Plans for bringing the Christian Church in line with the Congregational Church in providing for and meeting the needs of her aged and dependent ministers have not yet been presented to the Regional Convention by the General Convention. Owing to this fact, it is necessary that we hold in abeyance any further steps to secure funds to assist those who may be in need until such action is taken and given to the Church at large. This matter will, in all probability, be worked out and settled definitely at the Seattle Convention, and at the next meeting of this Conference it will be necessary for us to take definite action. In the meantime, should any one have any plan or suggestion to offer, the committee would be glad to receive same.

Respectfully submitted,

L. E. SMITH.
F. C. LESTER.

Upon a report of the Nominating Committee, Dr. C. C. Ryan and Mr. P. J. Carlton were elected on the Board of the Lord's Day Alliance, as provided for in the report of the Committee on Moral Reform.

It was moved and carried that the minutes of this session be printed in THE ANNUAL and that 600 copies be purchased and distributed pro rata among the Churches, and the Secretary be authorized to draw draft on the Conference fund to pay for same.

It was moved and carried that the Secretary be authorized to employ a stenographer to assist in preparing the minutes at a cost of not more than $25.00.

Address by Dr. L. E. Smith, "The Supreme Business of the Church."

A general discussion of "Evangelism and Church Growth" followed this address.

The following resolution was adopted:

RESOLUTION.

Resolved, That the Churches of this Conference be requested to make a survey of their respective fields, locating the people living within their fields who do not belong to the Church, on or before January 30, 1931, and the ministers be requested to report the results of this canvass to the February meeting of the ministers; and that we seek an increase of at least 500 in the total membership of the Churches of this Conference during the next Conference year; and to this end, we suggest that the Churches devote at least one week during the year to the study of evangelism, and that we designate the first Wednesday night in January, 1931, as a time for special prayer for this purpose.

Report of the Committee on Resolutions was read by Chaplain H. E. Rountree, chairman, and adpoted, as follows:

REPORT OF COMMITTEE ON RESOLUTIONS.

We, your Committee on Resolutions, beg leave to submit the following recommendations:

1. That the Conference acknowledge the excellent and faithful service of the officers, Executive Committee, and all Conference workers in promoting the interest of the Church toward the highest ideals and demands of the kingdom, and that we extend to them our sincere thanks.

2. That the Conference extend to its host, the South Norfolk Christian Church, pastor and people, their profound appreciation and unmitigated gratitude for the cordial and delightful reception so generously and hospitably extended.

3. That we thank the local press heartily for its courteous daily accounts of the Conference proceedings.

H. E. ROUNTREE.
F. M. BREWER.
MRS. I. W. JOHNSON.
MRS. W. B. WILLIAMS.

The report of the Committee on Finance was read by Mr. E. T. Holland, chairman, and adopted, as follows:

REPORT OF COMMITTEE ON FINANCE.

We have examined the report of W. E. MacClenny, Treasurer, and find same correct.

We recommend the payment of the following amounts from the Conference Fund:

I. W. Johnson, Secretary, salary...............$ 50.00
Stationery and supplies 4.00
Central Publishing Co., programs.............. 4.00

We recommend the following division of funds:

Conference Fund ....$ 400.00
Education Fund 200.00
Home Mission Fund 1,500.00

We recommend that after the above amounts have been deducted from the amounts paid in for Conference apportionments that the Secretary be instructed to forward draft to Dr. W. C. Wicker, Treasurer Southern Christian Convention, Inc., for the remainder on hand from Conference apportionments for this year.

We further suggest that the balances on hand for foreign missions and Convention missions also be forwarded to the Treasurer of the Southern Christian Convention.

Total Conference apportionment collection for this year, $8,318.

Respectfully submitted,
E. T. HOLLAND.
OLLIE V. COCKES.

It was moved and carried that $15.00 be paid from the Conference Fund for the expenses of Dr. Warren H. Denison in attending this session of Conference.

It was moved and carried that all departments or committees wishing to secure speakers for Conference, where expenses are to be incurred, shall make known such purpose to the Executive Committee, for approval, before the session of Conference.

It was moved and carried that the Secretary of Conference be authorized to receive the amount paid in for Conference apportionments and deliver same to the Treasurer of Conference.

The President appointed the following standing committees for the ensuing year:

Executive—H. S. Hardcastle, J. W. Manning, I. W. Johnson.

Education—W. W. Staley, N. C. Newman, I. W. Johnson.

Home Missions—J. E. West, E. E. Holland, E. T. Holland, I. T. Byrd.

Foreign Missions—L. E. Smith, Mrs. R. T. Bradford, M. J. W. White, J. M. Darden.

Christian Education—J. E. McCauley, J. F. West, Jr., R. E. Brittle, W. H. Baker, F. C. Lester.

Religious Literature—W. M. Jay, F. M. Brewer, Charles Eldred Shelton, C. E. Gerringer, B. E. White.

Evangelism—H. C. Caviness, J. F. Morgan, O. D. Poythress, W. H. Garman.

Stewardship—J. W. Fix, Warren H. Denison.

Temperance and Moral Reform—W. D. Harward, C. C. Ryan, M. F. Allen, E. B. White.

Superannuation—L. E. Smith, J. A. Williams, J. M. Darden.

Ministerial Ethics—N. G. Newman, M. W. Hollowell, T. N. Lowe.

It was moved and carried that, after adjournment of this session, the Conference will attend the laying of the corner-stone of Rosemont Christian Church, at 3 P. M. today, where an appropriate program will be rendered by members of Conference.

On motion, Conference adjourned, and the next session is to be held at Cypress Chapel Christian Church, Nansemond County, Va., beginning Wednesday before the first Sunday in November, 1931, at 10:30 o'clock A. M.

Closing service conducted by Rev. E. B. White.

REV. H. S. HARDCASTLE, *President.*

I. W. JOHNSON, *Secretary.*

MINISTERIAL REPORTS.

M. F. Allen—Churches in charge: Newport News, Mt. Zion. Sermons, 121; conversions, 21; members received, 47; marriages, 12; addresses, 4; baptisms, 21; visits, 1,122; funerals, 15. Salary, $2,000.

R. E. Brittle—Churches in charge: Cypress Chapel, Bethlehem, Union (Southampton). Sermons, 146; conversions, 28; members received, 45; marriage, 1; addresses, 5; baptisms, 36; visits, 1,512; funerals, 18. Salary, $1,500.

H. C. Caviness—Church in charge: First, Portsmouth. Sermons, 200; conversions, about 200; members received, 22; marriages, 4; baptisms, 10; visits, 450. Salary, $2,760.

J. N. Cutchin—No charge; preached in ten Churches. Sermons, 21; conversions, 5; funeral, 1. Salary, $25.

Warren H. Denison—Secretary General Convention. Sermons and addresses, 93; marriages, 3; funerals, 3. Salary, $3,600.

Joseph W. Fix—Church in charge: Franklin. Sermons, 100; members received, 3; marriages, 6; addresses, 10; visits, 300. Salary, $2,400.

A. R. Flowers—No report.

J. L. Foster—No report.

W. H. Garman—Church in charge: Old Zion. Sermons, 210; conversions, 53; members received, 48; marriages, 20; addresses, 15; baptisms, 27; visits, 895; funerals, 19. Salary, $2,080.

C. E. Gerringer—Churches in charge: Wakefield, Burton's Grove, Barrett's, Ivor and New Lebanon. Sermons, 90; conversions, 34; members received, 32; marriages, 2; baptisms, 14; funerals, 20. Salary, $1,635.

H. S. Hardcastle—Church in charge: Suffolk Christian Church. Sermons, 90; conversions, 13; members received, 24; marriages, 15; baptisms, 16; visits, not known; funerals, 28. Salary, $2,500.

W. D. Harward—Church in charge: Mt. Carmel. Sermons, 30; conversions, 6; members received, 6; marriages, 7; baptisms, 4; funerals, 14. Salary, $500.

W. C. Hook—Church in charge: Holland. Sermons, 142; conversions, 61; members received, 31; marriages, 7; addresses, 5; baptisms, 26; visits, 1,057; funerals, 13. Salary, $2,500.

I. W. Johnson—Churches in charge: Berea (Nansemond), Liberty Spring and Oakland. Sermons, 76; conversions, 35; members received, 40; marriages, 111; baptisms, 27; visits, 400; funerals, 20. Salary, $1,850.

Elwood W. Jones—Church in charge: Webster. Sermons, 110; members received, 3; marriages, 18; addresses, 18; baptisms, 2; visits, 300. Salary, $1,800.

L. L. Lassiter—No charge.

Fletcher C. Lester—Churches in charge: Centerville, Spring Hill, Waverly. Sermons, 110; conversions, 3; members received, 2; addresses, 10; visits, 200; funerals, 8 Salary, $2,000.

T. N. Lowe—Church in charge: Elm Avenue. Sermons, 161; conversions, 9; members received, 15; marriages, 10; addresses, 2; baptisms, 8; visits, 1,285; funerals, 15. Salary, $1,600.

Joseph E. McCauley—Church in charge: First, Norfolk. Sermons, 113; conversions, 15; members received, 2; marriages, 8; addresses, 8; baptisms, 5; visits, 784. Salary, $2,500.

J. F. Morgan—Churches in charge: Berea (Norfolk), Rosemont. Sermons, 139; conversions, 10; members received, 10; marriages, 13; addresses, 13; baptisms, 9; visits, 1,460; funerals, 11. Salary, $2,680.

Wilson C. Moore—Church in charge—Epworth (Mission Point). Sermons, 60; conversions, 65; members received, 9; baptisms, 30; funerals, 20.

D. D. Nash—Supply: Dendron, Wakefield, Hopewell. Sermons, 22; conversions, 2; address, 1; visits, 68; funerals, 2. Salary (expenses), $60.

N. G. Newman—Church in charge—Holy Neck. Sermons, 48; conversions, 10; members received, 10; addresses, 3; baptisms, 9; visits, 330; funerals, 5. Salary, $2,000.

George A. Pearce—No charge. Sermons, 2.

O. D. Poythress—Church in charge: South Norfolk. Sermons, 198; conversions, 48; members received, 50; marriages, 25; addresses, 10; baptisms, 29; visits, 1,144; funerals, 43. Salary, $3,224.

J. M. Roberts—Churches in charge: Eure, Sarem, Oak Grove, Johnson's Grove. Sermons, 52; conversions, 60; members received, 52; marriages, 4; baptisms, 45; funerals, 10. Salary, $800.

H. E. Rountree—Chaplain, U. S. N., S. S. Utah. Sermons, 48; conversions, 6; members received, 3; baptisms, 3. Salary, $3,000 and allowances.

C. C. Ryan—Church in charge: First, Richmond. Sermons, 150; conversions, 8; members received, 15; marriages, 16; addresses, 20; baptisms, 7; funerals, 14. Salary, $2,400.

Leon Edgar Smith—Church in charge: Christian Temple. Sermons, 91; members received, 38; marriages, 21; addresses, 7; visits, 806; funerals, 13. Salary, $5,000.

D. M. Spence—Church in charge: Ocean View. Sermons, 105; conversions, 4; members received, 6; marriage, 1; visits, 610.

W. W. Staley—Pastor-emeritus, Suffolk. Sermons, 34; marriages, 31; funerals, 66; visits, 2,343. Salary, $2,500.

R. S. Stephens—Church in charge: St. Luke's. Sermons, 64; conversions, 15; members received, 4; marriages, 4; addresses, 5; baptisms, 5; visits, 188; funerals, 3.

M. W. Sutcliffe—No report.

E. B. White—Churches in charge: Antioch, Damascus, Isle of Wight, Windsor. Sermons, 115; conversions, 12; members received, 7; addresses, 5; baptisms, 4; visits, 150; funerals, 15. Salary, $1,500.

CHURCH.	PASTOR.	SECRETARY AND ADDRESS.	Members Reported Last Year.	Members Received.
Antioch	E. B. White	W. K. Saunders, Zuni, Va	303	2
Barrets	C. E. Gerringer	P. B. Barrett, Sebrell, Va	69	4
Berea, Nansemond	I. W. Johnson	Mrs. L. E. Hargraves, Driver, Va	88	4
Berea, Norfolk	J. F. Morgan	M. W. Hollowell, Portsmouth, Va	170	11
Bethlehem	R. E. Brittle	J. W. Folk, Suffolk, Va	311	30
Burton's Grove	C. E. Gerringer	E. W. Carroll, Wakefield, Va	66	7
Centerville	F. C. Lester	J. L. Moss, Disputanta, Va	83	....
Christian Temple	L. E. Smith	Herman Capps, Norfolk, Va	1,558	34
Cypress Chapel	R. E. Brittle	C. W. Rountree, Cypress Chapel, Va	170	51
Damascus	E. B. White	J. E. Corbitt, Sunbury, N. C	147	3
Dendron		W. S. Barrett, Dendron, Va	76	....
Elm Avenue	T. N. Lowe	B. P. Deans, Portsmouth, Va	177	15
Eure	J. M. Roberts	J. H. Lilley, Eure, N. C	274	20
Epworth	W. C. Moore	(Mission Point)	....	....
First, Norfolk	J. E. McCauley	W. J. Thomas, Norfolk, Va	305	2
First, Portsmouth	H. C. Caviness	C. J. Heath, Portsmouth, Va	226	22
First, Richmond	C. C. Ryan	D. W. Darden, Richmond, Va	162	15
Franklin	J. W. Fix	W. A. Daughtrey, Franklin, Va	275	5
Hobson	(No Pastor)	T. H. Beale, Hobson, Va	5	....
Holland	W. C. Hook	E. J. Norfleet, Holland, Va	473	31
Holy Neck	N. G. Newman	A. L. Norfleet, Holland, Va	347	10
Hopewell	J. W. Barrett	Mrs. G. A. Robertson, Hopewell, Va	106	3
Isle of Wight	E. B. White	M. T. Whitley, Windsor, Va	88	2
Ivor	C. E. Gerringer	Dona V. Williams, Ivor, Va	26	4
Johnson's Grove	J. M. Roberts	Mrs. B. F. Hancock, Sedley, Va	79	11
Liberty Spring	I. W. Johnson	F. F. Brinkley, Suffolk, Va	302	16
Mt. Carmel	W. D. Harward	Mrs. Julian Carr, Walters, Va	191	9
Mt. Zion	M. F. Allen	Mrs. E. E. Martin, Eclipse, Va	58	1
New Lebanon	C. E. Gerringer	Ollie V. Cockes, Elberon, Va	61	15
Newport News	M. F. Allen	Mrs. J. H. Duling, Newport News, Va	325	46
Oakland	I. W. Johnson	W. G. Saunders, Chuckatuck, Va	362	20
Oak Grove	J. M. Roberts	W. C. Beamon, Savage, N. C	89	12
Ocean View	D. M. Spence	Mrs. L. H. Snider, Ocean View, Va	45	6
Old Zion	W. H. Garman	W. W. Starnes, Norfolk, Va	611	48
Rosemont	J. F. Morgan	Mary E. Halstead, Buell, Va	281	10
St. Luke's	R. S. Stephens	G. W. Brown, Dover, Del	17	....
St. Paul's	J. B. Chadwick	S. S. Sapp, Wyoming, Del	22	....
Sarem	J. M. Roberts	W. J. Felton, Gates, N. C	33	....
Suffolk	H. S. Hardcastle and W. W. Staley	J. D. MacClenny, Suffolk, Va	1,303	24
South Norfolk	O. D. Poythress	Cecil E. Hollowell, South Norfolk, Va	636	50
Spring Hill	F. C. Lester	Mrs. E. B. Richardson, Wakefield, Va	65	1
Union, S'hampton	R. E. Brittle	R. H. Joyner, Franklin, Va	142	10
Union, Surry	J. M. Roberts	R. T. Brittle, Dendron, Va	48	6
Wakefield	C. E. Gerringer	A. H. Spivey, Wakefield, Va	84	8
Waverly	F. C. Lester	R. T. West, Waverly, Va	215	4
Windsor	E. B. White	J. G. Roberts, Windsor, Va	120	1
Webster	E. W. Jones	W. W. Walker, Havre de Grace, Md	86	2
Totals			10,680	575

Present Membership.	Paid on Conference Apportionments.	Mission Offerings.	Amount Raised for Orphanage.	All Other Benevolences.	Pastor's Salary.	All Other Expenses.	Total Amount Raised.	Value of Church Property.
200	$ 53.50	$ 80.00	$ 63.00	$ 45.00	$ 360.00	$ 114.00	$ 715.00	$ 5,000.00
70	50.00	....	1.00	....	200.00	....	251.00	1,000.00
88	200.00	318.00	120.00	58.00	600.00	254.00	1,550.00	10,000.00
173	150.00	73.00	67.00	100.00	600.00	321.00	1,311.00	3,000.00
317	200.00	368.00	75.00	250.00	600.00	281.00	1,775.00	21,000.00
53	25.00	5.00	8.00	....	151.00	28.00	217.00	500.00
80	45.00	9.00	29.00	30.00	200.00	11.00	324.00	1,200.00
1,585	1,200.00	2,860.00	430.00	1,248.00	5,000.00	24,119.00	34,857.00	325,000.00
196	150.00	168.00	77.00	170.00	455.00	800.00	1,820.00	25,000.00
148	31.50	90.00	12.00	....	360.00	225.00	718.00	1,200.00
76	....	....	....	....	....	....	....	4,000.00
177	50.00	283.00	74.00	160.00	1,600.00	410.00	2,577.00	11,000.00
294	25.00	....	20.00	30.00	250.00	30.00	355.00	3,500.00
.....	5.00							
303	125.00	148.00	230.00	109.00	2,291.00	3,400.00	6,303.00	42,650.00
248	175.00	575.00	135.00	75.00	1,707.00	959.00	3,626.00	75,000.00
166	200.00	469.00	429.00	246.00	2,400.00	9,453.00	13,197.00	178,000.00
247	350.00	522.00	314.00	555.00	2,400.00	940.00	5,081.00	47,000.00
5	....	....	....	....	....	....	....	2,000.00
484	450.00	710.00	370.00	170.00	2,500.00	965.00	5,165.00	53,000.00
337	300.00	559.00	222.00	36.00	2,000.00	687.00	3,774.00	16,000.00
106	25.00	46.00	....	....	841.00	406.00	1,293.00	7,000.00
87	40.00	68.00	30.00	....	350.00	200.00	688.00	3,000.00
28	15.00	18.00	21.00	20.00	200.00	130.00	405.00	1,500.00
90	45.00	4.00	4.00	42.00	165.00	86.00	346.00	2,000.00
314	295.00	470.00	126.00	144.00	600.00	365.00	2,000.00	20,000.00
198	150.00	102.00	92.00	....	500.00	237.00	1,081.00	7,000.00
59	40.00	....	15.00	20.00	100.00	54.00	229.00	1,500.00
73	30.00	18.00	34.00	75.00	150.00	128.00	435.00	2,500.00
369	75.00	515.00	129.00	125.00	2,000.00	6,051.00	9,120.00	30,000.00
377	225.00	165.00	85.00	....	600.00	449.00	1,524.00	20,000.00
100	....	....	....	....	150.00	....	150.00	5,000.00
48	....	8.00	....	....	440.00	132.00	580.00	4,000.00
600	285.00	79.00	101.00	185.00	2,080.00	1,567.00	5,492.00	20,000.00
288	250.00	560.00	176.00	....	2,080.00	10,984.00	14,050.00	25,000.00
17	....	....	....	....	....	....	....	3,000.00
22	....	....	....	....	....	50.00	50.00	500.00
33	....	....	....	....	100.00	15.00	115.00	1,000.00
1,312	2,000.00	2,346.00	1,555.00	865.00	5,000.00	18,484.00	30,250.00	180,000.00
656	500.00	228.00	285.00	189.00	3,224.00	6,345.00	10,771.00	125,000.00
66	50.00	43.00	36.00	....	246.00	50.00	425.00	3,000.00
149	29.00	....	....	29.00	211.00	....	280.00	1,500.00
50	50.00	32.00	24.00	....	96.00	139.00	341.00	1,000.00
84	28.00	....	....	....	900.00	....	900.00	5,000.00
218	325.00	360.00	140.00	132.00	1,554.00	360.00	2,871.00	20,000.00
98	100.00	248.00	140.00	278.00	450.00	90.00	1,206.00	5,500.00
88	....	21.00	12.00	....	1,570.00	1,947.00	3,550.00	40,000.00
10,777	$ 8,318.00	$12,582.00	$ 5,681.00	$ 5,386.00	$46,681.00	$91,266.00	$ 169,953.00	$ 1,336,550.00

SUNDAY SCHOOL.	SUPERINTENDENT AND ADDRESS.	Number of Officers and Teachers.	Total Enrollment.	Total Amount Raised during Year.
Antioch	J. T. Godwin, Windsor, Va.	14	146	$ 117.00
Barretts	J. I. Hancock, Sebrell, Va.	7	60	45.00
Berea, Nansemond	W. H. Brinkley, Driver, Va.	10	100	157.00
Berea, Norfolk	Frank Hall, Hickory, Va.	12	100	743.00
Bethlehem	W. E. White, Suffolk, Va.	20	240	383.00
Burton's Grove	E. W. Carroll, Wakefield, Va.	5	30	23.00
Centerville	G. W. Bain, Disputanta, Va.	9	60	74.00
Christian Temple	F. M. Brewer, Norfolk, Va.	59	742	1,322.00
Cypress Chapel	R. M. Jones, Suffolk, Va.	14	176	680.00
Damascus	J. E. Corbitt, Sunbury, N. C.	6	100	106.00
Dendron	No Report			
Elm Avenue	Ellsworth Savage, Portsmouth, Va.	13	146	440.00
Epworth	No Report			
Eure	T. A. Eure, Eure, N. C.	7	75	18.00
First, Norfolk	T. L. Fulcher, Norfolk, Va.	24	227	330.00
First, Portsmouth	H. W. Lee, Portsmouth, Va.	16	205	829.00
First, Richmond	F. M. Webb, Richmond, Va.	18	174	709.00
Franklin	L. R. Jones, Franklin, Va.	22	186	609.00
Hobson	No School			
Holland	E. L. Daughtrey, Holland, Va.	15	246	831.00
Holy Neck	A. L. Norfleet, Holland, Va.	14	164	193.00
Hopewell	F. N. Lowe, Hopewell, Va.	12	123	323.00
Isle of Wight	M. T. Whitley, Windsor, Va.	13	60	77.00
Ivor	B. H. Lane, Ivor, Va.	8	33	68.00
Johnson's Grove	B. F. Handcock, Sedley, Va.	8	46	43.00
Liberty Spring	I. T. Byrd, Holland, Va.	16	175	289.00
Mt. Carmel	Otis V. Joyner, Walters, Va.	23	170	395.00
Mt. Zion	J. B. Martin, Eclipse, Va.	10	36	54.00
New Lebanon	Ollie V. Cockes, Elberon, Va.	12	62	50.00
Newport News	R. C. Jarratt, Newport News, Va.	34	391	789.00
Oak Grove	W. K. Parker, Sunbury, N. C.	6	85	103.00
Oakland	W. K. Wagoner, Suffolk, Va.	14	209	246.00
Ocean View	R. M. Wilkerson, Ocean View, Va.	10	85	183.00
Old Zion	W. W. Starnes, Norfolk, Va.	16	339	674.00
Rosemont	R. H. Morrison, Norfolk, Va.	23	269	1,500.00
St. Luke's	No Report			
St. Paul's	No Report			
Sarem	No Report			
South Norfolk	H. A. Seymour, So. Norfolk, Va.	48	362	821.00
Spring Hill	J. J. Faison, Waverly, Va.	8	65	96.00
Suffolk	W. S. Beamon, Suffolk, Va.	50	790	2,290.00
Union, Southampton	R. H. Joyner, Franklin, Va.	9	110	101.00
Union, Surry	R. T. Brittle, Dendron, Va.	7	35	55.00
Wakefield	A. H. Spivey, Wakefield, Va.	9	87	50.00
Waverly	B. E. White, Waverly, Va.	23	209	391.00
Windsor	Ralph D. Woolard, Windsor, Va.	14	105	346.00
Webster	W. W. Walker, Havre de Grace, Md.	11	59	125.00
Totals		669	7,182	$ 1,635.00

Proceedings of the Sixtieth Annual Session of the Western North Carolina Christian Conference

HANK'S CHAPEL CHRISTIAN CHURCH (NEAR PITTSBORO), CHATHAM COUNTY, N. C.—NOVEMBER 5-6, 1930.

FIRST DAY—MORNING SESSION.

The Western North Carolina Christian Conference met today and was called to order by President T. J. Green at 10:30 A. M. Devotional services were conducted by Rev. John M. Allred.

The roll of ministers and Churches was called, and the President declared a quorum to be present. The complete enrollment is as follows:

ENROLLMENT.

Ministers—John M. Allred, Asheboro, N. C., R. 1; E. C. Brady, Hemp, N. C.; H. V. Cox, Ramseur, N. C.; W. J. Edwards, 211 Ward St., High Point, N. C.; J. U. Fogleman, P. O. Box 362, Graham, N. C.; T. J. Green, Ramseur, N. C.; W. H. Hayes, Seagrove, N. C.; G. O. Lankford, Burlington, N. C.; W. C. Martin, Candor, N. C.; D. R. Moffitt, Coleridge, N. C.; M. A. Pollard, Liberty, N. C.; A. K. Scotton, Coleridge, N. C.; G. R. Underwood, Pittsboro, N. C.; T. E. White, Elon College, N. C.

Licentiates—J. D. Fogleman, Liberty, N. C.; B. H. Lowdermilk, Ramseur, N. C.; V. D. Shepherd, High Point, N. C.; R. O. Smith, High Point, N. C.; Geo. M. Tally, Carbonton, N. C.

Churches and Delegates.

Antioch (C)—D. M. Fisher, Lonnie Oldham.
Antioch (R)—J. H. Fox, G. K. Needham.
Bennett—Miss Clara B. Bennett, Mrs. H. C. Bouthe.
Biscoe—O. H. Lambeth, W. I. Ashehill.
Big Oak—D. E. Cole, C. C. Lewis, Leroy Momas.
Brown's Chapel—J. M. Morgan, J. W. H. Moore.
Burlington—W. L. Cates, Mrs. W. L. Cates, Miss Jewel Hatch, M. C. Stafford.
Ether—W. H. Freeman, Marshall Hammer, Homer J. Cochran.
Glendon—G. M. Tally, Ernest Phillips.
Grace's Chapel—Miss Margaret Register, Miss Eunice Maddox.
Graham—Mrs. James P. Harden, Mrs. J. D. Kernodle.
Graham-Providence Memorial—R. H. Ferrell, J. B. Ferrell, Mrs. J. B. Montgomery.

Hank's Chapel—R. T. Ferrell, L. J. Riddle, R. T. O. Mann, W. F. Bland.

High Point—M. C. Dry, W. R. Bray.

Liberty—C. L. Bray.

Mt. Pleasant—E. M. Marks, Miss Agnes Marks.

Needham's Grove—No report.

New Center—Bascom Craven, Susan Lowdermilk.

Park's Cross Roads—R. D. Craven, J. C. Cox, Mrs. J. W. Parks.

Patterson's Grove—A. C. Chandler, J. A. Patterson, J. E. Martin.

Pleasant Cross—Fannie Ellison, Ethel Malone.

Pleasant Grove—T. M. Brady, E. A. Brady.

Pleasant Hill—Paul E. Coble, C. V. Teague.

Pleasant Ridge—Geo. T. Gunter, Herman Bell, Mrs. Herman Bell, James Newell.

Pleasant Union—E. S. McDowell, A. V. McDowell, A. R. McDowell, Ben McDowell.

Poplar Branch—No report.

Ramseur—Mrs. C. A. Ward, Mr. C. A. Ward, I. H. Foust, Mrs. I. H. Foust.

Randleman—W. G. Lamb, Mrs. W. G. Lamb.

Seagrove—Mrs. D. A. Cornelison, Mrs. A. C. Harris.

Shady Grove—Beldos F. Deaton, Percy Deaton.

Shiloh—J. E. Stout, J. B. Garner.

Smithwood—P. W. Humble, Thomas House.

Spoon's Chapel—No report.

Union Grove—T. F. Brown, C. A. Byrd, Edd Brown.

Zion—S. M. Johnson, D. T. Marks.

President T. J. Green then announced the appointment of the following committees:

Nomination—Dr. G. O. Lankford, Herbert C. Ferrell, J. E. Stout.

Resolutions—M. A. Pollard, W. C. Martin.

Press—E. C. Brady, T. E. White.

Finance—Luther Cates, I. H. Foust, R. D. Craven.

Place of Next Meeting—Paul E. Coble, Willie Freeman, E. M. Marks.

The report of the Program Committee was read and unanimously adopted.

Reception of visitors. Rev. T. E. White introduced the following visiting brethren, who were invited to seats as deliberative members of the Conference: Rev. Dr. J. O. Atkinson, C. D. Johnston, J. C. Cummings, J. A. Denton, J. S. Carden, J. L. Foster and Rev. F. W. Hancock, of the Methodist Church. These brethren thanked the President and the Conference for the recognition, and were seated in the Conference.

The President called for the report of the Executive Committee, but as no matter of business had demanded the attention of the committee the President reported that the committee had nothing to offer the Conference.

The Conference then heard the annual address by the President, Rev. T. J. Green, taking for his text the command of God to Moses to "Go Forward," when he and the Israelite host were confronted with the sea and no visible means of crossing. President Green brought the Conference a great message in faith and perseverance in the face of adversity, and the sweet, simple message was enjoyed by all.

On motion, the Conference adjourned for lunch, to resume its deliberations at 1:30.

FIRST DAY—AFTERNOON SESSION.

Called to order by the President. After a song and religious service by Rev. H. V. Cox, the President called for the report of the Nomination Committee, which was submitted and adopted, as follows:

President—Rev. E. Carl Brady.
Vice-President—Rev. J. M. Allred.
Secretary—Junius H. Harden.
Assistant Secretary—W. H. Freeman.
Treasurer—O. D. Lawrence.

The newly elected President accepted the honor conferred upon him with a few well-chosen remarks, which were happily received by the Conference, and immediately applied himself to the dispatch of the business of the body. He called for Church letters from the Churches that had not already delivered their letters to the Conference, and then called for the annual reports from ministers of the Conference, which were presented.

The report of the Committee on Religious Literature was submitted by the chairman, Rev. G. R. Underwood, and, after discussion by the chairman, Dr. J. O. Atkinson, and Bro. Chas. D. Johnston, was unanimously adopted, as follows:

REPORT OF COMMITTEE ON RELIGIOUS LITERATURE.

The literature read by a people is a fair index of their character. We recommend the following:

That our people subscribe to and read THE CHRISTIAN SUN, the organ of the Southern Christian Convention, edited by Dr. J. O. Atkinson, Elon College, N. C.

That our Sunday Schools use our own literature published at Dayton, Ohio.

That our people read the books by our own publishing-houses.

Respectfully submitted,

G. R. UNDERWOOD,
M. A. POLLARD,
G. M. TALLY,
Committee.

The Committee on Social Service, not being ready to report, Rev. T. E. White asked the privilege of introducing to the Conference Rev. Dr. M. J. Sweet and wife, Dr. Sweet being pastor-at-large in the Congregational Church; and at the same time extend the courtesies of the Conference to Rev. T. Fred Wright, also of the Congregational Church. These motions were duly made and carried and these brethren were invited to seats as deliberative members.

As Dr. Sweet was on the program for the evening session, he was invited, by motion, duly made, seconded and carried, to use the time just now available for his message on account of the absence of the chairman of the Committee on Social Service, and the report from that committee. Dr. Sweet's message was well conceived and well received. It was bubbling over with the heart-thoughts of Christian union.

On motion, the Conference determined to divide the evening program between this afternoon's session and the sessions for tomorrow. At this time, Rev. T. Fred Wright, of the Congregational Church at Sanford, who was on the evening program, brought the Conference a wonderful message.

Rev. T. E. White read the ministerial report of Rev. N. Hayes to the Conference, and, on his motion, the Conference instructed the Secretary to write Bro. Hayes a letter from the Conference.

Rev. J. L. Foster, of the Eastern Virginia Conference, at this time asked for the floor to tender his services to the Churches of this Conference.

The Entertainment Committee having made its report, and the program for the day having been completed, the Conference adjourned until 9:30 tomorrow morning.

SECOND DAY—MORNING SESSION.

The Conference was called to order at 9:30 A. M. by the President, Rev. E. Carl Brady. Devotional services were led by Rev. M. A. Pollard.

Minutes of the first day's proceedings were read and, after corrections, approved.

At this time, Rev. T. E. White presented to the Conference Rev. S. M. Penn, of the Congregational-Christian Church, and Rev. J. L. Neese, of the North Carolina Christian Conference. These brethren were invited to seats as deliberative members.

When ministers not enrolled on the first day were called for, Rev. J. U. Fogleman, of Providence Memorial Church, responded and read his report.

The report of the Committee on Evangelism was not discussed, and the time alotted for this discussion was given to Rev. T. Fred Wright.

After the address of Rev. Wright. the report of the committee was unanimously adopted, as follows:

REPORT OF COMMITTEE ON EVANGELISM.

Evangelism is to make known to others the gospel. To do this, we must have the spirit of Christ in our own lives. Then we must tell it to people, that they may hear. They that hear should tell it to those who have not heard. We should not forget, in our conversation, to speak of this great salvation. Every member of the Church should help do this work for the Lord.

We insist that our ministers preach the word in its purity, and not compromise with the world. When we cannot go, we may send the message by those who will go, with our prayers and our means. We, as Christians, may be so agreeable that the world will know that we have been with Jesus.

J. M. ALLRED,
D. R. MOFFITT,
Committee.

The report of the Committee on Home Missions was submitted by the chairman of that committee, Rev. H. V. Cox, and, after discussion, was adopted, as follows:

REPORT OF COMMITTEE ON HOME MISSIONS.

Your committee notes with interest marks of improvement within the bounds of our Conference. Some of our Churches have recently added Sunday School rooms to their equipment, which indicates that we are going forward in a material way, and we hope spiritually.

There has no word reached your committee to the contrary, but what our Churches have had regular preaching throughout the year. Several Churches have appealed to your committee for help to finance their Church work. But realizing that funds for this kind of work are very much limited, your committee regrets not being able to meet all requests for help. However, after duly considering the matter, we recommend the following, provided that pastors be secured that will meet the approval of the Home Mission Board:

That the Churches at Alder and Bennett receive a supplement from the Home Mission Board (to be applied on pastor's salary) equal to the amount that each Church raises for the same. This to be paid quarterly, provided that the amount given each Church shall not exceed one hundred dollars.

That Biscoe Christian Church receive the amount of two hundred dollars to help them on their Church debt.

That Smithwood Church be donated one hundred dollars when the Church has raised one hundred dollars toward the liquidation of the indebtedness of the Church, which we understand is two hundred dollars.

We wish to urge that all Churches endeavor to raise as much as one-third of the amount paid their pastors for missions. As we understand that missions no longer share in the Conference apportionment, may our people realize the very urgent need of money for this work and rally to the cause of missions not only with their means but with their prayers also. As the heart of our Lord's message was missions, it is the prayer of your committee that our Churches may be aroused to the meaning of the old prophet's message when he said, "Awake, awake, put on thy strength, O Zion; put on thy beautiful garments, O Jerusalem; shake thyself from the dust, and arise, go tell the people of this wicked world that there is balm in Gilead for their aching breasts, and a healing Physician for their sin-sick souls." That will destroy all this pride and selfishness, and that predominating spirit that seems to be getting into the hearts of the nations as well as individuals.

H. V. Cox,
J. C. Cox,
JUNIUS H. HARDEN,
Committee.

Rev. T. E. White introduced Dr. W. A. Harper and Mr. S. J. Heindel to the Conference, and these brethren were seated as deliberative members.

Th Committee on Nominations submitted a supplemental report, and named the Woman's Board, as follows: Mrs. I. H. Foust, Mrs. W. R. Sellars, Mrs. John B. Montgomery, Rev. E. C. Brady, Rev. M. A. Pollard.

The Chair then appointed two additional members on the Committee on Location. Those named were R. T. Ferrell and J. A. Morgan.

In the absence of Mrs. I. H. Foust, chairman, Mrs. Walter R. Sellars, treasurer, submitted the reports of the Woman's Missionary Society and the Woman's Mission Board.

Report of the Woman's Missionary Societies in the Western North Carolina Christian Conference:

REPORT OF WOMEN'S MISSIONARY SOCIETIES.

WOMEN'S SOCIETIES.

Burlington	$ 916.58	Providence Memorial	30.00
Graham	30.00	Ramseur	55.00
Grace's Chapel	10.85	Randleman	9.60
High Point	13.15	Shiloh	15.65
Park's Cross Roads	2.80		
Pleasant Hill	23.40	Total	$1,107.03

YOUNG PEOPLE'S SOCIETIES.

Burlington	$ 250.00	Pleasant Hill	10.00
Burlington Junior	100.91	Ramseur	5.00
Graham	8.09		
		Total	$ 374.00

WILLING WORKERS' SOCIETIES.

Burlington	$ 51.11

CRADLE ROLL SOCIETIES.

Burlington	$ 25.00	Ramseur	3.16
High Point	2.00		
Parks Cross Roads	4.25	Total	$1,566.55

WOMAN'S MISSION BOARD.

50 Women's Societies	$3,465.43
14 Young People's Societies	570.55
8 Willing Workers	184.86
15 Cradle Rolls	142.54
6 District Meetings	52.30
Conference Offering	27.42
Total	$4,443.10

Western North Carolina Conference $1,566.55
Eastern North Carolina Conference 1,007.23
North Carolina and Virginia Conference 1,789.60
District Meeting Offering 52.30
Conference Offering 27.42

Total $4,443.10

MRS. W. R. SELLARS, *Treasurer.*

Mrs. Sellars moved the adoption of the report and, in speaking to the motion, made a great impression on the Conference. She very graciously gave the most of her time, however, to Miss Graham Rowland, who held the meeting spellbound with the most charming address of the session. Both reports were enthusiastically adopted.

Mr. George T. Gunter being absent, the report of the Committee on Sunday Schools was submitted by B. S. Moffitt. After reading the report, Bro. Moffitt moved its adoption and spoke to the Conference interestingly and instructively. Dr. G. O. Lankford offered an amendment to the report, providing that it contain the recommendation of the Southern Christian Convention that the offering on the fifth Sunday be given to Elon College. After the adoption of the amendment, the report of the committee was unanimously adopted.

REPORT OF COMMITTEE ON SUNDAY SCHOOLS.

We, your committee, report:

There has been little improvement in our Sunday Schools since our last report. The annual Sunday School and Christian Endeavor Convention was held at this Church (Hank's Chapel) on Tuesday, June 10, 1930, with only sixteen schools represented by delegates or reports.

Your committee believes that this Convention should have the support of every school, society and Christian worker in this Conference.

The next Convention will be held on Tuesday after the second Sunday in July, 1931, the place of meeting to be announced later.

We recommend:

First: That each Sunday School not now doing so, send a monthly offering to the Orphanage and to missions.

Second: That we give the Board of Christian Education and the field secretary our financial support and all the encouragement we can.

Third: That each school send delegates to Elon Summer School.

Fourth: We recommend that each school have a teacher-training class.

Fifth: That each school have a cradle roll superintendent.

Sixth: We urge that enough money be paid into the Convention to enable us to have the minutes printed in pamphlet form and the same distributed to each school.

Seventh: We especially urge that each school use our own Sunday School literature.

Eighth: We especially urge that each school comply with the request of the Southern Christian Convention that the fifth Sunday offerings be taken for and given to Elon College.

GEO. T. GUNTER,
B. S. MOFFITT,
H. C. FERRELL,
Committee.

After amendment, the motion was adopted.

At this time, the President noted that there were delegates present who had not been enrolled, and the delegates from the following Churches were duly enrolled: Biscoe, Bennett, Providence Memorial.

Rev. T. E. White introduced Rev. Robert Lee House, of the North Carolina Conference, who is the pastor-elect for Hank's Chapel Church for the coming year.

The report of the Committee on Foreign Missions was submitted by the chairman of that committee, Rev. E. C. Brady, Rev. John M. Allred, the Vice-President of the Conference, having been called to the Chair. After a motion to adopt the report had been duly made and seconded and the report had been spoken to with marked ability and great fervor by Dr. Atkinson, the report was unanimously adopted, as follows:

REPORT OF COMMITTEE ON FOREIGN MISSIONS.

The supreme and most important command of our Lord was, "Go ye into all the world and preach the gospel to every creature, and lo, I am with you always, even unto the end of the world." The Christians have always been slow in obeying this command. This alone explains our slow growth as a Church. We have not been a missionary people, and God has never allowed a non-mission or anti-mission people to grow into prestige and power.

By the merger with the Congregationalists, we now come to have a part in missions throughout the world—China, Japan, Africa, India, Turkey, Greece, the Philippine Islands.

After January 1, 1931, our Foreign Mission Boards become one with the American Board, the oldest and most honorable mission board in America; our secretary, Rev. W. P. Minton, becoming one of the secretaries of the Commission on Missions. This larger work should give us the larger vision, as it gives us the larger opportunity and entails on us the larger responsibility.

We recommend:

First: That as the Southern Convention voted to raise this year the sum of fifty thousand dollars for missions, one-half for home and one-half for foreign, that we do our best in raising this amount.

Second: That we set as our goals for each Church, including our Sunday Schools, one-third as much for missions as we pay our pastors.

Respectfully submitted,
E. C. BRADY,
G. R. UNDERWOOD,
J. W. EDWARDS,
Committee.

Upon the adoption of this report, the Conference adjourned for luncheon.

SECOND DAY—AFTERNOON SESSION.

Devotional services by Rev. Robert Lee House; Scripture, John 3:16.

The first item of business on the afternoon program was the report of the Committee on Education, submitted by the chairman, Rev. T. E. White. The report was read, and motion having been made for its adoption, was spoken to by Dr. W. A. Harper, who introduced to the

Conference his assistant, S. J. Heindel, who will, among other duties, have charge of the handling of the million-dollar campaign for Elon College. Bro. Heindel made a favorable impression on the Conference, and his message was well received. After the speeches by Dr. Harper and Bro. Heindel, the Secretary of the Conference made a few remarks and the report of the committee was adopted, as follows:

REPORT OF COMMITTEE ON EDUCATION.

Christian education had its origin in Christ. It teaches humanity how to discover the truth freedom, and makes possible for us the abundant life. It enables men to understand the mind of Christ, and to apply Christian principles to every-day problems. In other words, it is living our lives as we believe Jesus would have us live them. The Christian colleges of our land all grew out of a need for the teaching of Christian education. Our own college is no exception to the rule. It was born out of a deep-felt need, much fervent prayer, great faith and heroic sacrifice. It has proven its right to be and the wisdom of its founders.

There is not an enterprise of our Church that our college has not blessed. Whenever there is an important meeting, Conference or Convention of our Church anywhere in the Southland, there you will find Elon College. Most of the leaders in our Church either had their training in our college or they are the heroes of faith who had a part in giving it birth. So close is the union of our Church and our college that to destroy the one would almost mean the destruction of the other. But Elon College cannot be destroyed. Storms of fire might destroy the buildings, but the college never. It is far more than buildings of brick and mortar. It is a spirit, a glorious idea of "Christian Character, First and Always" at Elon. It lives in the hearts of her alumni and the Church and faithful friends who have never failed her. She gracefully grows greater with the years. Her influence is always widening, and we rejoice in her growth and power.

We recommend that our Sunday Schools take the offering for Elon College on each fifth Sunday, as requested by the Southern Christian Convention.

We wish to express our appreciation for what the Committee of the Million-Dollar Campaign has already done, and we recommend that this Conference give its hearty co-operation and loyal support in every possible way, that the greatest undertaking for Elon College and Christian education in our Church may be successfully brought to a glorious achievement.

Licentiate B. H. Lowdermilk has been in charge of Pleasant Union and Spoon's Chapel during the past year, and has been called to the same field next year. We recommend that he be continued as a licentiate.

Licentiate Geo. M. Tally has preached wherever the providence of God has called him. We recommend that he be continued as a licentiate.

T. E. WHITE,
E. CARL BRADY,
G. O. LANKFORD,
Committee.

Dr. Atkinson asked for a few moments of the time of the Conference to present the matter of a small unpaid balance on the O'Kelly Memorial. Time was granted the doctor, and the Conference contributed the sum of $18.41, and Mrs. W. R. Sellars, in the name of the Woman's Bible Class of the Burlington Christian Church, pledged $5.00 to this fund.

Rev. J. U. Fogleman offered the report of the Committee on Social Service.

REPORT OF COMMITTEE ON SOCIAL SERVICE.

When we think of the words, "social" and "service," we realize that they are large words indeed, and embrace a great deal of meaning. The topic itself covers practical life in its entirety—the psysical, moral, educational, industrial, economic, political, recreational and spiritual. Some one has said that there are six schools of which the most of us at some time or another are bona fide members, namely: the home, the school, the Church, industry, practical experience, the proper use of leisure time.

In reflecting upon the moral condition of the present day, and comparing them with those of the past, we must agree that the morale of our youth in general should be improved upon. Our real problem is to train boys and girls to live better with and for each other. Such a life might be termed Christian citizenship. To do this, we must enrich their environment with an atmosphere pure, undefiled, vital and uplifting.

It behooves us older people to set forth an ideal standard of good morals after which our youth may pattern. We will need to use our better judgment in the things which we like and do.

Therefore, we, your Committee on Social Service, recommend:

That we who profess to be Christians and leaders, as parents and guardians, must live an upright, clean and godly life before those about us.

That every loyal Christian and Church worker exercise a greater faith in the eighteenth amendment—its real value to humanity, to see that the law is both observed and enforced—so that people may live happier and better.

That the pastors and Church members pray daily for a united spirit of love and loyalty to be established between employer and employee, so that industrial and economic conditions in general may be improved.

That on November 11th, at some convenient time during the day, pause be made for a few moments in thanksgiving to God for having brought to a close the World War with all its horror, bloodshed, grief, woe and the consequent loss of life and property; and for greater love and wisdom to be displayed by all men of all nations, that war may be forever abolished, and love and peace may reign supreme.

J. U. Fogleman,
W. R. Sellars,
W. R. Rightsell,
Committee.

After the report had been spoken to by Bro. Fogleman, Dr. Atkinson and others, was, on motion duly made and seconded, adopted.

Mr. Charles D. Johnston then, in his usual way, presented the cause of the Christian Orphanage. Bro. Johnston knows that times have been subnormal, and so much so that he made the unusual statement that he had been necessitated to borrow money for his current expenses. The Conference heard from none of its enterprises with more pride and joy than from the Orphanage. It is a noble and self-sacrificing service and will be supported by the Conference.

The Committee on Apportionments made its report, which was duly adopted, as follows:

REPORT OF COMMITTEE ON APPORTIONMENTS.

We recommend that one hundred and fifty dollars be retained in the treasury for Conference expenses. We appeal to the Churches most strenuously that they exert every means to meet the apportionments and co-operate with each department in raising goals for missions, for the college, the Orphanage, and Christian education, through offerings and individual gifts.

We recommend the following apportionments:

Antioch (C)	$ 55.00	New Center	$ 82.50
Antioch (R)	44.00	Park's Cross Roads	137.50
Addor	27.50	Patterson's Grove	49.75
Bennett	44.00	Pleasant Cross	60.50
Big Oak	88.00	Pleasant Hill	115.50
Biscoe	27.50	Pleasant Grove	159.50
Brown's Chapel	66.00	Pleasant Ridge	115.50
Burlington	550.00	Pleasant Union	55.00
Center Grove	55.00	Poplar Branch	44.00
Ether	55.00	Ramseur	88.00
Glendon	55.00	Randleman	55.00
Grace Chapel	55.00	Seagrove	49.50
Graham	82.50	Shady Grove	55.00
Graham-Providence Mem'l	82.50	Shiloh	55.00
Hank's Chapel	137.50	Smithwood	55.00
High Point	55.00	Spoon's Chapel	27.50
Liberty	27.50	Union Grove	71.50
Mt. Pleasant	27.50	Zion	77.00
Needham's Grove	27.50		

Respectfully submitted,
O. D. LAWRENCE,
P. D. TEAGUE,
JUNIUS H. HARDEN,
Committee.

On motion, duly made and seconded, the report was adopted.

On motion of Dr. G. O. Lankford, in the absence of a report from the Committee on Superannuation, this matter and such other business as might require the attention of this committee was referred to the same committee of the Southern Christian Convention.

O. D. Lawrence, the Treasurer of the Conference, submitted the following report, which was adopted without discussion:

TREASURER'S REPORT.

1929.
Nov. 7. Balance in treasury .... $ 44.50
Collection from Churches 1,630.47

$1,674.97

DISBURSEMENTS.

Nov. 11. To Dr. J. O. Atkinson, home missions........$ 500.00
To G. O. Lankford, programs................. 6.75
To Junius H. Harden, Secretary 25.00
25. To W. C. Wicker, Treas. S. C. C. Fund....... 1,025.00
1930.
Mar. 14. To Central Publishing Co., ANNUALS 100.00
To Junius H. Harden, printing & postage...... 5.14

$1,661.89

Balance in treasury .... $ 13.08
Collected from Conference 1,397.46

On hand $1,410.54

Rev. T. J. Green, chairman, submitted the report of the Finance Committee, which was adopted without discussion, as follows:

REPORT OF FINANCE COMMITTEE.

We have checked the accounts of O. D. Lawrence, Treasurer, and find the same correct.

We recommend that the Program Committee be reimbursed with cost of programs, $3.75; also that the Secretary be paid $25.00 from the Conference fund. Respectfully submitted,

T. J. GREEN, *Chairman.*

Rev. M. A. Pollard, chairman, submitted the report of the Committee on Resolutions, as follows:

REPORT OF COMMITTEE ON RESOLUTIONS.

Resolved, That the Conference extend a rising vote of thanks to the pastor, members and friends of Hank's Chapel Church for their generous hospitality in the entertainment of this Conference.

That we express to the officers of the Conference our appreciation of their efficient and faithful service.

That the Western North Carolina Conference co-operate with the Churches and ministers of the Congregational Church in the bounds of the Western North Carolina Conference, on such basis as may be mutually agreeable to the Western North Carolina Conference and to the Churches and ministers of the Congregational Church.

M. A. POLLARD,
W. C. MARTIN,
Committee.

The President then appointed the following standing committees:

Executive—E. C. Brady, G. O. Lankford, Junius H. Harden.
Home Missions—H. V. Cox, J. H. Harden, J. M. Allred.
Foreign Missions—T. J. Green, G. R. Underwood, J. W. Edwards.
Religious Literature—G. R. Underwood, M. A. Pollard, G. M. Tally.
Education—T. E. White, G. O. Lankford, T. J. Green.
Evangelism—M. A. Pollard, J. M. Allred, D. R. Moffitt.
Sunday Schools—Geo. T. Gunter, B. S. Moffitt, B. N. Lowdermilk.
Christian Endeavor—E. H. Thompson, W. C. Martin, M. C. Stafford.
Social Service—J. U. Fogleman, W. R. Sellars, W. R. Wrightsell.
Apportionments—J. H. Harden, O. D. Lawrence, P. E. Coble.
Superannuation—I. H. Foust, T. A. Moffitt, W. E. Allred.
Program—T. E. White, E. C. Brady, G. O. Lankford.

The Secretary was ordered to secure two hundred copies of THE ANNUAL and distribute the same from his office.

The Committee on Location reported that Shiloh, Randolph County, had been selected as the Church with which the Conference would meet next year.

On motion, the Conference adjourned, to meet with the Church at Shiloh, in Randolph County, N. C., on Tuesday after the first Sunday in November, 1931, at 10:30 o'clock.

E. C. BRADY, *President.*
JUNIUS H. HARDEN, *Secretary.*

MINISTERIAL REPORTS.

John M. Allred—Churches: Pleasant Ridge, Biscoe, High Point, Shady Grove, Ether. Sermons, 126; members received, 59; baptisms, 40; marriage, 1; converts, 81. Salary, $675.

E. Carl Brady—Churches: Big Oak, Brown's Chapel, Liberty, Damascus. Sermons, 57; members received, 24; baptisms, 20; pastoral calls, 150; wedding, 1; funeral, 1. Salary, $700.

H. V. Cox—Churches: Pleasant Cross, Patterson's Grove, Union Grove. Sermons, 55; conversions, 22; members received, 5; baptisms, 5; funerals, 2. Salary, $420.91.

J. C. Cummings—Churches: Parks Cross Roads, Ramseur, Shiloh, Seagrove, Glendon, Ebenezer, Cary. Sermons, 166; professions, 50; members received, 17; marriages, 5; baptisms, 14; funerals, 10. Salary, $1,950.

J. U. Fogleman—Churches: Graham-Providence Memorial. Sermons, 60; conversions, 27; members received, 17; baptisms, 7; pastoral visits, 40; funerals, 5. Salary, $500.

T. J. Green—Churches: Bennett, Pleasant Grove, Pleasant Hill. Sermons, 84; members received, 23; marriages, 2; baptisms, 22; pastoral visits, 200; funerals, 11. Salary, $700.

W. N. Hayes—Reported that he had no charge;. that he preached sometimes in the near-by Churches and assisted in four protracted meetings; officiated at two burials. He writes that he feels that the Lord is very near him all the time, and requested the prayers of the Conference. The Secretary was instructed to write Bro. Hayes a letter.

G. O. Lankford—Church: Burlington. Sermons, 85; members received, 76; marriages, 6; addresses, 15; baptisms, 39; pastoral visits, 1,019; funerals, 22. Salary, $3,300.

W. C. Martin—Sermons 2; funeral, 1.

D. R. Moffitt—Coleridge, N. C., Sermons, 60; conversions, 26; members received, 4; addresses, 3; baptism, 1; funerals, 5. Salary, $153.25.

M. A. Pollard—Churches: Smithwood, Randleman. Sermons, 108; conversions, 51; members received, 10; marriage, 1; addresses, 4; baptisms, 15; pastoral visits, 200; funerals, 7. Salary, $450.

G. E. Underwood—Reported personally that he had no regular charge. He is still chairman of the Committee on Religious Literature and delivered the report of this committee and spoke to the resolution for adoption with his usual enthusiasm and vigor.

T. E. White—Elon College N. C. Had no pastoral charge; preached occasionally and taught at Elon College.

LICENTIATES.

G. M. Tally—Carbonton, N. C. Not serving any Churches. Sermons, 55; conversions, 25; addresses, 6; funerals, 6.

B. H. Lowdermilk—Churches: Pleasant Union, Spoon's Chapel. Sermons, 83; addresses, 5; pastoral calls, 25; funerals, 4. Salary, $116.50.

CHURCH.	PASTOR.	SECRETARY AND ADDRESS.	Members Reported Last Year.	Present Membership.
Antioch (C.)	J. S. Carden	Mrs. Grace Tysor, R. 3, Pittsboro, N. C.	70	64
Antioch (R.)	D. R. Moffitt	Fletcher Hayes, Moffitt, N. C.	74	74
Bennett	T. J. Green	L. M. Murray, Bennett, N. C.		19
Biscoe	J. M. Allred	O. H. Lambert, Biscoe, N. C.	33	57
Big Oak	E. C. Brady	D. E. Cole, Biscoe, N. C.	177	190
Brown's Chapel	E. C. Brady	Iola Sanders, Speeds, N. C.	91	167
Burlington	G. O. Lankford	E. H. Wilkins, Burlington, N. C.	611	671
Ether	J. M. Allred	C. C. Phillips, Ether, N. C.	81	83
Glendon	J. C. Cummings	G. M. Tally, Carbonton, N. C.	95	90
Grace's Chapel	J. A. Denton	R. B. Coggins, Sanford, N. C., R. 1	127	138
Graham	W. C. Wicker	J. D. Kernodle, Graham, N. C.	26	25
Graham-Prov. Mem.	J. U. Fogleman	Mrs. W. H. Holt, Graham, N. C.	83	89
Hank's Chapel	R. L. House	Mrs. Sam M. White, Pittsboro, N. C.	167	170
High Point	J. M. Allred	Mrs. M. D. Woodell, High Point, N. C.	77	91
Liberty	E. C. Brady	C. L. Bray, Liberty, N. C.	22	20
Mount Pleasant	H. V. Cox	Y. V. Brooks, R. 2, Vass, N. C.		65
Needham's Grove			84	
New Center	D. R. Moffitt	Helen Garner, Seagrove, N. C.	81	79
Parks Cross Roads	J. C. Cummings	W. R. Rightsell, Ramseur, N. C., R. 2	157	153
Patterson's Grove	H. V. Cox	J. T. Ellison, Franklinville, N. C.	35	36
Pleasant Cross	H. V. Cox	Fannie Ellison, R. 1, Asheboro, N. C.	64	61
Pleasant Grove	T. J. Green	J. M. Browne, Bennett, N. C.	294	285
Pleasant Hill	T. J. Green	Paul E. Coble, Liberty, N. C., R. 3	176	185
Pleasant Ridge	J. M. Allred	W. E. Allred, Asheboro, N. C., R. 1	206	214
Pleasant Union	B. H. Lowdermilk	A. V. McDowell, Mechanic, N. C.	19	19
Poplar Branch				
Ramseur	J. C. Cummings	T. A. Moffitt, Ramseur, N. C.	95	96
Randleman	M. A. Pollard	W. G. Lamb, Randleman, N. C.	108	111
Seagrove	J. C. Cummings	Mrs. A. C. Harris, Seagrove, N. C.	36	37
Shady Grove	J. M. Allred	Mrs. D. F. Hulin, Martin's Mills, N. C.	52	55
Shiloh	J. C. Cummings	F. L. Tedder, Asheboro, N. C., R. 1	113	114
Smithwood	M. A. Pollard	W. D. Humble, Liberty, N. C., R. 2	136	138
Union Grove	J. M. Allred	W. R. Brown, Asheboro, N. C., R. 1	76	79
Zion	J. A. Denton	T. E. Farrell, Sanford, N. C., R. 5	196	179
Totals			3,662	3,854

Paid on Pastor's Salary.	Special Mission Offering.	Special Orphanage Offering.	All Other Benevolences.	Conference Apportionment.	Paid on Conference Apportionment.	All Other Expenses.	Total Amount Raised.	Value of Church Property.
$ 44.00	......	$ 13.50	......	$ 8.00	$ 100.00	$ 10.00	$ 131.50	$ 1,500.00
55.00	$ 7.75	3.71	$ 2.59	22.57	54.80	6.15	97.57	500.00
44.00	14.18	6.27	3.00	......	75.00	......	98.45	2,650.00
27.00	27.50	50.00	41.11	100.75	150.00	98.15	467.51	4,885.00
88.00	22.46	14.36	11.00	......	134.60	82.00	264.42	500.00
66.00	15.00	1.80	......	15.00	69.70	......	101.50	600.00
550.00	550.00	2,929.97	2,146.18	1,282.00	3,300.00	5,903.26	16,111.41	100,000.00
55.00	21.00	25.00	25.00	......	100.00	25.10	196.10	1,250.00
55.00	......	11.01	55.45	......	400.00	......	466.46	3,500.00
55.00	26.14	......	......	66.00	124.82	10.00	226.96	1,500.00
82.00	25.00	54.43	17.64	20.00	120.00	139.49	376.56	2,400.00
82.00	41.00	22.23	17.40	......	500.00	72.88	653.51	5,000.00
137.00	46.43	28.24	23.22	26.94	300.00	175.41	600.24	7,000.00
55.00	55.00	91.25	132.00	12.83	400.00	39.86	730.94	3,750.00
27.00	20.00	5.00	124.00	32.75	91.73	124.00	397.48	3,500.00
27.00	10.00	......	......	......	200.50	81.78	292.28	1,000.00
......								700.00
82.00	10.00	......	3.00	......	74.85	......	87.85	
137.00	45.70	20.16	......	190.04	300.00	22.50	578.40	3,000.00
49.00	11.79	5.00	2.75	14.34	82.85	15.35	132.08	800.00
60.00	60.50	46.76	......	56.95	196.25	22.50	382.96	1,200.00
115.00	35.00	4.00	8.00	69.00	200.00	......	316.00	2,000.00
68.00	56.16	78.86	94.84	256.00	250.00	181.56	927.42	3,000.00
115.00	115.00	96.88	64.65	240.28	2o0.00	138.75	905.56	4,500.00
115.00	5.00	4.25	3.05	......	61.50	10.40	84.20	550.00
......								3,
88.00	23.00	133.33	155.95	480.09	350.00	190.81	1,333.18	
55.00	35.00	34.10	35.95	64.00	250.00	127.00	546.05	2,
49.00	50.00	10.00	14.75	61.15	200.00	24.25	360.15	3,'5
55.00	17.00	4.00	15.00	47.00	57.00	23.00	163.00	9oo.
55.00	30.75	15.00	12.00	82.80	200.00	......	340.55	1,000.
55.00	55.00	......	......	160.00	200.00	......	415.00	6,5,0.
71.00	40.00	14.50	12.00	103.70	131.00	2.90	304.10	1 230.00
77.00	25.25	55.60	40.00	60.00	200.00	30.00	410.85	2,000.00
$ 2,695.00	$ 1,506.61	$ 3,779.21	$ 3,060.53	$ 3,472.19	$ 9,124.60	$ 7,556.10	$28,499.24	$ 176,235.00

SUNDAY SCHOOL.	SUPERINTENDENT AND ADDRESS.	Number Officers and Teachers.	Number in Cradle Roll.	Number in Home Department.	Total Number on Roll.	Amount Raised During Year.
Antioch (C.)	W. C. Thomas, Cumnock, N. C.	9	7	76	....	$ 10.00
Antioch (R.)	G. K. Needham, Erect, N. C.	8	....	117	....	18.07
Biscoe	J. A. Dunlap, Biscoe, N. C.	8	25	118	....	92.80
Big Oak	D. E. Coles, R. 1, Biscoe, N. C.	4	....	35	....	....
Brown's Chapel	No Report	....	....	....	....	....
Bennett	A. B. Phillips, Bennett, N. C.	5	....	42	....	22.50
Burlington	J. M. Fix, Burlington, N. C.	45	15	515	15	4,018.16
Ether	W. H. Freeman, Star, N. C.	6	....	54	....	65.12
Glendon	L. G. Phillips, Putnam, N. C.	4	20	76	56	50.29
Graces Chapel	C. L. McDuffie, Jonesboro, N. C.	10	....	166	....	66.00
Graham	Mrs. M. R. Rivers, Graham, N. C.	9	8	55	....	99.74
Graham-Prov. Memor.	Robt. Russell, Graham, N. C.	11	....	117	....	....
Hank's Chapel	H. C. Ferrell, Pittsboro, N. C.	9	....	105	....	139.51
High Point	No Report	....	....	....	....	....
Liberty	W. A. Fergerson, Liberty, N. C.	8	3	63	....	124.00
Mount Pleasant	E. M. Marks, Overhills, N. C.	5	....	64	....	41.78
Needham's Grove	No Report	....	....	....	....	....
New Center	A. F. Garner, Seagrove, N. C.	4	....	....	....	....
Parks Cross Roads	W. S. Cox, Ramseur, N. C.	8	15	150	....	170.66
Patterson's Grove (R)	J. E. Martin, Franklinville, N. C.	6	....	59	....	14.34
Pleasant Cross	J. Q. Pugh, Franklinville, N. C.	6	6	73	....	54.35
Pleasant Grove	Albert Brown, Bennett, N. C.	6	....	113	....	50.00
Pleasant Hill	W. A. Hornaday, R. 3, Liberty, N. C.	9	....	188	....	232.00
Pleasant Ridge	J. M. Newell, Ramseur, N. C.	10	14	146	....	240.28
Pleasant Union	E. G. McDowell, Mechanic, N. C.	6	....	40	....	18.00
Ramseur	E. A. Cox, Ramseur, N. C.	14	15	175	....	480.09
Randleman	S. G. Robbins, Randleman, N. C.	10	....	150	....	150.00
Seagrove	O. D. Lawrence, Seagrove, N. C.	6	....	60	....	55.00
Shady Grove	B. B. Martin, Ether, N. C.	6	10	76	....	33.00
Shiloh	F. L. Tedder, Asheboro, N. C., R. 1.	7	8	96	....	32.80
Smithwood	J. M. Smith, R. 2, Liberty, N. C.	8	13	107	....	160.00
Union Grove	W. E. Brown, Asheboro, N. C. Star R.	8	13	90	....	69.70
Zion	T. E. Farrall, Sanford, N. C.	7	....	100	....	60.00
Totals		262	172	3226	71	$ 6,568.19

Proceedings of the One Hundred and Fifth Annual Session of the North Carolina and Virginia Christian Conference

FIRST DAY—MORNING SESSION.

The One Hundred and Fifth Annual Session of the North Carolina and Virginia Christian Conference met with Long's Chapel Christian Church, Alamance County, N. C., on November 11, 1930, and was called to order at 10:30 A. M. by the President, Dr. C. H. Rowland.

Devotional services were conducted by Rev. J. W. Patton.

The roll of ministers and Churches was called and a quorum was found present. The complete enrollment for the session follows:

Enrollment.

Ministers—Revs. J. F. Apple, J. O. Atkinson, S. A. Bennett, J. S. Carden, G. C. Crutchfield, T. B. Dawson, J. H. Dollar, P. H. Fleming, Stanley C. Harrell, S. E. Madren, J. L. Neese, C. E. Newman, J. U. Newman, C. H. Rowland, W. T. Scott, R. A. Whitten, L. L. Wyrick, Roy Coulter.

Churches and Delegates.

Apple's Chapel—R. E. Apple, R. C. Apple, Robert Murrell.
Belew Creek—Mrs. Zeb Strader, Mrs. Annie Preston.
Berea—Miss Frona Taylor, Mrs. B. M. Bennett, J. U. Sutton.
Bethel—L. M. Pettigrew, Joe H. King.
Bethlehem—Mr. and Mrs. R. V. Moore, Mr. and Mrs. G. E. Brown.
Concord—W. B. Allred.
Carolina (Congregational-Christian)—John W. Trollinger.
Danville—Ed Harris, Miss Argene Harris, Miss Linner McClanahan, Mrs. Verlie Townsend.
Durham—Dr. W. H. Boone, J. L. Cash, Mrs. J. P. Avent, Mrs. A. T. Crutchfield.
Elk Spur—By letter.
Elon College—J. C. McAdams, Chas. D. Johnston, Dr. W. A. Harper.
Greensboro, First—W. B. Truitt, Mrs. Grace Stewart, H. V. Simpson, J. R. Truitt.
Greensboro, Palm Street—Miss Fannie Gillis, Miss Ophelia Morris, Mrs. J. L. Neese.
Happy Home—E. M. Gunn, R. J. Hudson.
Haw River—Miss Emma Thomas, W. E. Cook.
Hebron—W. C. Williamson, J. G. Williamson.

Hines Chapel—A. D. Gerringer, Holt R. Gerringer, R. W. Iseley.

Hopedale—Mrs. R. L. Gerringer, Mrs. C. B. Sumner.

Howard's Chapel—J. M. Lambeth, J. W. Madison, Mr. and Mrs. J. R. Stewart.

Ingram—Mrs. C. V. Dunn, Mrs. W. B. Alderson, Harry Henderson, Dr. S. T. A. Kent.

Kallam Grove—Miss Pauline Washburn, Mr. and Mrs. Ralph McCollum, J. W. Wilson.

Lebanon—By letter.

Liberty—By letter.

Long's Chapel—W. L. Barnette, B. T. Hester.

Lynchburg—Miss Maggie Hight, Miss Odessa Tolley, W. T. Dunn.

Monticello—By letter.

Mt. Bethel—Mrs. Clara Moricle, J. W. Moricle, J. G. Price.

Mt. Zion—Julius Pace, Zeb H. Lynch.

New Hope—J. H. Carroll.

New Lebanon—Miss Virginia Moore, Mrs. G. C. Moore, Miss Bernice Moore.

Pleasant Grove—By letter.

Pleasant Ridge—W. M. Crutchfield.

Reidsville—Mrs. J. H. Dollar, Mrs. Ed Chilton, D. E. Mitchell, W. H. Smith.

Rocky Ford—By letter.

Salem Chapel—By letter.

Salisbury—Mrs. W. T. Scott.

Shallow Ford—R. P. Iseley, Miss Mabel Iseley.

Union (N. C.)—J. P. Bowland, G. R. Graham, M. R. Kirkman.

Union (Va.)—J. E. Goode, A. J. Wilson, J. R. Murray, Mrs. Alfred Hayes.

The following petition was presented:

PETITION.

We, whose names are hereunto affixed, members, as we trust, of the body of Christ, having exercised repentance towards our Lord Jesus Christ, being desirious of association ourselves together as a Church, agree to be governed by the Cardinal Principles of the Christian Church, as set forth in Chapter III of Government and Principles of the Christian Church.

We, the officers of the Carolina Congregational-Christian Church—John W. Trollinger, Secretary; Lonnie Thomas, Treasurer; E. D. Paylor and Royal Councilman, Deacons—do hereby request admittance to the North Carolina and Virginia Christian Conference, and promise to comply with all requests of said Conference.

On motion, the Carolina Congregational-Christian Church was received into Conference membership, and the delegates enrolled.

The minutes of the United Church (Congregational-Christian), of Salisbury, N. C., in which the Church voted to request membership in the North Carolina and Virginia Christian Conference, was read before Conference.

It was moved and carried that the United Church (Congregational-Christian), of Salisbury, N. C., be received to Conference membership and that formal application be filed with the Secretary.

On motion, the pastors and delegates from the two Churches received to membership were presented to Conference—Rev. W. T. Scott, pastor, and Mrs. W. T. Scott, delegate from the Salisbury Church; Rev. Roy Coulter, pastor, and Mr. John W. Trollinger, delegate, from the Carolina Congregational-Christian Church.

Moved and carried that the printed program be adopted as the official order of business for this session, subject to such changes as Conference may elect.

Words of welcome by Bro. J. W. Fonville, of Long's Chapel. Response by Rev. R. A. Whitten.

The report of the Executive Committee was presented, as follows:

REPORT OF EXECUTIVE COMMITTEE.

We, your Executive Committee, have transacted the following business for Conference since the last session:

We gave the First Christian Church of Greensboro the authority to collect from the city for damage done to the Church property.

We granted a letter of transfer to Dr. W. S. Alexander to unite with the New York Christian Conference.

A letter of transfer from Miami Ohio Christian Conference to Rev. W. T. Scott received, and he was enrolled as an ordained minister.

C. H. ROWLAND,
STANLEY C. HARRELL,
R. A. WHITTEN,
Committee.

Moved and carried that the report of the Executive Committee be adopted.

The Treasurer presented the following report:

1929. REPORT OF TREASURER.

Nov. 1.	Balance in treasury	$ 82.30
	Received from Secretary, 1929 collections.............	4,248.46
	Total	$4,330.76

DISBURSEMENTS.

Nov. 29.	To W. C. Wicker, Tr. S. C. C................$3,559.76		
	To Central Publishing Co., programs..........	4.90	
	S. C. Harrell, Sec. work	25.00	
Dec. 20.	J. O. Atkinson, home missions................	100.00	
1930.			
Feb. 5.	J. O. Atkinson, home missions................	400.00	
Mar. 27.	Central Publishing Co., ANNUALS.............	100.00	
			4,189.66
Nov. 1.	Balance in treasury		$ 141.10

W. WALDO BOONE, *Treasurer.*

Moved and carried that the report of Treasurer be received and referred to the Auditing Committee.

The President appointed the following special committees:

Nominations—C. D. Johnston, C. E. Newman, P. H. Fleming, W. B. Truitt, W. M. Crutchfield.

Resolutions—J. H. Dollar, J. W. Patton, G. C. Crutchfield.

Collectors—H. V. Simpson, S. E. Madren, W. T. Scott.

Auditing—R. A. Whitten, W. E. Cook, J. C. McAdams.

Press—S. A. Bennett, W. A. Harper, J. O. Atkinson.

Memoirs—J. O. Atkinson, W. B. Madison, P. T. Klapp, J. S. Carden, J. U. Newman.

Place for Next Session—J. L. Neese, J. W. Fonville, Mrs. Grace Stewart.

During Conference sessions, the following were presented to Conference as visitors and, by motion, invited to seats as deliberative members: Rev. J. L. Foster and Dr. C. C. Ryan, of Eastern Virginia Conference; Dr. W. C. Wicker, president, and Revs. T. F. Wright, M. T. Sorrell and R. L. House, of Eastern North Carolina Conference; Dr. G. O. Lankford and Col. J. H. Harden, secretary, of Western North Carolina Conference; Miss Jewel Truitt, secretary of the Board of Religious Education; Rev. L. A. Nall, of the Baptist Church, and Rev. A. L. Lucas, of the M. E. Church, South.

The President, Dr. C. H. Rowland, delivered the Conference address, using the subject, "The Christian a Marked Man."

Dr. J. O. Atkinson conducted the administration of the Lord's Supper.

Closing prayer by Dr. J. U. Newman.

FIRST DAY—AFTERNOON SESSION.

Conference called to order at 1:45 P. M. Devotional service led by Rev. J. S. Carden.

The report on Sunday Schools and Christian Endeavor was presented, as follows:

REPORT ON SUNDAY SCHOOLS AND CHRISTIAN ENDEAVOR.

Your committee makes the following recommendations:

1. The support and co-operation of all our Churches in making the Sunday School and Christian Endeavor Convention an instructive and useful agency in promoting our young people's work.

2. We urge the financial support of the program and work of the Southern Christian Convention through its Board of Religious Education.

3. Pastors and Churches are encouraged to have well-selected groups of young people in attendance at the Elon Summer School of Methods.

4. It is recommended that our Churches co-operate in community training schools whenever and wherever available.

5. Parents, pastors and Church leaders are urged to study the courses in leadership training that are offered in the curriculum of Elon College, and to encourage their young people to attend Elon and avail themselves of these college courses.

6. It is recommended that our Churches give careful consideration to the possible improvements in plant and equipment for Sunday School and Young People's work.

> Simon A. Bennett,
> L. L. Wyrick,
> Mrs. Grace Stewart,
> *Committee.*

Address on "Sunday School Work," by Mr. W. B. Truitt.

Address by Miss Jewel Truitt.

On motion, the report of the Committee on Sunday Schools and Christian Endeavor was adopted.

The report of the Committee on Moral Reform was presented, as follows:

REPORT OF COMMITTEE ON MORAL REFORM.

In view of the present conditions, we ask for the adoption of the following • resolutions:

First: Be it resolved, That we, as ministers, delegates, and Church-folks of the North Carolina and Virginia Christian Conference, deplore the present "hysteria" of the "wet" propaganda and declare that we believe it to be "all bunk"; that it is absolutely false.

Second: We, your committee, believe that the Church should present a solid front against the organized forces of evil, so we plead with every voter of our constituency to exercise his or her full power of selecting for public office men and women of character and ability who are willing to support the Constitution of the United States, including the eighteenth amendment.

Third: That we acknowledge the worth of the Anti-Saloon League as a forceful and righteous agency in the great fight for God, home, and humanity and that we acknowledge the faithful servants of the Most High in the faithful against the demon liquor, and that we pledge to it our whole-hearted support, defense of home and nation, namely: the W. C. T. U.

Fourth: We recommend that each minister in the Conference preach a sermon between now and January 1st, if possible, on "Making Prohibition Permanent and Effective," or some similar subject; that we memorialize the Southern Convention to change the name of the Conference Committee on Moral Reform to the "Committee on Temperance and Moral Reform," and that the Convention provide for a board of that body to be known as the "Board on Temperance and Moral Reform."

We recommend further that the Committee on Moral Reform which the President of this Conference will appoint be requested to give its effort during the coming year to the organization of temperance societies and the holding of temperance meetings, as far as possible, in all the Churches.

> G. C. Crutchfield,
> J. S. Carden,
> *Committee.*

Address by Dr. C. C. Ryan.

On motion, the report of the Committee on Moral Reform was adopted.

Recognition of Armistice Day by the Conference standing in silent prayer. Rev. Stanley C. Harrell led the Conference in a prayer for world peace.

On motion, the Conference adjourned for the day. Closing prayer led by Dr. C. C. Ryan.

SECOND DAY—MORNING SESSION.

Conference called to order at 9:30 A. M. Devotional services led by Rev. Roy Coulter.

Minutes of previous day's sessions were read and adopted.

The Nominating Committee reported as follows:

REPORT OF NOMINATING COMMITTEE.

Your committee submits the following nominations:

President—Dr. C. H. Rowland.
Vice-President—Rev. R. A. Whitten.
Secretary—Rev. Stanley C. Harrell.
Assistant Secretary—Mrs. Grace Stewart.
Treasurer—Dr. W. Waldo Boone.
Home Mission Board—W. B. Truitt, A. W. Hurst, Stanley C. Harrell, C. E. Newman; Dr. C. H. Rowland, ex-officio.

The committee recommends that the Conference elect some one as "Musical Director" for the Conference session, and suggests the name of Rev. Jesse H. Dollar for that position.

CHAS. D. JOHNSTON,
C. E. NEWMAN,
W. B. TRUITT,
P. H. FLEMING,
G. C. CRUTCHFIELD,
Committee.

Moved and carried that the report of the Nominating Committee be adopted, and that the Secretary be instructed to cast the ballot of the Conference in favor of the nominees. The nominees were elected to their respective offices by ballot.

The President requested Revs. G. C. Crutchfield and R. A. Whitten to act as a Committee on Grouping Churches and report to Conference at this session.

Moved and carried that this Conference elect two publicity men to serve between sessions. Dr. J. O. Atkinson and Rev. W. T. Scott were elected to handle Conference publicity.

The report on home missions was presented as follows:

REPORT OF HOME MISSION BOARD.

As a Conference, we seem to have lost our initiative in home mission work. There are places within our borders that ought to have Christian Churches, but we seem to be satisfied with holding to the places we have. Two Churches joined the Conference this year, but without our help. Our Conference should add one or more Churches to our number each year. As a local Church grows by adding individual members, a Conference grows by adding Churches and congregations.

At the last session of Conference, it was voted, upon the recommendation of this board, that, out of the funds sent up to Conference by the Churches, $500.00 be retained for home mission work, same to be turned over to the Secretary of the Southern Christian Convention Mission Board, to be expended within the bounds of this Conference upon recommendation of this board. Of this amount, the Conference voted that $100.00 be appropriated to the Lynchburg Church. Upon recommendation of this board, $150.00 was applied to the rent of a parsonage for the Lynchburg Church. The balance of $250.00 remains in the hands of the S. C. C. Mission Board.

On petition of the Lynchburg Church, we recommend an appropriation of $300.00 on parsonage rent and $100.00 on pastor's salary at Lynchburg, parsonage rental to be paid monthly, salary appropriation to be paid quarterly.

We recommend that, of the funds sent to this Conference by the Churches, $150.00 be paid to the Secretary of the S. C. C. Mission Board, which, together with the $250.00 now in hand, will cover appropriations herein made to the United Church, Lynchburg, and that the Secretary of Missions pay out same as provided in this report.

The Southern Christian Convention voted at its last session to raise $50,000 a year for each year of the present biennium, one-half for home and half for foreign missions. We recommend that, as a Conference, we do our part in this undertaking, and that our goal for the Churches be as last year—one-third of the amount of the pastor's salary.

W. B. Truitt,
C. E. Newman,
Stanley C. Harrell,
C. H. Rowland, ex-officio,
Home Mission Board.

After general discussion, the report of the Home Mission Board was adopted by motion.

The report of the Committee on Foreign Missions was presented by Rev. J. W. Patton, acting chairman, as follows:

REPORT OF COMMITTEE ON FOREIGN MISSIONS.

We, of the Christian Church, have not been a missionary people. We have neglected, to our own hurt, economically, morally and spiritually, the fundamental cause for which the Church was founded. Our Saviour established the Church that, as an institution, it might bear His name and declare His message to the uttermost parts. This neglect has resulted in slow growth to us as a people and in an appalling indifference to the demands of the kingdom of our Lord. God allows a people to grow only as that people is missionary in spirit and in activity. In these latter days, however, God seems to be calling us again and giving us a challenge to new duties, heavier responsibilities and enlarged opportunities. The merger of the Christian and Congregational Churches, now effective through a unanimous vote of both national assemblies, has resulted in uniting our forces, Christian and Congregational, on the foreign field and thus giving to us Christians, representatives as missionaries, and missions to be helped in China, Japan, India, Africa, Turkey, Greece, the Philippine Islands, and in other remote parts.

Therefore, be it resolved, That as the challenge to this larger service seems to be of divine appointment, we do our best as Churches, Sunday Schools and individuals to meet the new obligations and responsibilities as laid upon us, and to enter with whole heart into this program of kingdom enlargement.

Second: That we, as Churches, Sunday Schools and individuals, through prayer, consecration and sacrifice, pledge to do our part in helping to raise $50,000 for missions this year—half for home, and half for foreign—as unanimously voted at the last session of the Southern Christian Convention.

Third: That in the forefront of all our missionary undertakings and activities, we put prayer, consecration and devotion to our Lord, in whose name and for whose sake the missionary enterprise is carried on. Our Lord, and not we ourselves, instituted missions, and what we do for missions we do in loving loyalty to Him, that the goodness and the glory of His life and love may be shared with all peoples everywhere.

P. T. Klapp,
C. E. Newman,
J. W. Patton,
J. L. Neese,
W. T. Dunn,
Committee.

Address by Rev. J. W. Patton.

Address by Dr. J. O. Atkinson.

On motion, the report of the Committee on Foreign Missions was adopted.

The report of the work of the Woman's Missionary Conference of North Carolina was presented, as follows, by the president, Mrs. C. H. Rowland:

REPORT OF WOMAN'S MISSIONARY CONFERENCE.

The annual meeting of the Woman's Missionary Conference was held with the women of Liberty, Vance, Church, on October 17th. There was a good attendance, a good program, and a fine spirit was manifested. A number of new societies were reported—the total number of W. M. S. in the Woman's Conference being 50, as against 43 of last year; Young People, 14 as against 13 of last year; Willing Workers, 8 as against 6 of last year; Cradle Roll, 15 as against 11 of last year. There are in this Conference 22 W. M. S., 6 Y. P., 8 W. W., and 5 Cradle Rolls. The next annual session of the Conference will meet with the society at Elon College, N. C.

Some of our pastors have been most active in promoting our work in their Churches, and there was a fine representation of pastors present at our annual meeting. There were seven district meetings held in the spring, and these were well attended and full of interest.

The total amount raised during the year was $4,443.10, of which amount $1,814.60 came from the societies in this Conference. While we do stress the financial side of our work, because there is an ever-increasing cry for means to further the missionary work, yet, through our Spiritual Life Department, we are seeking to develop, through prayer and Bible study, the spiritual side of missions. All of our societies are asked to make a study of Romans, a letter written by the greatest missionary since Christ Himself.

The following officers were elected, to be approved by this body: Mrs. C. H. Rowland, President; Mrs. S. C. Harrell, Vice-President; Mrs. J. P. Barrett, Secretary; Mrs. W. R. Sellars, Treasurer; Mrs. W. H. Carroll, Superintendent of Spiritual Life; Miss Lucile Mulholland, Superintendent of Young People; Mrs. R. M. Rothgeb, Superintendent of Cradle Roll; Mrs. W. T. Scott, Superintendent of Literature.

Address, "Marching With Youth," by Miss Graham Rowland.

On motion, the report from the Woman's Missionary Conference was adopted and the election of officers approved.

The report of the Committee on Budget was presented, as follows:

REPORT OF COMMITTEE ON APPORTIONMENTS.

For some time there has been a feeling that the apportionments for the Churches of the Conference have been too high, and this feeling has been accentuated by the general depression from which our territory is suffering. On the other hand, the Southern Christian Convention has requested this Conference to apportion to its Churches $7,500 for the Convention, and the North Carolina and Virginia Conference has never failed to meet any request of the Southern Christian Convention. The committee has made it its policy to add 10 per cent to the apportionment for the Convention for Conference purposes. Last year, accordingly, the budget was $8,250. One Church, of its own accord, asked for an increase in its apportionment, bringing the total up to $8,265.

In view of the facts stated above, the committee recommends that a minimum and a maximum apportionment be suggested to the Churches. If a Church raises the minimum it will be considered as having raised its Conference apportionment, but it is earnestly hoped that it will do its best to raise the maximum which will enable the Conference to discharge its full obligation to the Southern Christian Convention.

We, therefore, recommend the following apportionments for the coming year:

	Minimum.	Maximum.
Apple's Chapel	$ 150.00	$ 415.00
Belew Creek	100.00	185.00
Berea	100.00	165.00
Bethel	100.00	150.00
Bethlehem	200.00	415.00
Carolina	10.00	25.00
Concord	50.00	75.00
Danville, Va.	100.00	185.00
Durham	500.00	650.00
Elk Spur	10.00	20.00
Elon College	500.00	650.00
Greensboro, First	500.00	650.00
Greensboro, Palm Street	100.00	165.00
Happy Home	100.00	185.00
Haw River	125.00	220.00
Hebron, Va.	125.00	240.00
Hines Chapel	200.00	305.00
Hopedale	25.00	45.00
Howard's Chapel	75.00	85.00
Ingram	200.00	280.00
Kellam Grove	20.00	45.00
Lebanon	200.00	370.00
Liberty, Va.	75.00	110.00
Lynchburg, Va.	45.00	75.00
Long's Chapel	75.00	140.00
Monticello	50.00	85.00
Mt. Bethel	100.00	165.00
Mt. Zion	75.00	95.00
New Hope	20.00	45.00
New Lebanon	100.00	205.00
Pleasant Grove	200.00	555.00
Pleasant Ridge	100.00	130.00
Reidsville	150.00	200.00
Rocky Ford	10.00	20.00
Salem Chapel	75.00	120.00
Salisbury	20.00	40.00
Shallow Ford	100.00	185.00
Union (N. C.)	250.00	415.00
Union (Va.)	200.00	325.00
Totals	$5,135.00	$8,435.00

W. A. HARPER,
J. C. McADAMS,
R. A. WHITTEN,
Committee.

On motion, the report of the Committee on Apportionments was adopted.

Conference adjourned. Benediction by Dr. W. C. Wicker.

SECOND DAY—AFTERNOON SESSION.

Conference called to order at 1:30.   Devotional services conducted by Rev. C. E. Newman.

The officers elected at the morning session were presented to Conference, pledging their services to Conference, and the Conference pledging support to the officers.   Consecration prayer led by Rev. R. A. Whitten.

The President added Rev. W. T. Scott and Bro. J. W. Madison to the Committee on Religious Literature.

The report of the Committee on Stewardship was presented as follows:

REPORT OF COMMITTEE ON STEWARDSHIP.

The United Stewardship Council, representing thirty-four denominations in the United States and Canada, declared it to be their belief that the time is ripe for a nation-wide emphasis on Christian stewardship, and recommended that the respective communions so plan their programs as to give, unitedly, emphasis to this important subject in 1930-'31.

We begin the emphasis of this in our own Church with November. It will accomplish little, however, for the life of our people unless there is wholehearted observance of it by all our pastors and Churches. When God planted His Church, He gave a plan for its support. When we recognize this plan, our financial problems will be solved in a spiritual way. We need to recognize the claims of stewardship for all of life, and especially should this be presented to our young people in Sunday Schools and Christian Endeavor Societies.

We recommend—First: That our young people's societies plan stewardship programs in connection with their work, and secure literature from our publishing house to give them.

Second: That they stress not only the habit of tithing, but the consecration of their talents, their special training for service, and their Christian influence as a sacred trust to be used in the kingdom service.

Third: That the young people teach and promote the every-member canvass in meeting the financial needs of the Church.

Fourth: That our pastors co-operate with the young people in this undertaking by studying several books on stewardship during the year, and assisting them in the promotion of their programs.

S. T. A. KENT,
MRS. C. H. ROWLAND,
Committee.

General discussion on stewardship.   On motion, the report on stewardship was adopted.

Bro. Chas. D. Johnston presented a group from the Orphanage family, which presented a program of music and recitations.   Upon the invitation of Bro. Johnston, Rev. J. L. Foster presented the Orphanage work.

Moved and carried that an offering be taken for the Orphanage. The offering amounted to $38.50.

The report of the Committee on Education was presented, as follows:

REPORT OF COMMITTEE ON EDUCATION.

The recent session of the Southern Christian Convention adopted the following under the report of Board of Education:

"We recommend that the Convention endorse again the raising of a million dollars for Elon College, $400,000 of which shall be used to liquidate the debt of the college for which the Convention gave its bonds; and that when this $400,000 has been raised, the college surrender these bonds to the Convention; the remaining $600,000 to be raised in the campaign, we recommend, to be added to the permanent invested funds of the college."

Resolved: That, as a Conference, we ratify the same, and do what we can to aid in this great undertaking.

We recommend that a loan of $250.00 be made to Rev. Roy Coulter, now in his junior year at Elon College, and that the Georgia and Alabama Conference be requested to grant him ordination papers, in lieu of those lost.

Rev. W. S. Smith, a licentiate from the Pilgrim Holiness Church, came before the committee for admission into the Christian Church. He has served several months as pastor in Christian Churches. It is recommended that he be licensed as a probationer for a year, and that Revs. I. T. Underwood and R. H. Coble be continued as licentiates. Since the last session of Conference is advised that Licentiates H. Geo. Robertson and G. D. Underhill have been ordained elders in other Conferences and are, therefore, no longer members of or responsible to this Conference.

J. O. ATKINSON,
P. H. FLEMING,
J. U. NEWMAN,
Committee.

Dr. W. A. Harper presented the members of the Elon College faculty who were present. Dr. J. U. Newman, Mr. S. C. Heindel and Col. J. H. Harden spoke on the work of Elon College and the campaign to raise a million dollars for the college.

On motion, the report of the Committee on Education was adopted.

Moved and carried that Conference adjourn. Benediction by Rev. J. L. Foster.

THIRD DAY—MORNING SESSION.

Conference called to order at 9:30. Devotional services conducted by Rev. S. E. Madren.

Minutes of Wednesday's session were read and approved.

The reports from pastors and Churches were read. (For details of reports, see "Ministerial Reports" and "Statistical Tables.)

Moved and carried that the Secretary be requested to write letters to Churches not represented in Conference by delegates, expressing regret that they were not officially represented and urging the importance of all Churches being represented in Conference.

The Committee on Superannuation reported as follows:

REPORT OF COMMITTEE ON SUPERANNUATION.

We are not doing for our superannuates what duty enjoins we should do. Faithful pastors give the best years of their lives to the service of the Church on small salary, and in old age and declining health find themselves without support. Out of sheer gratitude to these soldiers of the cross, we ought to largely increase our annual offering in their behalf. The Convention has called upon us to raise at least 10 cents per Church member and send up to our annual Conferences to the support of our superannuated ministers and the widows of deceased ministers. It should be a privilege to do this much. As beneficiaries in this Conference, we have Rev. P. T. Klapp, Mrs. L. I. Cox, Mrs. J. P. Barrett, Mrs. C. C. Peele, Mrs. W. S. Long, and Mrs. J. W. Knight.

We recommend to the Board of Superannuation of the Southern Christian Convention that these be retained on the list, and that they share with others of the Convention such competence as resources will justify.

CHAS. D. JOHNSTON,
H. V. SIMPSON,
W. E. COOK,
Committee.

On motion, the report of the Committee on Superannuation was adopted.

The Committee on Religious Literature reported, as follows:

REPORT OF COMMITTEE ON RELIGIOUS LITERATURE.

There is a wealth of good reading material available for the reading public. An increasing amount of reading is now being done, and there are at least two questions which should be considered as we attempt to evaluate as to the time spent and the material covered: Are we reading the books and papers that are most helpful? Do we provide time and purpose?

The books which are sold through our publishing houses are selected with care and may be relied upon as being among those most desirable for our people. Therefore, we recommend:

First: The use of our Sunday School literature as prepared by the Joint Boards of Publication of the Congregational-Christian Churches.

Second: That the pastors co-operate with those in charge in getting Church papers into every Church home. The *Congregationalist and Herald of Gospel Liberty*, being the official organ of the Church at large, should be read for its instruction as to the general program of the Church. *The Christian Sun*, as the official organ of the Southeastern Convention of Congregational and Christian Churches, should be read for acquaintance and co-operation with the program of Church promotion in this section. We must heartily recommend the plan as outlined by our circulation manager, Mr. Chas. D. Johnston, to get this information into the homes of our constituency, and we beg that the pastors give their loyal support to this matter.

Third: Since it is important and to be expected that our young people read other literature than that published by our Church, and on various subjects, we recommend that the pastors read more widely in order that they may be able to give intelligent guidance to our youth; that the pastors keep before their congregations suggestions for reading, either through their Church bulletins or other effective mediums. -

Fourth: That the office of the Christian Education Board be asked to supplement the page in *The Christian Sun*, now devoted to religious education, with suggested books, articles and programs which will encourage and make more effective the third recommendation.

W. M. JAY,
J. H. DOLLAR,
W. T. SCOTT,
Committee.

Address on "Religious Literature" by Rev. J. H. Dollar. General discussion of the report.

On motion, the report on religious literature was adopted.

An offering for the balance due on the O'Kelly Memorial was taken, which amounted to $20.00.

The Committee on Resolutions reported as follows:

REPORT OF COMMITTEE ON RESOLUTIONS.

We, your Committee on Resolutions, recommend that the Conference extend a rising vote of thanks to the pastor and Church for their invitation to meet with them and for their generous hospitality shown during this session of Conference.

That we express to the officers of Conference our appreciation for their efficient and faithful efforts and service.

That we express our pleasure in the presence and participation of visiting speakers and deliberative members of this Conference.

That this Conference, through its Secretary, send fraternal greetings and sympathy to Revs. P. T. Klapp and A. W. Hurst.

J. H. DOLLAR,
G. C. CRUTCHFIELD,
J. W. PATTON,
Committee.

On motion, the report of the Committee on Resolutions was adopted.
The Collectors reported as follows:

REPORT OF COLLECTORS.

Thirty-three out of the thirty-seven Churches in the Conference sent remittances to Conference. The total collections from the Churches amounted to $2,875.74. (See "Statistical Table" for the amount sent to Conference by each Church.)

H. V. SIMPSON,
S. E. MADREN,
W. T. SCOTT,
Collectors.

Moved and carried that the report of Collectors be admitted to record and that the Secretary be instructed to amend if additional remittances be received.

The Auditing Committee reported as follows:

REPORT OF AUDITING COMMITTEE.

We, your Auditing Committee, have examined the accounts of the Treasurer, Dr. W. Waldo Boone, and checked same with vouchers and receipts. We find same to be correct, with a balance of $141.10, $10.00 of which was received from the Lynchburg Church after THE ANNUAL was printed. We recommend that this $10.00 be credited to this year's Lynchburg report, and that the Treasurer's balance appear as $131.10.

We commend our Treasurer for the efficient manner in which his records have been kept.

R. A. WHITTEN,
J. C. McADAMS,
W. E. COOK,
Committee.

On motion, the report of the Auditing Committee was adopted.

It was moved and carried that, of the funds sent to this Conference by the Churches, together with the balance now in the hands of the Treasurer, the Secretary draw draft for the $150.00 provided by the Home Mission Board report; that $175.00 be retained for Conference expenses, and that the Secretary draw draft for the balance payable to the Treasurer of the Southern Christian Convention, to be distributed as voted by the Convention.

It was moved and carried that the minutes of this session be printed in THE CHRISTIAN ANNUAL, this Conference taking 200 copies for pro rata distribution among the Churches; that the Secretary be paid $25.00 for his services, and that a bill of $3.75 be paid to the Central Publishing Company for printing programs.

The Committee on Grouping Churches reported as follows:

REPORT OF COMMITTEE ON CHURCH GROUPING.

We, your Committee on Grouping the Churches into Pastorates, find that, of the suggested groups, two are operating as suggested by the committee, and approved by the Conference last year. They are groups five and seven.

Delegates from the various Churches in Conference, with your committee, have agreed to go back to their Churches and see to it that a like committee from the Churches of other suggested groups be appointed to investigate the possibilities of perfecting the groups.

Therefore, we recommend that a committee be appointed from this Conference to assist these committees in solving their problems.

G. C. CRUTCHFIELD,
R. A. WHITTEN,
Committee.

On motion, the report of the Committee on Church Grouping was adopted.

It was moved and carried that the Advisory Committee on Church Grouping be composed of laymen.

The Committee on Place of Next Meeting reported invitations to hold the next session with Mt. Bethel, Berea, and Concord, with recommendation that the invitation from Mt. Bethel be accepted.

On motion, Conference voted to adopt the report and to hold the next session at Mt. Bethel Church.

The Committee on Memoirs reported as follows:

REPORT OF COMMITTEE ON MEMOIRS.

On September 10, 1930, Rev. J. W. Knight, Stokesdale, N. C., a beloved and faithful member of this Conference, passed from labor to reward. For thirty years he had served as a devout minister of the gospel, revealing both by word and deed the spirit of his Lord and Master. While we of this Conference shall see his face no more, all of us who knew him realize that if we are faithful, as we all feel that he was, we shall meet him in the better world. One of the highest testimonies to his Christian walk and work was that his home people and those about him believed in him and took note of him that he walked with Jesus. At the time of his death he was serving, as pastor, his own home Church, Mt. Bethel, also nearby Churches—New Lebanon, Howard's

Chapel, and New Hope. These Churches, as well as others he served, loved him and he loved them, and in the fellowship of devoted service they took sweet counsel together as they went up from time to time to the house of the Lord.

The funeral service was conducted by Rev. P. T. Klapp and others from Mt. Bethel Church, on September 12th, in the presence of a great host who gathered to do honor to the last remains and memory of a man beloved in Christ.

Resolved, That we express to the bereaved wife, five sons and five daughters our sympathy in the going away of their loved one.

Resolved, second, That this memoir be made a part of our minutes.

J. O. ATKINSON,
J. U. NEWMAN,
J. S. CARDEN,
Committee.

Moved and carried that report of the Committee on Memoirs be adopted.

Moved and carried that the Secretary inform the Churches as to Conference apportionments for the coming year, and the distribution of the same.

Moved and carried that Chas. D. Johnston, Dr. W. A. Harper and Mrs. C. H. Rowland be elected as the Advisory Committee on Grouping Churches.

The President appointed the following standing committees:

Executive—C. H. Rowland, Stanley C. Harrell, R. A. Whitten.

Education—J. O. Atkinson, P. H. Fleming, J. U. Newman, A. W. Hurst, J. H. Dollar.

Home Missions—W. B. Truitt, Stanley C. Harrell, C. E. Newman, A. W. Hurst, C. H. Rowland, ex officio.

Foreign Missions—P. T. Klapp, C. E. Newman, J. W. Patton, J. L. Neese, W. T. Dunn.

Sunday Schools and Christian Endeavor—S. A. Bennett, S. E. Madren, Roy Coulter, W. T. Scott, W. T. Dunn.

Moral Reform—G. C. Crutchfield, J. S. Carden, J. R. Truitt, J. F. Apple, L. L. Wyrick.

Religious Literature—J. H. Dollar, Dr. W. H. Boone, Mrs. C. H. Rowland, J. W. Fonville.

Apportionments—W. A. Harper, J. C. McAdams, J. W. Patton.

Program—C. H. Rowland, Stanley C. Harrell, R. A. Whitten.

Stewardship—A. W. Hurst, W. T. Scott, W. E. Cook.

Superannuation—C. D. Johnston, H. V. Simpson, W. E. Cook.

Minutes of today's session were read and approved.

Moved and carried that we adjourn, to meet with the Church at Mt. Bethel, Rockingham County, N. C., on Tuesday after the second Sunday in November, 1931.

Closing worship service conducted by Dr. C. H. Rowland.

C. H. ROWLAND, *President.*
STANLEY C. HARRELL, *Secretary.*

MINISTERIAL REPORTS.

J. F. Apple—Churches: Bethel, Mt. Zion, Hopedale. Sermons, 53; members received, 42; marriages, 2; addresses, 3; baptisms, 36; visits, 75; funerals, 3. Salary, $448.76.

J. O. Atkinson—Mission Secretary, Southern Christian Convention. Sermons, 30; addresses, 20; funerals, 2. Salary, $3,000.

S. A. Bennett—Professor at Elon College.

J. S. Carden—Churches: Mt. Pleasant, Antioch, Morrisville. Sermons, 80; members received, 4; marriages, 4; baptisms, 4; funerals, 4. Salary, $379.00.

Roy Coulter—Churches: Haw River, Hopedale, Carolina. Sermons, 24; members received, 2; addresses, 2; visits, 12. Salary, $115.00.

G. C. Crutchfield—Church: United Christian, Lynchburg. Sermons, 155; members received, 6; marriages, 4; addresses, 10; baptisms, 6; visits, 1,000; funeral, 1. Salary, $1,368.

T. B. Dawson—No charge.

J. H. Dollar—Churches: Reidsville, Kallam Grove. Sermons, 170; conversions, 22; members received, 48; marriage, 1; addresses, 17; baptisms, 27; visits, 842; funerals, 17. Salary, $1,860.50.

P. H. Fleming—Churches: Union (Va.), Long's Chapel. Sermons, 33; members received, 16; marriages, 2; addresses, 2; baptisms, 12; funerals, 4. Salary, $700.00.

S. C. Harrell—Churches: Durham, O'Kelly's Chapel. Sermons, 135; conversions, 24; members received, 43; marriages, 4; addresses, 14; baptisms, 19; visits, 300; funerals, 8. Salary, $3,000.

A. P. Hurst—Supply work. Sermons, 38; conversions, 24; addresses, 2; visits, 64; funerals, 2. Salary, $49.00.

A. W. Hurst—No report on account of illness.

W. M. Jay—Church: Berea. Sermons, 30; conversions, 12; members received, 7; addresses, 8; baptisms, 7; funeral, 1.

P. T. Klapp—Supply work. Sermons, 50; professions in meetings held, 60; funerals, 4.

D. A. Long—No report.

S. E. Madren—Churches: Rocky Ford, Elk Spur. Sermons, 62; conversions, 24; members received, 17; marriages, 2; addresses, 4; baptisms, 17; visits, 510; funerals, 3. Salary, $1,200.

J. L. Neese—Churches: Palm Street (Greensboro), Hines Chapel, Monticello. Sermons, 115; conversions, 265; members received, 108; marriages, 2; addresses, 4; baptisms, 80; visits, 825; funerals, 17. Salary, $1,350.

C. E. Newman—Churches: Hebron, Union (Va.), Liberty, Lebanon. Sermons, 91; conversions, 40; members received, 31; marriages, 6; addresses, 12; baptisms, 25; visits, 400; funerals, 20. Salary, $1,125.

J. U. Newman—Professor, Elon College. Marriages, 2; addresses, 5; funerals, 2.

J. W. Patton—Church: Bethlehem. Sermons, 29; members received, 14; marriage, 1; baptisms, 14; funerals, 8.

C. H. Rowland—Church: First, Greensboro. Sermons, 98; conversions, 15; members received, 28; marriages, 7; addresses, 12; baptisms, 14; visits, 1,080; funerals, 8. Salary, $3,000.

W. T. Scott—Churches: Walnut Hills (6 mos.), United (Salisbury, 6 mos.). Sermons, 80; conversions, 25; members received, 54; marriages, 5; addresses, 3; baptisms, 4; visits, 500; funerals, 3. Salary, $2,300.

H. Shelton Smith—No report.

R. A. Whitten—Churches: Hanks' Chapel, Mebane, Apple's Chapel, Shallow Ford, Mt. Bethel, New Lebanon. Sermons, 151; conversions, 57; members received, 30; marriages, 4; addresses, 5; baptisms, 26; funerals, 14. Salary, $2,000.

L. L. Wyrick—Churches: Concord, Bethel, New Hill. Sermons, 40; conversions, 3; members received, 2; addresses, 3; baptisms, 2; visits, 119; funerals, 2. Salary, $350.00.

LICENTIATES.

R. H. Coble—Church: Carolina Mills. Sermons, 12; address, 1; visits, several.

I. T. Underwood—Supply work with Presbyterian and Methodist Churches. Sermons, 20; addresses, several.

W. S. Smith—Received to membership at present session.

CHURCH.	PASTOR.	SECRETARY AND ADDRESS.	Members Reported Last Year.	Present Membership.
Apple's Chapel........	R. A. Whitten.....	Mrs. R. E. Apple, Brown Summit, N. C.......	413	304
Belew Creek.........	W. C. Wicker......	Jas. G. Fulton, Belew Creek, N. C.	130	129
Berea...............	A. P. Hurst.......	W. S. Simpson, Altamahaw, N. C............	102	110
Bethel..............	J. F. Apple........	Mrs. Ida Pinnix Murray, Corbitt, N. C.......	146	147
Bethlehem...........	J. W. Patton......	Clyde Iseley, R. 6, Burlington, N. C........	428	432
Carolina............	Roy Coulter.......	J. W. Trollinger, R. 3, Burlington, N. C.......	......	......
Concord.............	L. L. Wyrick.....	G. G. Anderson, Altamahaw, N. C............	91	94
Danville............	M. T. Sorrell.....	Miss L. McClanahan, 1349 Myrtle Ave........	266	300
Durham.............	S. C. Harrell.....	A. T. Crutchfield, 523 Warren St., Durham....	386	420
Elk Spur............	S. E. Madren.....	Mrs. S. E. Madren, Fancy Gap, Va........	59	68
Elon College........	A. W. Hurst......	J. C. McAdams, Elon College, N. C..........	386	455
Greensboro, First....	C. H. Rowland....	R. G. Moffitt, 813 Vance St., Greensboro, N. C.	447	456
Greensboro, Palm St.	J. L. Neese........	A. H. Hinshaw, B. 1402, Greensboro, N. C....	138	206
Happy Home........	M. T. Sorrell.....	Mrs. Geo. W. Hill, R. 3, Ruffin, N. C........	171	186
Haw River..........	Roy Coulter......	Mrs. Rosa B. Thomas, Haw River, N. C......	173	171
Hebron.............	C. E. Newman....	Alden Williamson, Nelson, Va., R. 2........	123	134
Hines' Chapel.......	J. L. Neese.......	L. V. Smith, McLeansville, N. C.............	222	217
Hopedale...........	Roy Coulter.......	P. R. Long, R. 5, Burlington, N. C...........	81	80
Howard's Chapel.....	W. S. Smith.......	W. B. Madison, Wentworth, N. C...........	87	97
Ingram.............	M. T. Sorrell.....	J. K. Landrum, Vernon Hill, Va.............	147	146
Kellam's Grove......	J. H. Dollar......	Mrs. Ralph McCollum, Madison, N. C........	45	45
Lebanon............	C. E. Newman....	T. J. Earp, Milton, N. C....................	121	126
Liberty.............	C. E. Newman....	Jas. T. Whitt, Nathalie, Va.................	148	152
Long's Chapel.......	P. H. Fleming....	J. W. Johnston, R. 5, Burlington, N. C.......	151	164
Lynchburg..........	G. C. Crutchfield.	Miss Ettie Harvey, R. 1, Lynchburg, Va......	108	114
Monticello..........	J. L. Neese.......	Miss Russell McKinney, Brown Summit, N. C.	55	63
Mt. Bethel.........	R. A. Whitten....	Miss Ethel Friddle, Stokesdale, N. C........	66	62
Mt. Zion...........	J. F. Apple........	Zeb Lynch, Mebane, N. C...................	99	123
New Hope..........	W. S. Smith.......	Miss Gladis White, Stokesdale, N. C.........	25	23
New Lebanon.......	R. A. Whitten....	Miss Carrie Sharpe, Summerfield, N. C.......	132	130
Pleasant Grove......	W. C. Wicker......	Mrs. D. J. Sipe, News Ferry, Va...........	385	376
Pleasant Ridge......	J. L. Neese........	O. D. Nelson, B. 1080, Greensboro, N. C......	90	95
Reidsville..........	J. H. Dollar......	Mrs. C. W. Gerringer, Reidsville, N. C......	305	337
Rocky Ford.........	S. E. Madren.....	Mrs. Flora McCrary, Cana, Va.............	48	53
Salem Chapel.......	J. L. Foster.......	Miss Selma Marshall, Walnut Cove, N. C.....	131	135
Salisbury...........	W. T. Scott.......	No Report.............	......	......
Shallow Ford........	R. A. Whitten....	W. E. Walker, R. 4, Burlington, N. C........	152	159
Union (N. C.).......	P. H. Fleming....	G. R. Graham, R. 3, Burlington, N. C........	299	295
Union (Va.).........	C. E. Newman....	J. R. Murray, Virgilina, Va.................	347	357
Totals.........	....	....	6,703	6,961

Conference Apportionments.	Amount Paid on Apportionment.	Special Mission Offering.	Special Orphanage Offering.	All Other Benevolences.	Paid on Pastor's Salary.	All Other Expenses.	Total Amount Raised.	Value of Church Property.
$ 415.00	$ 72.50	$ 17.56	$ 20.22	$ 90.50	$ 500.00	$ 603.00	$ 1,303.78	$ 12,000.00
185.00	15.20	9.40	....	10.50	300.00	46.00	381.10	800.00
165.00	10.00	25.00	52.18	15.36	250.00	125.00	477.54	2,500.00
150.00	55.40	....	....	23.30	200.00	22.30	301.00	1,700.00
415.00	133.00	70.00	55.50	....	350.00	598.67	1,207.17	5,000.00
....								....
75.00	35.48	11.82	....	....	150.00	31.00	228.30	800.00
185.00	....	89.12	103.07	490.00	850.00	848.13	2,380.32	10,000.00
650.00	650.00	1,144.69	647.27	336.82	3,000.00	2,363.60	8,142.38	57,500.00
20.00	10.00	2.00	2.00	4.50	10.25	1.00	29.75	3,500.00
650.00	325.00	479.00	207.92	794.92	1,000.00	873.16	3,680.00	7,500.00
650.00	200.00	700.00	351.00	100.00	2,900.00	5,522.29	9,773.29	60,000.00
165.00	13.50	73.00	84.00	18.00	600.00	763.07	1,551.57	10,000.00
185.00	45.00	43.31	40.05	81.00	250.00	73.86	533.22	1,500.00
220.00	80.00	63.00	87.85	135.00	252.00	645.62	1,263.47	5,000.00
240.00	20.00	23.00	25.00	....	200.00	75.00	343.00	1,500.00
305.00	120.00	50.75	26.68	....	400.00	192.57	790.00	3,500.00
45.00	5.00	2.32	10.00	64.00	32.31	....	113.63	3,500.00
85.00	65.00	30.00	25.00	25.00	126.00	45.00	316.00	1,500.00
280.00	105.00	112.00	45.00	47.50	400.00	53.20	762.70	2,500.00
20.00	22.26	7.91	3.41	5.51	75.00	42.37	156.46	750.00
370.00	....	11.44	22.40	....	300.00	170.50	504.34	2,300.00
110.00	20.00	8.31	....	....	124.00	16.94	169.25	1,350.00
140.00	32.46	11.81	31.56	....	200.00	166.00	441.83	4,000.00
45.00	55.00	163.00	48.00	48.00	993.00	470.00	1,767.00	7,000.00
85.00	21.65	55.35	17.92	183.65	182.50	⸮ 35.00	496.07	2,000.00
165.00	55.00	55.12	41.32	60.65	250.00	....	462.09	3,000.00
95.00	53.28	19.46	32.73	43.69	200.00	45.94	395.10	1,500.00
45.00	....	1.60	....	....	29.00	10.75	41.35	1,500.00
205.00	67.25	22.00	33.70	....	200.00	43.75	366.70	2,000.00
555.00	....	70.40	56.22	30.00	400.00	28.80	585.42	4,000.00
130.00	52.00	70.00	16.50	43.00	250.00	55.00	486.50	1,000.00
150.00	150.00	211.30	121.00	170.00	1,150.00	5,543.50	7,345.80	29,000.00
20.00	10.00	3.00	4.59	2.00	16.35	....	35.94	3,000.00
120.00	51.00	8.77	19.67	193.66	200.00	....	473.10	2,000.00
....					....			....
185.00	61.00	14.75	46.19	....	250.00	286.83	658.77	2,500.00
415.00	164.76	21.25	75.75	....	500.00	42.00	803.76	6,000.00
325.00	100.00	81.00	26.00	325.00	500.00	550.00	1,582.00	15,000.00
$ 8,265.00	$ 2,875.74	$ 3,782.44	$ 2,379.70	$ 3,341.56	$17,590.41	$20,389.85	$50,359.70	$ 278,200.00

SUNDAY SCHOOL.	SUPERINTENDENT AND ADDRESS.	Number of Officers and Teachers.	Number on Cradle Roll.	Number in Home Department.	Total Enrollment.	Total Amount Raised during Year.
Apple's Chapel	J. A. Cook, Brown Summit, N. C.	12	16	....	218	$ 146.94
Belew Creek	J. W. Strader, Belew Creek, N. C.	8	10	....	83	26.00
Berea	W. L. Iseley, R. 1, Elon College, N. C.	11	....	....	140	218.43
Bethel	M. S. Walker, Union Ridge, N. C.	6	....	....	66	30.00
Bethlehem	C. H. Sutton, R. 1, Altamahaw, N. C.	15	12	....	142	119.80
Carolina		....	....	....	....	....
Concord	W. L. Miles, Altamahaw, N. C.	6	....	....	35	....
Danville	J. E. Jones, Myrtle Ave., Danville, Va.	18	15	....	318	....
Durham	R. J. Kernodle, 1013 Watts St., Durham, N. C.	36	14	38	374	1,192.26
Elk Spur	S. E. Madren, Fancy Gap, Va.	3	....	....	35	9.50
Elon College	C. M. Cannon, Elon College, N. C.	27	....	....	225	350.00
Greensboro, First	S. D. Scott, Scott Ave., Greensboro, N. C.	25	40	....	300	885.44
Greensboro, Palm Street	S. C. Brady, Poplar St., Greensboro, N. C.	26	48	....	389	592.99
Happy Home	R. J. Hudson, Reidsville, N. C.	6	....	....	88	67.96
Haw River	Herma Neese, Haw River, N. C.	14	....	....	161	290.89
Hebron	W. P. Williamson, R. 2, Nelson, Va.	9	....	....	90	27.00
Hines' Chapel	L. V. Smith, McLeansville, N. C.	6	....	....	160	113.56
Hopedale	B. F. Blanchard, Burlington, N. C., R. 3	8	....	....	101	70.44
Howard's Chapel	J. C. Madison, Wentworth, N. C.	7	....	....	45	50.00
Ingram	J. K. Landrum, Ingram, Va.	7	18	....	120	42.75
Kallam Grove	J. F. Foulks, Madison, N. C.	6	....	....	55	19.88
Lebanon	H. G. Earp, Milton, N. C.	7	....	....	43	106.56
Liberty	Edd Tuck, Nathalie, Va.	12	....	....	126	86.00
Long's Chapel	R. W. Barnette, Mebane, N. C.	11	18	....	140	100.00
Lynchburg	W. T. Dunn, R. 1, Lynchburg, Va.	11	....	15	106	249.00
Monticello	J. E. Cumbie, Brown Summit, N. C.	8	....	....	70	74.50
Mt. Bethel	L. P. Rippey, Wentworth, N. C.	5	....	....	60	95.87
Mt. Zion	Julius Pace, R. 3, Mebane, N. C.	6	....	....	75	35.94
New Hope	E. P. Smith, R. 1, Stokesdale, N. C.	6	....	....	60	9.93
New Lebanon	W. T. Moore, Wentworth, N. C.	10	....	....	117	181.04
Pleasant Grove	Miss Nannie B. Farmer, News Ferry, Va.	8	....	....	120	133.91
Pleasant Ridge	C. B. Higgins, Guilford College, N. C.	8	10	....	90	65.00
Reidsville	T. J. Mitchell, Reidsville, N. C.	22	....	....	312	455.00
Rocky Ford	Walter Edwards, Cana, Va.	7	....	....	55	13.25
Salem Chapel	W. L. Marshall, Walnut Cove, N. C.	7	....	....	50	62.76
Salisbury		....	....	....	....	....
Shallow Ford	J. L. Loy, Burlington, N. C.	15	....	....	149	114.08
Union (N. C.)	W. H. Garrison, R. 2, Burlington, N. C.	10	14	....	161	156.40
Union (Va.)	Alfred Hayes, Virgilina, Va.	10	6	....	100	200.00
Totals		419	221	53	4979	$ 6,393.08

Proceedings of the One Hundred and Fifth Annual Session of the Eastern North Carolina Christian Conference

CATAWBA SPRINGS CHRISTIAN CHURCH—NOVEMBER 18-20, 1930.

FIRST DAY—MORNING SESSION.

The One Hundred and Fifth Annual Session of the Eastern North Carolina Christian Conference met with the Catawba Springs Christian Church. The Conference was called to order at 10:30 o'clock by Dr. W. C. Wicker, President.

Song service conducted by Mr. George McCullers. Prayer by Rev. Geo. R. Underwood. Devotional by Rev. T. Fred Wright.

Roll of ministers and Churches was called, and the following were present

ENROLLMENT.

Ministers—Revs. J. A. Denton, W. C. Wicker, R. L. House, Herbert Scholz, H. E. Crutchfield, J. Lee Johnson, T. Fred Wright, J. C. Cummings, J. E. Franks, B. J. Howard.

Churches and Delegates.

Amelia—M. C. Smith.

Antioch—Mr. and Mrs. J. B. Moseley, Mr. J. W. Reed, Mrs. S. R. Jones.

Auburn—Mr. and Mrs. E. J. Poole.

Bethel—Aaron Holleman, C. B. Holland.

Bethlehem—

Beulah—J. B. Edwards, C. J. Perry.

Caroleigh—R. L. Johnson.

Cary—J. F. Hilliard, M. J. Carlton, J. C. Mathews.

Catawba Springs—B. F. Branch, D. L. Mann, M. C. Sorrell, J. T. Carroll.

Chapel Hill—

Christian Chapel—B. N. Dickens, W. E. Peele, J. C. Ellis, Merry Callan.

Christian Light—T. R. Brown.

Clayton—W. C. Bundy, C. P. Hill.

Damascus—

Ebenezer—J. E. Dillard, J. W. King.

Fuller's Chapel—W. S. Briggs, Miss Gladys Woodlief, Miss Clara Coghill.

Good Hope—

Hayes Chapel—Lee Hatcher, W. Stone, Mrs. Frank Carroll.

Henderson—W. A. Newman, Mrs. E. T. Vickers, Mrs. D. L. Langston.

Lebanon—Alvis Holder, Ruford Spivey.

Lee Chapel—

Liberty—C. O. Wrenn, G. W. Eaves, Mr. and Mrs. Murdock Newman.

Martha's Chapel—

Mebane—T. C. Ferrell, Miss Dela Fowler.

Moore's Union—

Morrisville—E. W. Clements, Mrs. G. J. Green.

Mt. Auburn—A. P. Read, W. A. Hilliard, Miss Ella Hilliard, J. A. Kimball.

Mt. Carmel—Mrs. A. W. Sandling, Miss Emma Mitchell.

Mt. Gilead—

Mt. Hermon—

New Elam—R. L. Trotter, W. M. Goodwin, Miss Lola Jones, Miss Blanche Holt.

New Hill—Mrs. E. M. Holt, Mrs. W. G. Wilson.

New Hope—W. M. King, P. J. King, Mrs. Pope.

Oak Level—W. H. Hudson.

O'Kelly's Chapel—

Piney Plains—G. C. Oliver, W. R. Horton, H. G. Franklin.

Pleasant Hill—Booker Creech, Berkly Barbour.

Pleasant Union—Mrs. M. E. Wilder, Miss Iva McKinnie, Hugh Greene, Malcone Upchurch.

Plymouth—Miss Nora Partin.

Pope's Chapel—J. W. House.

Raleigh—Mrs. E. W. Boshart, Mr. and Mrs. C. H. Stephenson, L. L. Vaughan.

Sanford—C. C. Way, Mrs. C. L. Wicker, K. B. Way.

Shallow Well—Mrs. Doyle Mc Farland, Mrs. L. J. Sloan, L. J. Sloan, B. W. Thomas.

Six Forks—

Turner's Chapel—C. S. Kelly, Mrs. J. W. Myers, Mrs. R. L. Ross.

Wake Chapel—N. B. Hester, K. B. Johnson.

Wentworth—W. M. Rowland, Mrs. G. M. Williams.

Youngsville—

Address of welcome was made by Mr. John Murray.

Dr. Wicker introduced Mr. Herbert Scholz, who responded to the address of welcome.

On motion, the following were recognized by the Conference and invited to seats as deliberative members: Revs. D. M. Spence, E. M. Carter, Geo. R. Underwood, J. L. Foster, W. Sykes Smith, J. Edward Kirbye, F. C. Lester, Mrs. Lester, Dr. J. O. Atkinson, Miss Jewel

Truitt, Miss Priscilla Chase and Bro. C. D. Johnston. Each one responded to the recognition.

On motion, Rev. E. M. Carter was voted a member of the Eastern North Carolina Christian Conference, having been transferred from the Alabama Christian Conference.

Report of Executive Committee. Dr. Wicker, President, stated that at the last Conference the business was transacted so well that the Executive Committee had no report to make at this time.

Prayer.

The annual address by the President was delivered by Dr. W. C. Wicker.

On motion, the Conference adjourned.

FIRST DAY—AFTERNOON SESSION.

The Conference was called to order at 1:30 o'clock by the President. Song service conducted by Mr. Geo. McCullers. Devotional by Rev. J. A. Denton. Prayer by Mr. David Mann.

Appointment of committees as follows:

Rev. R. L. House was appointed chairman of the Committee on Home Missions to take the place of Rev. M. T. Sorrell.

Rev. E. M. Carter was appointed chairman of the Committee on Foreign Missions to take the place of Rev. B. J. Howard.

Press Committee—Rev. Herbert Scholz.

Resolutions Committee—Rev. T. F. Wright, H. E. Crutchfield, J. E. Franks.

Place of Meeting—W. A. Newman.

Report of Committee on Education by Rev. J. Lee Johnson.

In the absence of Dr. W. A. Harper, Dr. J. E. Kirbye was asked to introduce Mr. S. C. Heindel, business manager of Elon College, who gave the address on "Education and Elon College."

On motion, the report of the Committee on Education was adopted, and is as follows:

REPORT OF COMMITTEE ON EDUCATION.

We believe in education and would urge upon our people the necessity of obtaining a Christian education. This is perhaps better done, at least among our own people, in their own institutions. This might apply all the more to young men preparing themselves to preach the gospel. Elon College is ours, and should be used by our people in preparing for life's great work.

A movement is on foot to better finance Elon College, known as the "Million Dollar Campaign." We recommend its endorsement by this Conference.

Bro. Jones Lee, who was licensed by this Conference two years ago, has been examined for ordination. As to the requirements laid down in Government and Principles of our Church—that is, to the very letter of law—Bro. Lee was hardly prepared to pass the examination, but the committee finds that he is a great reader and on many subjects, and is what we would term a well-read man. He has proven himself useful; his Church urges, and we recommend, his ordination.

J. May Dickens, Sam B. Wilson, and Raymond T. Grissom, each students in Elon College, and having passed a satisfactory examination, we recommend that they be licensed as probationers.

We recommend a loan of $150.00 to Mr. Raymond T. Grissom.

We recommend that Bro. Hilliard continue his studies in Elon College as a licentiate.

> J. LEE JOHNSON,
> HERBERT SCHOLZ,
> H. E. CRUTCHFIELD,
> *Committee.*

Report of Committee on Religious Literature, by Rev. H. E. Crutchfield. Discussion by Dr. J. E. Kirbye and Dr. J. O. Atkinson. On motion, the report was adopted, as follows:

REPORT OF COMMITTEE ON RELIGIOUS LITERATURE.

As long as the Church continues to hold before the people the highest ideals in life, there will be a place in its program for religious literature. There is an abundant supply of religious literature that is helpful in the development of Christian character. It is evident that the press, to a large extent, controls the public mind. This being true, it is all the more important that the right kind of literature be printed and distributed among the people. Every kind of literature is being distributed. It is our duty as followers of Jesus Christ to do all we can to encourage the people to read more literature that will be an aid in the development of the Christian life. We, therefore, recommend:

1. That we devote more time to the reading and study of the Bible.

2. That we, as a Conference, strive to place *The Christian Sun* in every home within the bounds of this Conference. We feel that this is the only way by which the members of the local Church may adequately be informed as to the program and procedure of the various enterprises of the Church.

3. That more of our members subscribe to and read the *Congregationalist and Herald of Gospel Liberty* than heretofore.

4. That we also subscribe to and study the *Missionary Herald*, which will inform us of the mission work in the United Church.

5. That each Church urge the Sunday School to use our denominational literature.

6. That we patronize our own publishing house, and keep in touch with the best literature available.

> H. E. CRUTCHFIELD,
> HERBERT SCHOLZ,
> *Committee.*

Mr. Chas. D. Johnston asked the chairman of the Board of Publication, L. L. Vaughan, to make a short talk with reference to *The Christian Sun* prior to his address.

Address, "The Christian Sun," by Mr. Chas. D. Johnston.

Report of Committee on Sunday Schools and Christian Endeavor Societies, by Mr. C. H. Stephenson. Discussion. On motion, the report was adopted, as follows:

REPORT OF SUNDAY SCHOOL AND CHRISTIAN ENDEAVOR SOCIETIES.

The Sunday School being an institution for creating, and the Christian Endeavor Society an institution for applying spiritual energy, activities and ambition, we feel that both these organizations are essential and necessary to progressive and intelligent Church work.

It is gratifying to note the increase in attendance, annual reports, and Convention dues at our last Convention, held at Liberty Vance, over the previous year. In 1929, two Christian Endeavor Societies and fourteen Sunday Schools reported $91.10; while in 1930, three Christian Endeavor Societies and twenty-one Sunday Schools reported $119.46 to the Treasurer; a gain in finances alone of $28.36.

Your committee is thoroughly convinced that better and more permanent results might be obtained if our individual schools and societies could fully realize their connections with and individual responsibilities to the entire organization of the young people's work in the Church.

The Board of Religious Education is composed of eight busy members, elected by the Southern Christian Convention, and does practically all kinds of Christian educational work. Therefore, we would recommend that each school and society give this organization its full and hearty support, and strive to maintain and keep alive a Sunday School and Christian Endeavor Society in every Church in the Conference. That every Church be represented at the next Sunday School and Christian Endeavor Convention, and Summer School at Elon College. That the work of our Mission Board and Christian Orphanage be recognized, endorsed, and helped financially each month.

That the Conference donate as liberally as possible to the work of the Board of Christian Education.

Respectfully submitted,

C. H. STEPHENSON,
T. FRED WRIGHT,
Committee.

Rev. F. C. Lester, chairman of the Board of Christian Education, gave a short talk.

Miss Jewel Truitt was introduced.

Report of Committee on Social Service, by Rev. R. L. House. The chairman read an amendment to the report on social service, which was accepted, and the report, as amended, was adopted.

REPORT OF COMMITTEE ON SOCIAL SERVICE.

We, the Committee on Social Service, would like to have it understood in the beginning that, although we are placing great emphasis on social service, we realize that this is not the only problem which the Church has to face. The Church must give its attention to organization, finance, missions, etc. Neither have we been carried away by the tide of humanism to the extent that our God is merely a projection of the highest known social values. We do not claim that social service is a panacea for all ills. Certainly we realize that the ideal society is not to be built merely on reformed government, but on transformed lives. This should be understood. We have presupposed all this and taken it for granted there are yet those who preach as if the two texts in the Bible to be taken literally are these: "Except a man be born again, he cannot see the kingdom of God," and "Believe on the Lord Jesus Christ, and thou shalt be saved." Those extensive portions of Scripture which deal with social interest being treated apparently as if they were all more or less figurative, or else simply explanatory of the one idea of individual piety. Personal piety is a foundation. The kingdom of God is a super-structure. It has been justly said that many people have been more ready to trust Jesus to deliver them from a hell of which He spoke but little rarely, than to believe Him competent to establish that finer social order on which He dwelt habitually in His utterances regarding the kingdom.

We need to remember that we are citizens of a commonwealth, and, as such, have grave and weighty responsibilities which we can neither shirk nor ignore. Our membership in the Church of Jesus Christ, our citizenship in the kingdom of heaven, does not destroy our citizenship in the State and nation to which we belong. "Render unto Caesar the things which be Caesar's, and unto God the things which be God's," is the sweeping positive commandment of our Master to all His followers. As citizens of the State, therefore, we consider ourselves responsible to the extent of our influence and power for the character of the laws of the State in which we live.

No man can be Christian in fact who does not carry the great principles of the religion of Jesus Christ into every relation of life. Be it urged, therefore, that we, as Christian citizens, both ministers and laymen, be active advocates of civic righteousness and determined opponents of civic corruption and of civil laws.

In the midst of the present financial depression, we urge that the ministers of this Conference co-operate with the deacons of their respective Churches, whose duty it is to supply the needs of the poor. In cases of extreme poverty, the minister should endeavor to co-operate with the proper welfare official. Ministers should also spend more time on their respective fields in order that no needy case may be overlooked.

We also recommend the endorsement of a portion of the report of Committee on Social Service in the last session of the Southern Christian Convention, namely: "Pastors, in their teaching and preaching, should emphasize the place and importance of the Christian home and family, the advancement of social education, the application of the Golden Rule in industry and economic life, the maintenance of purity in sex relationships, the appalling prevalence of divorce and its evils, the seeming increase of disregard for the Lord's Day, the observance and enforcement of law, the application of Christian principles to political life, the abolition of war and the promotion of peace, the practice of Christian principles in all our relations with other peoples and nations."

The Christian Conference, meeting at Catawba Springs, November 18th, urges the North Carolina Legislature to enact the following goals for working-children under sixteen years, as advocated by the Legislative Council of North Carolina Women, together with fourteen other State-wide groups:

1. Maximum of eight-hour working day for children under sixteen.

2. Completion of the sixth grade for children between fourteen and sixteen leaving school for work.

3. Prohibition of employment of children under sixteen in oiling and cleaning hazardous machinery in motion, in working around exposed electric wires, working with poisonous acids and dyes, and running elevators; and the granting of power to the appropriate commission to extend this list.

Respectfully submitted,

R. L. HOUSE,
J. A. KIMBALL,
J. F. HILLIARD,
Committee.

Report of Committee on Entertainment.

On motion, the meeting adjourned.

SECOND DAY—MORNING SESSION.

Song service. Devotional by Rev. E. M. Carter. Reading of the minutes of the previous day. Minutes adopted.

Ministerial and Church reports were received, and the following ministers reported: Revs. J. A. Denton, B. J. Howard, H. E. Crutchfield, R. L. House, E. M. Carter, J. C. Cummings, W. C. Wicker, T. Fred Wright, J. Lee Johnson, M. T. Sorrell, J. E. Franks, G. J. Green.

Special music by four ministers—R. L. House, J. A. Denton, E. M. Carter and T. F. Wright—who were dubbed by the President as the "Apollo Quartette."

Report of Treasurer W. J. Ballentine was read by the Secretary. This report was referred to the Committee on Finance, K. B. Johnson, chairman. Mr. J. A. Kimball was appointed to substitute for W. H. Wicker on the Finance Committee.

Report of Committee on Foreign Missions was read by Rev. E. M. Carter. Discussion of report by the chairman, the President, and Rev. G. R. Underwood.

Dr. J. O. Atkinson delivered the address on "Missions."

Song and prayer.

Report of woman's work was read by Mrs. D. I. Stephenson.

The reports of the Committee on Foreign Missions and Woman's Work were adopted, and are as follows:

REPORT OF COMMITTEE ON FOREIGN MISSIONS.

We, of the Christian Church, have not been a missionary people. We have neglected, to our own hurt economically, morally and spiritually, the fundamental cause for which the Church was founded. Our Saviour established the Church that, as an institution, it might bear His name and declare His message to the uttermost parts. This neglect has resulted in slow growth to us as a people and in an appalling indifference to the demands of the kingdom of our Lord. God allows a people to grow only as that people is missionary in spirit and in activity. In these latter days, however, God seems to be calling us again and giving us a challenge to new duties, heavier responsibilities and enlarged opportunities. The merger of the Christian and Congregational Churches, now effective through a unanimous vote of both national assemblies, has resulted in uniting our forces, Christian and Congregational, on the foreign field, and thus giving to us Christians representatives as missionaries and missions to be helped in China, Japan, India, Africa, Turkey, Greece, the Philippine Islands, and in other remote parts.

Therefore, be it resolved, That as the challenge to this larger service seems to be of divine appointment, we do our best as Churches, Sunday Schools, and individuals to meet the new obligations and responsibilities as laid upon us, and to enter with whole heart into this program of kingdom enlargement.

Second, That we, as Churches, Sunday Schools and individuals, through prayer, consecration and sacrifice, seek to do our part in helping to raise $50,-000 for missions this year—half for home and half for foreign—as unanimously voted at the last session of the Southern Christian Convention.

Third, That in the forefront of all our missionary undertakings and activities, we put prayer, consecration and devotion to our Lord, in whose name and for whose sake the missionary enterprise is carried on. Our Lord, and not we ourselves, instituted missions, and what we do for missions we do in loving loyalty to Him, that the goodness and the glory of His life and love may be shared with all peoples everywhere.

Respectfully submitted,

E. M. CARTER,
J. E. FRANKS,
Committee.

REPORT OF N. C. WOMAN'S MISSIONARY CONFERENCE.

A noted thinker of today says: "I am convinced that there is no more evil thing in this present world than race prejudice." And another has said: "One of the greatest agencies in the world to diminish race hatred is the foreign missionary enterprise." It has done and is doing much to promote understanding, respect, and good will throughout the world. The Woman's Missionary Society in the Church fosters and promotes this spirit and seeks to train the young in missionary thinking and giving.

When the women in every Church shall become interested in missionary work in a special way, then all of our Churches will be quickened into a new life. Our aim is that the women in all our Churches shall become engaged in this the greatest business of the Church. It is not enough that just about one-third of the Churches in this Conference should have their women identified with our work. We call on our pastors to help us change this record.

Our treasurer gives us the following as the financial report for this Conference:

Woman's Missionary Societies ....$ 935.70
Young People's Societies 10.00
Cradle Roll 36.53

Total ....$ 982.23

From the North Carolina Missionary Societies:

50 Women's Societies $3,465.43
14 Young People's Societies 570.55
8 Willing Workers' Societies 184.86
15 Cradle Rolls 142.54
6 District Meetings 52.30
Conference offering 27.42

Total $4,443.10

Respectfully submitted,

MRS. D. I. STEPHENSON.

Address on "Progress in Our United Work," by Rev. J. Edward Kirbye, pastor of United Church, Raleigh.

Committee on Nomination of Officers of the Conference was appointed, as follows: Revs. H. Scholz, E. M. Carter, J. Lee Johnson.

Announcements.

Rev. J. Lee Johnson announced that the Pleasant Union Church was destroyed by fire early in March. It was suggested that an offering be taken for the building fund of this Church. The offering amounted to $44.76.

On motion, the meeting adjourned.

SECOND DAY—AFTERNOON SESSION.

Song service. Special music by members of the Catawba Springs Church. Devotional by Rev. H. E. Crutchfield. Special music by the "Apollo Quartette."

Report of Committee on Apportionments by L. L. Vaughan. On motion, the report was adopted, as follows:

REPORT OF COMMITTEE ON APPORTIONMENTS.

The Southern Christian Convention, in session at Raleigh, April 29th to May 2, 1930, through its Apportionment Committee, apportioned the Eastern North Carolina Conference $2,500 as a Convention fund. The Eastern North Carolina Conference is requesting a Conference fund of $500. Therefore, in order to take care of the Convention fund and the Conference expenses, it is necessary to apportion $3,000 among the forty-eight Churches of this Conference, as follows:

Church	Amount	Church	Amount
Amelia	$ 40.00	Moore Union	$ 45.00
Antioch	65.00	Mt. Auburn	100.00
Auburn	70.00	Mt. Carmel	50.00
Bethel	40.00	Mt. Gilead	75.00
Bethlehem	30.00	Mt. Herman	30.00
Beulah	35.00	New Elam	125.00
Caroleigh	20.00	New Hill	25.00
Cary	25.00	New Hope	85.00
Catawba Springs	90.00	Oak Level	75.00
Chapel Hill	60.00	O'Kelly's Chapel	40.00
Christian Light	65.00	Piney Plains	75.00
Christian Chapel	80.00	Pleasant Hill	40.00
Clayton	50.00	Pleasant Union	85.00
Damascus	65.00	Plymouth	40.00
Ebenezer	60.00	Pope's Chapel	60.00
Fuller's Chapel	60.00	Raleigh	125.00
Good Hope	50.00	Sanford	90.00
Hayes Chapel	30.00	Shallow Well	110.00
Henderson	100.00	Six Forks	50.00
Lebanon	30.00	Turner's Chapel	40.00
Lee Chapel	30.00	Wake Chapel	160.00
Liberty	225.00	Wentworth	50.00
Martha's Chapel	30.00	Youngsville	35.00
Mebane	25.00		
Morrisville	15.00	Total	$3,000.00

We, your committee, recommend the distribution of the Conference assessments as follows:

1. Four hundred dollars to Conference missions.

2. Expenses of the Conference, including the printing of minutes in THE ANNUAL, the programs and Secretary's salary, and the balance to be sent to the Treasurer of the Southern Christian Convention.

Respectfully submitted,
L. L. VAUGHAN,
J. A. KIMBALL,
K. B. JOHNSON,
Committee.

Rev. J. L. Foster spoke on "The Place and Purpose of the Orphanage"; Mr. Chas. D. Johnston on "The Needs of the Orphanage."

REPORT OF TREASURER.

1929.		
Nov. 15.	Balance on hand	$ 423.41
	Collection for Conference	1,545.72
	Total	$1,969.13
Dec. 21.	R. L. House	$ 37.50
1930.		
Jan. 22.	Central Publishing Co.	4.75
23.	L. L. Vaughan	27.50
27.	Rev. W. C. Wicker, Treas.	1,000.00
Feb. 22.	M. J. Carlton	100.00
Mar. 29.	R. L. House	25.00
Apr. 6.	J. A. Denton	25.00
20.	Central Publishing Co.	100.00
May 8.	J. A. Denton	25.00
June 25.	R. L. House	25.00
Aug. 19.	J. A. Denton	25.00
Oct. 3.	R. L. House	25.00
Nov. 8.	J. A. Denton	25.00
17.	Balance on hand	524.38
	Total	$1,969.13

W. J. BALLENTINE, *Treasurer.*

Report of Committee on Finance was read by Mr. J. A. Kimball. On motion, the report was adopted, as follows:

REPORT OF COMMITTEE ON FINANCE.

We, your Committee on Finance, beg to report that we have examined the books of W. J. Ballentine, Treasurer, and found them correct. We recommend that $25.00 be paid our Conference Secretary for his services for the year, and also that a bill of $3.75 for programs and $8.37 for postage be paid.

K. B. JOHNSON,
J. A. KIMBALL,
J. F. HILLIARD,
Committee.

Report of Committee on Stewardship was read by the Secretary. On motion, the report was adopted, as follows:

REPORT OF COMMITTEE ON STEWARDSHIP.

Since stewardship occupies such a large place in the Bible, since faithful stewards were praised and blessed by our Lord and unfaithful ones could, by our Lord's own words, "be no longer stewards," and since such great blessings are derived by every one who puts into practice the teachings concerning stewardship, we, therefore, recommend:

1. That every pastor acquaint himself and his people as much as possible with the biblical teachings on stewardship, and especially on the point of tithing.

2. That every lay member begin themselves to study this important truth and put into practice the teaching of the Bible on the same, and especially that which relates to tithing, not only tithing the money, but time, energy, etc. If this be practiced, the question of visitation of the needy, sympathy to the unfortunate, and the financing of the Church would be solved.

CHAS. N. JOHNSON.

The report of the Committee on Evangelism was read by Rev. T. Fred Wright. On motion, the report was adopted, as follows:

REPORT OF COMMITTEE ON EVANGELISM.

We, your Committee on Evangelism, submit the following report:

Evangelism is the recruiting work of the Church, the winning of souls for the Master, helping people to the experience of salvation.

We should not depend only on a revival in the Church. The fires of evangelism should be kept burning every day in the year.

Soul-winning should not be left to the pastor alone, but members of the local Church should share with the pastor the responsibility of winning souls to Christ. The business of the Church is to bring men to a saving knowledge of Jesus Christ.

There are three recognized forms of evangelism, namely: educational, mass evangelism, personal visitation evangelism.

Educational evangelism is carried on mainly through the Sunday School and Young People's Societies of the Church. Our aim should be to win the boys and girls for Christ before they become hardened sinners.

Mass evangelism is the form most of us are familiar with and resort to in our work; however, we believe it fails to reach the unsaved in any large number.

Personal visitation evangelism is, we believe, the Jesus way. Teams of personal workers visiting men, women and children in their homes, getting decisions for Christ, can be more than one man from the pulpit.

We recommend that our Churches give more thought to the work of evangelism the year around and not confine our efforts to one or two weeks each year.

T. FRED WRIGHT.
J. A. DENTON.

Dr. Atkinson made an appeal to the Conference for $20.00, the balance needed to complete payment on the James O'Kelly Monument, which is located on the Elon College campus. An offering was taken, which amounted to $20.45, which was given to Dr. Atkinson, treasurer of this fund.

The report of the Committee on Place of Meeting was called for. In the absence of the chairman, Mr. W. A. Newman, Rev. T. F. Wright invited the Conference to meet with the Shallow Well Christian Church. On motion, the Conference voted to accept the invitation. The time of the meeting will be Tuesday after the third Sunday in November, 1931.

Dr. J. Edward Kirbye brought to the attention of the Conference the meeting of the Conference of the Carolinas of the Congregational Churches which would be held in the spring. He requested that fraternal delegates be sent to that Conference from this Conference. A motion was made and carried that delegates be sent and that we name ten ministers and ten laymen. The names of the delegates be presented by the Nominating Committee.

On motion, the Conference voted to subscribe for the same number of ANNUALS. The mailing of THE ANNUALS was left to the Secretary.

Announcements.

On motion, the meeting adjourned.

THIRD DAY—MORNING SESSION.

The Conference was called to order by President W. C. Wicker. Song service. Devotional by Rev. R. Lee House. Reading of the minutes of the previous day. Minutes adopted.

The President appointed Revs. J. Lee Johnson, J. E. Franks and E. M. Carter as an ordaining presbytery to attend to licensure or ordination of candidates for the ministry.

Report of Committee on Home Missions was read by Rev. R. Lee House, who was appointed chairman of the committee by the President, in the absence of Rev. M. T. Sorrell. Discussion of the report by chairman, Rev. H. E. Crutchfield, Rev. J. E. Frank and Rev. E. M. Carter. Report adopted as amended, as follows:

REPORT OF COMMITTEE ON HOME MISSIONS.

The Committee on Home Missions is pleased to report that Bethlehem has been reorganized and contributed a small amount to the Conference this year.

We are also gratified to know that Pleasant Union Church is to be rebuilt in the near future. As an expression of sympathy, a collection of $44.76 was taken in this Conference for this purpose.

We heartily endorse the assistance being given to Caroleigh by the Raleigh United Church, under the able direction of Dr. Kirbye. Weekly preaching, Sunday School, and prayer services are being conducted. We recommend that Dr. Kirbye be authorized and urged to promote, if possible, at Six Forks and at any other point where such procedure may be possible and desirable.

Four hundred dollars of the Conference assessments have been appropriated for Conference missions. We are persuaded that this amount is needed for home missions, and, therefore, recommend:

1. That Cary be granted $100 to apply on Church indebtedness, to be paid at once.

2. That Antioch be granted $50 on pastor's salary next year, same to be paid semi-annually.

3. That Clayton be granted $50 on pastor's salary next year, same to be paid semi-annually.

4. That $200 be appropriated to repair and recover the Franklinton Church, thus making it possible for services to be held. At the present time, the property is in rapid decay, and complaints are to the effect that it is a menace to the health of the community. This amount is to be placed at the disposal of the committee. The committee to investigate conditions with respect to securing help from former members of the Church before any expenditure is made.

We would also like to urge that the members of this Conference, and especially the ministers, endeavor to ascertain if there be any unchurched territory within the bounds of this Conference, and if so, report same to some member of this committee.

R. L. HOUSE,
W. A. NEWMAN,
K. B. JOHNSON,
Committee.

Rev. J. Lee Johnson presented to the Conference Messrs. J. Ray Dickens and Sam B. Wilson, both of Holly Springs, and now students at Elon College, and requested that they be licensed as probationers, which was done. Certificates to be given by Conference Secretary.

Rev. J. A. Denton presented Rev. J. H. Lee for ordination by the presbytery. Rev. J. Lee Johnson questioned the candidate, Rev. J. E. Franks offered the prayer, and Rev. E. M. Carter delivered the charge.

Report of Committee on Nominations read by Rev. H. Scholz. The report was adopted, as follows:

REPORT OF COMMITTEE ON NOMINATIONS.

Your Committee on Nominations nominate the present officers of the Conference to succeed themselves.

As fraternal delegates to the Congregational Conference, we nominate all the ordained ministers of this Conference and the following laymen: W. A. Newman, L. L. Vaughan, J. A. Kimball, Mrs. R .L. Ross, Mrs. R. J. Newton, W. J. Ballentine, Geo. McCullers, C. H. Stephenson, K. B. Johnson.

HERBERT SCHOLZ,
E. M. CARTER,
J. LEE JOHNSON,
Committee.

Rev. R. Lee House, president of the Sunday School and Christian Endeavor Convention of the Eastern North Carolina Conference, presented the following names to represent our Conference at the Young People's Meeting at Elon College: Mr. Stanley Pattishal, Sanford; Miss Lizzie Bell Newman, Henderson. Elected.

Report of Resolutions Committee was read. Report adopted, and is as follows:

REPORT OF COMMITTEE ON RESOLUTIONS.

Whereas, the Conference could not have been successful without the laborious efforts of its officers, the hospitality of its host and the loyal co-operation of those who have done so much to make it a success, we, your committee, beg leave to submit the following resolutions:

1. That we extend to the Executive Committee a vote of thanks for the planning and presenting of such an excellent program, and for their excellent service during the session.

2. That we express our appreciation to Bro. McCullers for the splendid music rendered.

3. That we express our appreciation to the Catawba Springs Church and community for its royal entertainment and generous hospitality during the session.

T. F. WRIGHT,
H. E. CRUTCHFIELD,
J. E. FRANKS,
Committee.

Motion made and carried that the Program Committee arrange for a Communion service at the next Conference.

The President presented the standing committees for the ensuing year, and are as follows:

STANDING COMMITTEES FOR 1931.

Executive—W. C. Wicker, L. L. Vaughan, J. E. Franks.
Education—J. Lee Johnson, Herbert Scholz, E. M. Carter.
Home Missions—R. Lee House, K. B. Johnson, W. A. Newman.
Foreign Missions—E. M. Carter, J. E. Franks, Mrs. L. L. Vaughan.
Evangelism—T. Fred Wright, M. T. Sorrell, J. A. Denton.
Sunday School & *C. E.*—B. J. Howard, R. Lee House, T. Fred Wright.
Social Service—Herbert Scholz, J. A. Kimball, W. A. Newman.
Religious Literature—H. E. Crutchfield, J. Lee Johnson, J. A. Denton.
Stewardship—M. T. Sorrell, J. C. Cummings, B. J. Howard.
Apportionment—L. L. Vaughan, K. B. Johnson, W. H. Hudson.
Finance—K. B. Johnson, J. A. Kimball, J. Milton Banks.
Program—W. C. Wicker, L. L. Vaughan.

Helpful suggestions were offered by several members of the Conference.

Song, "On Jordan's Stormy Banks," was sung at the request of Bro. Council, who is ninety-six years old.

Conference adjourned.

W. C. WICKER, *President.*
L. L. VAUGHAN, *Secretary.*

MINISTERIAL REPORTS.

E. M. Carter—Churches: Mt. Gilead, Good Hope, Mt. Carmel, New Elam, New Hope, Youngsville, Pope's Chapel. Sermons, 136; conversions, 41; members received, 36; baptisms, 42; pastoral visits, 403; funerals conducted, 18. Salary, $1,375.

H. E. Crutchfield—Churches: Fuller's Chapel, Henderson, Liberty, Oak Level. Sermons, 131; Conversions, 30; members received, 24; baptisms, 19; pastoral visits, 300; funerals conducted, 10. Salary. $1,485.

J. C. Cummings—Churches: Parks Cross Roads, Ramseur, Shiloh, Sea Grove, Glendon, Ebenezer, and Cary. Sermons, 166; conversions, 50; members received, 17; baptisms, 14; pastoral visits, many; funerals conducted, 10. Salary, $1,950.

J. A. Denton—Churches: Auburn, Clayton, Zion, Lee's Chapel, Lebanon, Turner's Chapel, Grace's Chapel. Sermons, 160; conversions, 40; members received, none; baptisms, 34; pastoral visits, many; funerals conducted, 10. Salary, $1,200.

J. E. Franks—Churches: Christian Chapel, Hayes Chapel. Sermons, 35; conversions, 50; members received, 24; baptisms, 18; pastoral visits, 100; funerals conducted, none. Salary, $350.

B. J. Howard—Churches: United Church of Chapel Hill. Sermons, 60; conversions, none; members received, 6; baptisms, none; pastoral visits, none; funerals conducted, 8. Salary, $751.

R. L. House—Churches: Antioch, Amelia, Bethlehem, Beulah, Martha's Chapel. Sermons, 149; conversions, 20; members received, 26; baptisms, 21; pastoral visits, 415; funerals conducted, 2. Salary, $424.

J. L. Johnson—Churches: Catawba Springs, Plymouth, Wentworth, Piney Plains, Wake Chapel, Christian Light, Pleasant Union, Pleasant Hill. Sermons, 175; conversions, 55; members received, 27; baptisms, 23; pastoral visits, 160; funerals conducted, 15. Salary, $1,600.

M. T. Sorrell—Churches: Third Avenue, Danville; Happy Home, Ruffin, N. C.; Ingram, Ingram, Va. Sermons, 220; conversions, 267; members received, 60; baptisms, 30; pastoral visits, 1,922; funerals conducted, 10. Salary, $1,500.

W. C. Wicker—Churches: Mt. Auburn, Graham, Pleasant Grove (Va.), Pleasant Ridge, Belews Creek. Sermons, 140; conversions, 30; members received, 25; baptisms, 20; pastoral visits, 440; funerals conducted, 6. Salary, $1,550.

T. F. Wright—Churches: Sanford, Shallow Well. Sermons, 120; conversions, 21; members received, 59; baptisms, 25; pastoral visits, 688; funerals conducted, 8. Salary, $1,500.

CHURCH.	PASTOR.	SECRETARY AND ADDRESS.	Members Reported Last Year.
Amelia	R. L. House	Miss Iola Eatman, Clayton, N. C., R. 1	85
Antioch	R. L. House	H. L. Wall	97
Auburn	J. A. Denton	J. Edward Branch	130
Bethel	J. E. Franks	Clarine Holleman	61
Bethlehem	R. Lee House	Mrs. J. H. Shearin, Littleton, N. C	
Beulah	R. Lee House	J. B. Edwards, Wake Forest, N. C	99
Caroleigh	J. H. Lee		40
Cary	J. C. Cummings	M. J. Carlton, Cary, N. C	28
Catawba Springs	J. L. Johnson	B. F. Branch, R. 2, Raleigh, N. C	198
Chapel Hill	B. J. Howard	Mrs. Annie N. Farrell, Chapel Hill, N. C	
Christian Chapel	J. E. Franks	Royce B. Dickens, Corinth, N. C	163
Christian Light	J. L. Johnson	E. M. Blanchard, Varina, N. C	102
Clayton	J. A. Denton	Herman Moore, Clayton, N. C	47
Damascus		Miss Lillian Bowden, Chapel Hill, N. C	97
Ebenezer	J. C. Cummings	Miss Mattie Carpenter, R. D., Cary, N. C	197
Fuller's Chapel	H. E. Crutchfield	J. C. Woodlief, R. 4, Henderson, N. C	106
Good Hope	E. M. Carter	Miss Nola Woodlief, Youngsville, N. C	92
Hayes' Chapel	J. E. Franks	Lee Hatcher, Garner, N. C	65
Henderson	H. E. Crutchfield	C. D. Newman, Henderson, N. C	107
Lebanon	W. Sykes Smith	Mrs. B. L. Mansfield, R. 2, Sanford, N. C	36
Lee Chapel			
Liberty (Vance)	H. E. Crutchfield	J. D. Newman, R. 6, Henderson, N. C	390
Martha's Chapel			
Mebane	R. A. Whitten	Mrs. J. O. Fowler, Mebane, N. C	23
Morrisville		E. W. Clements, Morrisville, N. C	25
Moore's Union	W. Sykes Smith	D. J. Womack, Sanford, N. C	122
Mt. Auburn	W. C. Wicker	A. P. Read, Norlina, N. C	171
Mt. Carmel	E. M. Carter	Miss Eva May, Franklinton, N. C	105
Mt. Gilead			
Mt. Hermon			
New Elam	E. M. Carter	Miss Blanch Holt, New Hill, N. C	288
New Hill	L. L. Wyrick	Miss Carey Welch, New Hill, N. C	25
New Hope	J. Howard Smith	John Chamblee, Louisburg, N. C	225
Oak Level	H. E. Crutchfield	J. W. Hudson, Youngsville, N. C	145
O'Kelley's Chapel	S. C. Harrell	J. D. Harward, R. 3, Durham, N. C	29
Piney Plains	J. L. Johnson	Mrs. D. I. Stephenson, R. 3, Raleigh, N. C	105
Pleasant Hill	J. L. Johnson	J. W. Neighbors, Benson, N. C	95
Pleasant Union	J. L. Johnson	W. S. Long, Lillington, N. C	115
Plymouth	J. L. Johnson	B. G. Partin, R. 1, McCullers, N. C	112
Pope's Chapel	E. M. Carter	H. G. Holmes, R. 2, Youngsville, N. C	111
Raleigh	J. E. Kirbye	R. M. Rothgeb, Raleigh, N. C	217
Sanford	T. F. Wright	Miss Stella A. Stout, Sanford, N. C	156
Shallow Well	T. F. Wright	L. J. Sloan, Jonesboro, N. C	183
Turner's Chapel	J. A. Denton	Mrs. R. L. Ross, R. 5, Sanford, N. C	68
Wake Chapel	J. L. Johnson	H. W. Johnson, Fuquay Springs, N. C	196
Wentworth	J. L. Johnson	Mrs. Geo. Williams, McCullers, N. C	79
Youngsville	E. M. Carter	W. G. Scarborough, Youngsville, N. C	47
Totals			4,782

47

Present Membership.	Conference Apportionment.	Paid on Conference Apportionment.	Special Mission Offering.	All Other Benevolences.	Paid on Pastor's Salary.	All Other Expenses.	Total Amount Raised.	Value of Church Property.
100	$ 40.00	$ 5.00	$ 9.31	....	$ 104.00	....	$ 118.31	$ 1,500.00
100	65.00	7.00	18.50	$ 17.00	125.00	$ 100.00	267.50	1,500.00
141	70.00	....	10.25	15.25	185.00	21.40	231.90	800.00
53	40.00	17.00	....	24.00	100.00	24.00	165.00	1,000.00
20	30.00	4.50	....	....	15.00	....	19.50	800.00
99	35.00	15.00	....	....	....	....	15.00	500.00
60	....	....	7.20	....	....	32.00	39.20	1,000.00
27	25.00	25.00	17.72	24.03	150.00	100.26	317.01	2,700.00
201	90.00	50.00	61.03	154.63	....	300.00	565.66	200.00
88	60.00	25.00	65.00	25.00	751.00	838.40	1,704.40	40,000.00
169	80.00	14.00	25.00	18.30	200.00	....	257.30	300.00
113	65.00	30.00	20.75	60.00	100.00	....	210.75	800.00
47	50.00	10.00	....	4.80	36.00	58.00	108.80	4,000.00
93	65.00	18.38	18.58	14.32	153.91	42.06	247.25	2,000.00
206	60.00	....	35.83	....	....	....	35.83	3,000.00
104	60.00	35.50	29.38	79.47	150.00	33.01	327.36	1,500.00
98	50.00	12.00	3.20	....	116.50	....	131.70	500.00
73	30.00	30.00	20.00	10.00	150.00	....	210.00	950.00
105	100.00	75.00	132.85	144.80	420.00	479.72	1,252.37	12,000.00
32	30.00	20.00	3.00	5.00	70.00	....	98.00	....
394	225.00	125.00	180.13	135.85	700.00	359.70	1,500.68	6,000.00
25	15.00	15.00	39.00	65.00	177.50	384.85	681.35	5,000.00
21	25.00	7.65	12.09	35.13	79.00	18.32	152.19	1,500.00
137	45.00	33.30	....	15.00	130.00	....	178.30	1,000.00
177	100.00	100.00	202.35	146.14	400.00	67.25	915.74	4,000.00
105	50.00	12.00	....	....	86.50	....	98.50	500.00
287	125.00	40.00	4.60	11.25	300.00	54.55	410.40	2,500.00
19	25.00	15.00	....	34.00	100.00	....	149.00	600.00
224	85.00	12.62	....	....	131.50	51.70	195.82	2,500.00
147	75.00	....	13.86	14.83	215.00	24.00	267.69	4,000.00
28	40.00	40.00	....	....	46.00	....	86.00	1,000.00
107	75.00	11.65	44.75	87.06	200.00	7.50	350.96	1,800.00
95	40.00	21.00	8.55	70.00	100.00	....	199.55	1,000.00
105	85.00	21.00	4.78	53.40	275.00	....	354.18	....
110	40.00	15.00	....	18.47	120.45	....	153.92	400.00
111	60.00	15.00	4.25	....	225.00	....	244.25	2,500.00
238	125.00	....	315.00	30.00	3,000.00	1,287.46	4,632.46	175,000.00
190	90.00	90.00	200.93	98.89	950.00	173.52	1,513.34	10,000.00
201	110.00	....	88.60	35.22	550.00	1,318.00	1,991.82	4,000.00
70	40.00	26.50	90.00	12.50	250.00	....	379.00	1,000.00
195	160.00	150.00	253.33	262.54	300.00	40.00	1,005.87	15,000.00
85	50.00	50.00	50.00	149.78	210.45	26.00	486.23	1,500.00
44	35.00	14.00	43.00	36.00	....	77.00	170.00	3,000.00
5,044	$ 2,765.00	$ 1,208.10	$ 2,032.82	$ 1,907.66	$11,372.81	$ 5,918.70	$ 22,440.09	$ 318,850.00

SUNDAY SCHOOL.	SUPERINTENDENT AND ADDRESS.	Number Officers and Teachers.	Number on Cradle Roll.	Total Number on Roll.	Amount Raised During Year.
Amelia	B. H. Phelps, R. 2, Clayton, N. C	6			$ 69.92
Antioch	S. B. Spragins, Gasburg, Va	7		56	26.19
Auburn	Douglas Branch, R. 2, Raleigh, N. C	15		92	71.99
Bethel	R. R. Marks, New Hill, N. C	6		31	14.00
Bethlehem					
Beulah	A. W. Watkins, R. 3, Wake Forest, N. C	4		64	12.50
Caroleigh	W. O. Murchison, Raleigh, N. C., R. 3	5		69	80.20
Cary	R. F. Braswell, Box 122, Cary, N. C.	6		50	154.05
Catawba Springs	Geo. McCullers, McCullers, N. C	7		129	84.78
Chapel Hill	Grady H. Leonard, Chapel Hill, N. C	10		86	125.00
Christian Chapel	Elmer Peele, Merry Oaks, N. C	7		74	20.00
Christian Light	J. R. Brown, Fuquay Springs, N. C	6		80	30.00
Clayton	J. B. Harrison, Clayton, N. C., R. 1	8		100	23.96
Damascus	T. C. Lindsay, Chapel Hill, N. C	5		70	46.80
Ebenezer	J. W. King, R. 1, Cary, N. C	10		136	38.28
Fuller's Chapel	W. S. Briggs, Henderson, N. C	8		56	121.86
Good Hope	Z. T. May, Youngsville, N. C	7		55	10.00
Hayes' Chapel	Lee Hatcher, Garner, N. C	6		56	
Henderson	C. D. Newman, Henderson, N. C	10		93	242.28
Lebanon	E. L. Pattishall, R. 2, Sanford, N. C	7	10	50	11.00
Lee Chapel					
Liberty (Vance)	G. W. Macon, Jr., Henderson, N. C., R. 1	18	35	240	342.95
Martha's Chapel					
Mebane	J. O. Fowler, Mebane, N. C	6		35	35.00
Morrisville	E. W. Clements, Morrisville, N. C	3		16	55.72
Moore's Union	G. E. Moore, Broadway, N. C	5	20	86	
Mt. Auburn	J. A. Kimball, Manson, N. C	10		107	83.18
Mt. Carmel	R. N. Evans, Franklinton, N. C	14		54	11.20
Mt. Gilead					
Mt. Hermon					
New Elam	W. A. Drake, R. 2, New Hill, N. C	7		95	50.81
New Hill					
New Hope	M. H. Privett, Youngsville, N. C	14		158	56.75
Oak Level	J. W. Hudson, Youngsville, N. C	8		79	79.75
O'Kelley's Chapel					
Piney Plains	J. B. Stephens, R. 2, Cary, N. C	4	16	65	15.60
Pleasant Hill	J. B. Barbour, Benson, N. C	7		60	28.00
Pleasant Union					
Plymouth	D. G. Partin, McCullers, N. C	4		41	14.75
Pope's Chapel	J. W. Suit, Youngsville, N. C	6		55	75.00
Raleigh	R. M. Rothgeb, Raleigh, N. C	26	8	209	254.04
Sanford	J. S. Truitt, Sanford, N. C	18	25	264	283.88
Shallow Well	F. F. Watson, Jonesboro, N. C	12		142	131.63
Turner's Chapel	C. S. Kelly, Colon, N. C	9		89	52.00
Wake Chapel	D. J. Ellis, Varina, N. C	12		122	234.14
Wentworth	B. L. Brown, R. 3, Raleigh, N. C	7		122	71.29
Youngsville	L. H. Ragan, Youngsville, N. C	10		50	75.00
Totals		340	114	3436	$ 3,133.50

Proceedings of the Eighty-fifth Annual Session of Georgia and Alabama Christian Conference

FIRST DAY—MORNING SESSION.

The Georgia and Alabama Christian Conference met in its Eighty-fifth Annual Session with the Oak Grove Christian Church on October 7th, at 10 A. M.

Song led by Mr. Claude Sorrell.

Session called to order by President Rev. J. D. Dollar.

Enrollment of ministers and delegates.

Election of officers for ensuing year:

President—Rev. J. D. Dollar.

Vice-President—Rev. C. W. Hanson.

Secretary—Mrs. J. O. Mabry.

Assistant Secretary—Rev. W. C. Carpenter.

Treasurer—Mr. H. B. Floyd.

By motion, the following were invited to be seated as deliberative members: Miss Dora C. Brackin, C. E. & S. S. worker of the Congregational Church; Rev. W. H. Spear, pastor of Methodist Church; Rev. G. S. Hunt, of Alabama Conference; Dr. McQuarrie, of Congregational Church.

Welcome by Rev. C. W. Hanson. Response by Rev. H. M. Gray.

Motion that program be adopted as order of business. Adopted.

Report of Executive Committee read by Rev. J. D. Dollar, and discussed by Rev. J. D. Dollar, Rev. H. M. Gray, Rev. G. D. Hunt.

Resolution read by Rev. W. C. Carpenter and discussed by Miss Brackin, Rev. Neil McQuarrie.

Report adopted.

By rising vote, the Conference endorsed the report of the Executive Committee.

REPORT OF EXECUTIVE COMMITTEE.

We, your committee have had the following business to claim our attention this year:

On October 19, 1929, we received by transfer Rev. Myron Tyler, from the Philadelphia Christian Conference.

Early in the year, Rev. H. R. Heard, having been called to the service of, and his ordination asked for by, the Church at Bethany, in the Alabama Christian Conference, we ordained him to the full work of the ministry.

We were called upon by the Church at Rosehill to help them to adjust some troubles that arose between them, which we did, and we are glad to note progress made by them since that time, and the outlook for that Church is very encouraging.

We have also prepared a program for this session of Conference.

We recommend that the Executive Committee of this Conference be empowered with authority to act with a like committee from the Georgia State Conference of the Congregational Church to arrange a time, program, and place for a joint meeting next year.   J. D. DOLLAR,

H. M. GRAY,

Committee.

Annual address by President J. D. Dollar.

On motion, the Conference adjourned for lunch. Benediction by Rev. Spear.

FIRST DAY—AFTERNOON SESSION.

Conference was called to order at 1:30 P. M. by President Rev. J. D. Dollar. Song service led by Mr. Claude Sorrell. Prayer by Dr. S. L. Beougher.

Motion made that Dr. S. L. Beougher and Dr. Jenkins be invited to be seated as deliberative members. Adopted.

Appointment of committees:

Resolutions—W. C. Carpenter, D. S. Hogg, G. D. Hunt.

Publicity—Mrs. J. O. Mabry, Ollie Bell Dollar, Lucile Slaughter.

Nominating—Claude Swanson, C. R. Rutledge, Estell McClendon.

Apportionments—H. M. Gray, Walter Hand, A. B. Smith.

Report of Committee on Education read by Rev. W. C. Carpenter.

REPORT OF COMMITTEE ON EDUCATION.

We rejoice that such wonderful progress has been made of late in our school system generally, and especially of our Church schools and colleges. We wish to call especial attention to our Piedmont Junior College at Wadley, Ala., and commend it for the thorough work that it has done, in spite of serious handicaps. We wish to urge a more faithful patronage of it by our people.

In behalf of Piedmont Junior College, we would, therefore, recommend:

1. That we give our loyal support toward our denominational schools and colleges.

2. That all our people, who feel themselves called of God to preach the gospel, train for His work in one of our Church schools.

3. That we approve the methods of securing $25,000 for current expenses for Piedmont Junior College, and $35,000 for completing and equiping and beautifying the campus and indebtedness by Dr. Frank E. Jenkins, who is now employed by the institution to raise its finances.

4. That the Georgia and Alabama Conference accept as their share of the offerings from the Sunday Schools $100.00.

5. That the usual offering to be taken for Piedmont Junior College by the Georgia and Alabama Conference during the Conference session of $100.00, and that all money subscribed by the Sunday Schools be applied on the $100.00 to be raised by fifth-Sunday offerings, and all money raised on pledges by missionary societies, Christian Endeavor Societies, Churches or individuals be applied on the interest on the endowment note.

6. That every Church of the Conference observe "Piedmont Junior College Day" with a suitable program this Conference year.

7. That a suitable person be chosen by each Church in the Conference to look after the interest of education and Piedmont Junior College as to publicity, students and finances.

8. We recommend that all our Churches send representatives to our Summer School of Religious Education at Wadley.

9. That we express our appreciation to Dr. Frank E. Jenkins for what he has already done for Piedmont Junior College, and pledge our loyal support to him in all his future plans and endeavors in his work for building up Piedmont Junior College.

10. That we will do our best as a Conference to raise the interest ($375) on the endowment note ($7,500) held by the college from the Georgia and Alabama Conference, and approve of having the interest amount apportioned to the Churches of the Conference.

We recommend that Mr. J. R. Prince, who comes with a recommendation from North Highlands Church, and his pastor, Rev. H. R. Heard, be granted a certificate of licensure to preach the gospel wherever the providence of God may call for a period of one year.

We further recommend that Mr. B. F. Doggett, who has come with a recommendation from Rose Hill Church and his pastor, Rev. Neil McQuarrie, be granted a certificate of licensure to preach the gospel wherever the providence of God may call for a period of one year.

We heartily recommend these young men for their ambition to follow such a high and noble calling, and recommend that they pursue their studies for their educational improvement in some regular institution of learning, or take such extension work by correspondents as this Conference may recommend, to the end that their license may further be extended if desired.

We recommend that the license of Rev. J. C. Short be renewed for a period of one year.

The license of Revs. A. B. Moore and W. W. Willingham being expired, and no report being in hand from them or a request for license to be extended, we recommend that their names be dropped from our ministerial roll.

We recommend that the name of Rev. H. A. Screws be dropped from our ministerial roll, he having joined another Church.

> W. C. CARPENTER, *Chairman,*
> THOMAS W. GRAY,
> A. H. SHEPPARD,
> *Committee.*

Motion to adopt report.

Address by Dr. Jenkins. Discussed by Dr. S. L. Beougher.

A subscription of $100 was taken for Piedmont Junior College.

Report adopted.

Reading of ministerial reports and Church letters. Motion to adopt. Adopted.

Assignment of delegates to homes.

Adjournment of afternoon session. Benediction by Rev. A. H. Sheppard.

FIRST DAY—EVENING SESSION.

Meeting of Missionary Association at 7:30 P. M. Song service led by Mr. McClendon. Prayer by Rev. A. H. Sheppard.

The work of Rev. H. W. Elder was discussed by Rev. W. C. Hanson and Miss Frances Floyd.

Prayer by Rev. J. D. Dollar.

Resolution read by Mr. D. S. Hogg. By rising vote the resolution was ordered published in the minutes.

RESOLUTION.

Resolutions of respect to the memory of Rev. Hilliard Walter Elder:

Whereas, Rev. H. W. Elder was the originator of our missionary association; and whereas, he was president of the organization while he lived; and whereas, he was ever ready to spend and be spent for the missionary cause; and whereas, he spent his whole life giving the gospel of love to those who needed it; therefore, be it resolved by the missionary association:

1. That we bow in humble submission to the will of Him who doeth all things for the best; and further:

2. That we double our diligence in missionary effort and contribution; and further:

That all our missionary efforts and contributions through this association be given as a memorial to the faithfulness of Rev. H. W. Elder.

REV. G. D. HUNT,
D. S. HOGG,
H. M. GRAY,
Committee.

IN MEMORIAM.

In memory of Rev. Hilliard Walter Elder, who departed this life August 30, 1930:

Bro. Elder was, from young manhood, a faithful minister in the Christian Church for more than forty years. He was a very prominent minister of the Christian Church in Georgia and Alabama.

Almost all the Churches in the Georgia Conference were either built or rebuilt by him. He organized more Churches and built more houses of worship than any other man in the South. Very few homes in this beautiful Southland that he has not visited. His appearance and fellowship were so gentle and sweet that even the children found in him a companion and friend. For more than three years Bro. Elder was afflicted and could not preach with his voice, but he preached with his life. No man ever lived among us who was more universally loved, and none have departed from us who will be more universally missed. But our loss is his eternal gain. Earth is poorer for his going. Heaven is richer for his coming. Life is more lonely for us since his departure. But heaven and glory will be so much sweeter to him that our sorrow and grief will be turned into joy.

Let us, brethren of the ministry, close up the rent in our ranks. Let us seek to emulate the many noble virtues of our fallen comrade. Let us continue to give to the host of earth and to the sorrowing and suffering the same salvation and comfort that he preached.

G. D. HUNT.

Election of officers for the ensuing year:

President—Rev. C. W. Hanson.

Vice-President—Rev. A. H. Sheppard.

Secretary-Treasurer—Mrs. J. O. Mabrey.

Total amount collected		$ 47.83
Paid for wreath for Rev. Elder	$10.00	
Paid to Secretary, for service	3.00	
		13.00
Total amount in treasury		$ 34.83

Song. Sermon by Dr. Neil McQuarrie. Song. Adjournment. Benediction by Rev. H. M. Gray.

SECOND DAY—MORNING SESSION.

Song. Devotional by Rev. A. H. Sheppard.
Report of Foreign Mission Committee read by Rev. A. H. Sheppard.

REPORT OF COMMITTEE ON FOREIGN MISSIONS.

Paul and his fellow-apostles were the first great missionaries. After them came a succession of heroic men who carried the doctrine of the early Church into foreign lands with the greatest zeal and devotion.

We, as Christian Churches in the Georgia and Alabama Conference, have our part to do in spreading the gospel of Christ among the peoples who do not know Him. Until we realize this fact more forcefully and support missions in purse and prayer, part of our mission work will remain undone.

We recommend that we, the Georgia and Alabama Christian Conference, inform ourselves better on the subject of missions by reading the department of missions in *The Christian Sun,* and that we subscribe for and read the *Missionary Herald.*

A. H. SHEPPARD.

Motion that report be adopted. Discussed by Rev. A. H. Sheppard, Dr. McQuarrie, Rev. J. D. Dollar. Adopted.
Report of Committee on Moral Reform read by Rev. T. W. Gray.

REPORT OF COMMITTEE ON MORAL REFORM.

We, your Committee on Moral Reform, beg leave to submit the following report:

1. That every minister live above reproach and absent himself from all kinds of worldly amusement where betting, gambling, profanity and every thing that degrades or lowers the standard of Christian living is carried on.

2. That the laity be instructed by their pastors to keep themselves unspotted from the world, so that sinners may see our good works and be constrained to glorify our Father which is in heaven.

3. We live in a day of increasing crime and lawlessness, and it seems like we have lost our grip on those things both civil and religious.

4. We all know that there is no power that can rebuke the evil spirit but the power of God. Now the question is, When do we hope to improve the morals of the nation? When the Church of God repents and gets right with God, then we will get results.

5. Why do the supreme judges ask the question, "Why are crimes committed, and what is the cause?" The answer is simply that we have left God out, and we have become powerless. That's the cause and the only cause. We see the power of evil growing stronger day by day, in the midst of all our knowledge and education, science and schools, colleges and Churches. Thousands of men are going to and fro, sea to sea. Millions of dollars are being spent on prohibition, trying to sober the world by the means of legislation, but we fail until Jesus comes the second time, without sin unto salvation.

So let us take everything to God and invoke His divine power. May God bless this world that's groping in darkness and don't know it.

T. W. GREY.

Motion made that report be adopted. Discussed by Rev. T. W. Gray, W. C. Carpenter, J. D. Dollar, H. M. Gray, A. H. Sheppard, Mr. Hand, Dr. McQuarrie. Report adopted.
Report on C. E. & S. S. read by Mrs. J. O. Mabry.

REPORT OF SUNDAY SCHOOL AND CHRISTIAN ENDEAVOR COMMITTEE.

Your Committee on Sunday School and Christian Endeavor wishes to submit the following report:

Since the Sunday School is recognized as a stepping-stone to the Church, realizing that the Church is depending for its growth and the enlargement of her borders, depends on the Sunday School, we should put forth every effort to rescue the children and interest them in Sunday School. Since the Christian Endeavor is a preparatory room, preparing the young people for their life's work in the Church, giving them a chance to express the fullness of their heart, and a rare opportunity of exercising in a public way, they are both great aids to the Church in a gentle way.

We, your committee, are happy to report that our interest in this work is growing. We had a wonderful convention at Rose Hill Christian Church. It was there that we planned for a greater year and undertaking in the Sunday School and Christian Endeavor. Realizing that a year ago our Sunday School work at Richland was divided in groups, but this year we are putting forth a consolidated effort both for the Christian and Congregational Churches. Hoping that our next convention, which was left in the hands of a committee, will be the best we have ever had. We wish to thank our President, Rev. W. C. Carpenter, and co-workers for the fine program they rendered at our last convention.

We want to recommend that all of our Churches have an evergreen Sunday School, and that each one strive to organize a Christian Endeavor Society, and that our pastors render to the young people every service possible in their work.

C. W. HANSON,

MRS. J. O. MABRY,

Committee.

Discussed by G. D. Hunt, D. S. Hogg, W. C. Carpenter, G. S. Hunt, H. M. Gray, H. R. Heard. Address by Miss Dora C. Brackin. Report adopted.

Report on Orphanage read by Rev. G. D. Hunt.

Motion that report be adopted. Discussed by Rev. G. D. Hunt. Report adopted.

Report of Resolutions Committee read by Rev. G. D. Hunt.

Motion made that the report be adopted. By a rising vote the report was adopted.

Motion made that we adjourn for lunch.

Sermon by Rev. G. D. Hunt. Song. Benediction by Rev. H. R. Heard.

SECOND DAY—AFTERNOON SESSION.

Devotional by Dr. McQuarrie.

Report on religious literature read by Rev. H. M. Gray.

REPORT OF COMMITTEE ON RELIGIOUS LITERATURE.

We, your Committee, knowing something of the powerful influence the reading of literature of any sort has in molding the character, shaping the belief and determining the conduct of those who read it, would urge our people to read more religious literature and give the Bible their greatest attention. The more we read the Bible, the better we can understand the reading of religious literature and the better we will like to read it. We cannot read the Bible too much, for when we read God's word it is God talking to us, and when we can understand Him we will know for ourselves how to live and how to teach others to live the good life that God would have us live. And when we have done that, we have done all that God would· have us do. If we read the Bible and learn God's will and do it, it will make us wise, and God has taught us that we should read the Bible from childhood. Read Timothy 3 chapter, 15-17 verses: "And that from a child thou hast known the Holy Scriptures which are able to make thee wise unto salvation through faith which is in Christ Jesus." All Scripture is given by inspiration of God, and is profitable for doctrine, for reproof, for correction, for instruction in righteousness, that the Man of God may be perfect, thoroughly furnished unto all good works.

So let us urge you to read the Bible. Let us hear the words of Solomon, how he admonished his people. He says, "And further, by these, my son, be admonished of making many books there is no end, and much study is a worriness of the flesh." Let us leave off the reading of trashy literature and read that kind that will lead us to higher and richer things in Christ Jesus.

H. M. GRAY,
T. J. DEAN,
Committee.

Motion that report be adopted. Discussed by Rev. H. M. Gray and Rev. G. D. Hunt. Report adopted.

Report on superannuation read by A. H. Sheppard.

REPORT OF COMMITTEE ON SUPERANNUATION.

We, your Committee on Superannuation, submit the following report:

Since a part of the Conference apportionment is set aside to help aged ministers and their widows, we should, as a Conference, endeavor to raise our quota in full.

We recommend that Mrs. P. L. Duke, the widow of the late Rev. P. L. Duke, be placed on the superannuated list.

A. H. SHEPPARD.

Motion made that report be adopted. Adopted.

Report on Home Mission Board read by Rev. J. D. Dollar.

REPORT OF HOME MISSION BOARD.

Your Board has done its work this year jointly with the Home Mission Board of the Alabama Christian Conference, and has been as follows:

We employed Rev. G. D. Hunt as field secretary, or superintendent of these two Conferences for his whole time. Bro. Hunt has been right on the job and has rendered us a valuable and faithful service, and we feel that both the Churches and pastors have been highly benefitted by his services. Bro. Hunt has gone from border to border of both our Conferences, and has done his part to educate and to enlarge the vision of our people for larger programs of service for the kingdom of God. But we have only made a beginning, and we feel that we cannot afford to let Bro. Hunt go after just one year of service for our Conferences, for he has just had time and opportunity this year to learn some of the needs of our work in these two Conferences, and we feel that he can render a more valuable service another year. We, therefore, recommend that we continue our work, as this year, with the Alabama Conference Home Mission Board.

We have several very inviting fields in the bounds of these two Conferences that seek attention at once, and we hear the Macedonian cry to come over and help. We also have some weak Churches in these two Conferences that need the assistance of a strong field-man to help them to strengthen their stakes.

Brethren, in this day of progress and development in every line, we cannot afford to slack our effort for the kingdom of God. We, therefore, recommend that we teach, preach and practice tithing next year, and that we raise next year for home missions in this Conference 50 cents per member.

J. D. DOLLAR.

A. H. SHEPPARD.

Motion made that report be adopted.

Rev. G. D. Hunt gave his report on the work of field worker.

Report adopted.

Report on resolutions read by Rev. W. C. Carpenter.

Motion made that report be adopted. Adopted.

Report on nominations read by Mr. C. S. Swanson.

Motion that report be adopted, with the following nominated to the Congregational Conference: Rev. J. D. Dollar, Rev. H. M. Gray, D. S. Hogg, T. W. Gray, H. B. Floyd. Report adopted.

Report on apportionments read by Rev. H. M. Gray.

REPORT OF COMMITTEE ON APPORTIONMENTS.

We, your committee, recommend that the apportionment for 1931 be as follows:

Ambrose	$ 55.00	Hillside	50.00
Beulah	45.00	Richland	50.00
North Highland	45.00	Enigma	55.00
East La Grange	35.00	Vanceville	75.00
Lanett	160.00	Providence Chapel	30.00
La Grange, First	160.00	Rose Hill	40.00
Oak Grove	110.00		
		Total	$910.00

We recommend that the Conference apportionments be divided as follows:

Superannuation ....15 per cent.
Piedmont Junior College ....25 per cent.
Home Missions ....25 per cent.
Conference Fund ....35 per cent.

H. M. GRAY,

WALTER HAND,

W. A. SMITH,

Committee.

Motion that report be adopted. Adopted.

Motion that we have our minutes published in THE ANNUAL, and the Georgia and Alabama Conference take 100 copies. Adopted.

Appointment of standing committees:

Executive—J. D. Dollar, C. W. Hanson, A. H. Sheppard.

Education—W. C. Carpenter, H. M. Gray, D. S. Hogg.

Foreign Mission—T. W. Gray, C. R. Rutledge, H. R. Heard.

Moral Reform—H. M. Gray, H. B. Floyd, Estell McClendon.

Religious Literature—W. C. Carpenter, Walker Pierson, T. J. Holland.

Superannuation—A. H. Sheppard, H. M. Gray, G. F. Partridge.

C. E. & S. S.—C. W. Hanson, Claude Swanson, Miss Lucile Slaughter.

Home Mission Board—J. D. Dollar, C. W. Hanson, A. H. Sheppard, G. F. Partridge, H. B. Floyd.

REPORT OF COMMITTEE ON NOMINATIONS.

We, your Committee on Nominations, wish to recommend the following names:

Home Mission Board—H. B. Floyd.

Delegates to Alabama Conference—Revs. C. W. Hanson, T. W. Gray, J. D. Dollar, H. M. Gray.

C. S. SWANSON,
C. R. RUTLEDGE,
H. E. McCLENDON,
Committee.

REPORT OF COMMITTEE ON RESOLUTIONS.

We wish to offer the following resolutions:

1. That our Conference express its appreciation, by a rising vote of thanks, to the pastor of Oak Grove Church and the community for their hospitality during this session of our Conference.

2. That we express our thanks and appreciation to Dr. Frank E. Jenkins, Dr. S. L. Beougher, Dr. Neil McQuarrie, and Miss Dora Brackin for their participation in our deliberations and for the forceful messages brought to the Conference.

3. That we send a letter of thanks to Mr. M. A. Atkinson for his generous gift of fish to our Conference.

4. That the Conference take note of the fact that Bro. J. H. Floyd, a member of our Home Mission Board, who for many years has been an honored member of our Church at Oak Grove, in Troup County, Ga., has passed from labor to reward since we last met. We will try to cherish in our memory the many noble virtues of our brother, we will emulate his noble character, and we bow in submission to the will of Him who gives and who takes away. We commend his loving family to our Heavenly Father, for He doeth all things well. May they find in Him just what they need in this sad hour.

5. Whereas, in almost every city where our Church has been established, the manufacturing interests have shown their appreciation of the same by contributing regularly to the pastor's salary, and also by aiding generously our building programs. Therefore, be it resolved by the Georgia and Alabama Christian Conference, in session at Oak Grove Church, That we hereby express our appreciation for the help rendered and the recognition given our pastors and Churches by these industries and manufacturing plants.

W. C. CARPENTER,
D. S. HOGG,
G. D. HUNT,
Committee.

Columbus, Ga., October 1, 1930.

This is to certify that Mr. B. F. Doggett, of Columbus, has asked the Rose Hill Christian Church to recommend him to the Georgia and Alabama State Conference for license to preach.

The Church has so voted, and takes pleasure in recommending him to the State committee for consideration and the granting of a license for one year to preach the gospel.

ELIZABETH HOUGHTON, *Church Clerk.*

North Highland, September 7, 1930.

We recommend Bro. J. R. Prince to this annual Conference for license to preach the gospel. Done by Church in Conference.

REV. H. R. HEARD, *Pastor.*
MRS. J. A. KIRKLAND, *Secretary.*

Since the South Georgia Congregational and Christian Churches have been fully united for one year, and all of our relations have been happy and harmonious; since from our experience, so far, we have had no reason to regret, and every reason to be proud of, this action; since the State Conferences of both the Congregational and Christian Churches of Georgia are to consider the matter of completely merging all of our interests at their next sessions; be it therefore,

Resolved, That we, the South Georgia Association of Congregational and Christian Churches, do urge our State bodies to complete the merger as speedily as they think it is expedient.

Done by order of the South Georgia Association of Congregational and Christian Churches.

REV. DAN PEARSON, *Moderator.*
MISS BESSIE JAMES, *Scribe.*

REPORT OF TREASURER.

HOME MISSION.

Received from Churches		$ 83.76
Paid to Mrs. Mabry	$ 18.05	
Paid to W. C. Edge	50.00	
Paid to C. W. Hanson	15.71	
		83.76

SUPERANNUATE FUND.

Received from Churches		$ 50.26
Paid to W. C. Wicker		50.26

COLLEGES.

Received from Churches		$ 83.76
Paid to Dr. S. L. Beougher		83.76

CONFERENCE FUND.

Received from Churches		$ 123.77
Rev. W. C. Carpenter, for ANNUALS		5.00
Total		$ 128.77
Paid to Mrs. Mabry, Secretary	$ 15.00	
Paid to H. B. Floyd, Treasurer	10.00	
Paid to Mrs. Mabry, stationery, stamps	1.30	
Paid to P. J. Kernodle, balance on ANNUALS	28.44	
Paid to Central Publishing Co., programs	2.65	
Paid to Central Publishing Co., for ANNUALS	50.00	
Paid to J. D. Dollar	16.38	
Total paid out		123.77
Balance		$ 5.00

COLLECTED THIS SESSION.

Home Missions		$ 68.24
Superannuation Fund		40.94
Colleges		68.24
Conference Fund		95.54
Total		$ 272.96

H. B. FLOYD, *Treasurer.*

Reading of Treasurer's report.

Adopted.

Motion that all bills against Conference be paid. Carried.

Motion that Conference stand adjourned until next annual Conference. Carried. Song. Benediction by Rev. W. C. Carpenter.

REV. J. D. DOLLAR, *President.*
(MRS.) J. O. MABRY, *Secretary.*

HISTORY OF OAK GROVE CHURCH, CHIPLEY, GA.

During the years between 1890 and 1898 the place now known as Oak Grove Community was in great spiritual need. At this time, there were several preachers of different denominations that were kind-hearted enough to come to the place and deliver the Gospel to the hungry people here.

Among the last of these years, during the season best loved by farmers who occupied this community, a preacher came, with his wife, who had relatives here, to visit them. He being a man who possessed a wonderful spiritual personality and was unusually quick to see the needs of any of his fellow-men, saw the vast opening for a great work.

While on this visit, the visiting Christian preacher, Rev. H. W. Elder, of Columbus, Ga., was asked to preach one sermon in the old, long one-room school-building, which he did. The congregation hearing this sermon was so appreciative that it inspired him to preach for them whenever he could conveniently come this way in filling his regular appointments.

In the summer and fall of 1898, Rev. H. W. Elder filled almost a regular pastor's place here, especially the latter part of the year. As David has said, "All great work must have a pleasant place in order to be carried on successfully."

Early in the spring of 1899, Bro. Elder, being a swift carpenter as well as an able preacher, set to work, with the help of the good people here, to erect a Church building. He even helped to cut the trees for the lumber. As some of our elderly people have said, he actually cut a number of the trees from which the lumber was sawed for the foundation of the Church before breakfast. Now that the lumber was ready for the building, Mr. West Smith, a citizen of the community who saw far into the future and knew the great need then, was liberal-hearted enough to contribute the spot of ground upon which the Church was built, the same to belong to the public as long as it was used for such a worthy cause.

The community of men, under the direction of Bro. Elder, completed the Church building quickly, despite a terrific wind which gave the building quite a jar, and the Church was dedicated on the third Sunday in April, 1899, and the services were continued in this building for fifteen years. During these years there were 172 men and 176 women converted, making a total of 348 members. Of this number, there have been 17 women and 22 men to die, and 46 women and 35 men who have seen fit to change their membership, which gives a total loss of 120 members, leaving 228 members in good standing under the leadership of Rev. H. W. Elder and his co-workers, who were called deacons and were appointed in 1899. They were Messrs. J. R. Highsmith, J. E. Smith, I. M. C. Bryant, and J. H. Floyd.

In the midst of this great progress on the road of great faith, a mighty storm rushed madly by in February, 1912, and gave the Church building such a smash until the people were very uneasy at every meeting for the next two years, when the members of said Church decided to build a new building, which we are now using. Even though Rev. H. W. Elder has been away for several years, he is still greatly loved by the people, and we think of him as the father of our Church.

MINISTERIAL REPORTS.

W. C. Carpenter—Churches: Ambrose, Enigma, Vanceville, Antioch. Sermons preached, 99; addresses, 12; members received, 21; baptised, 11; pastoral calls, 200; weddings, 8; funerals, 6; benevolences, $850.

W. T. Crowder—Churches: Forest Home, Mt. Zion. Sermons preached, 58; addresses, 3; members received, 18; baptisms, 11; pastoral calls, 40; weddings, 3; funerals, 2. Salary, $112.75.

T. J. Dean—Church: Beulah. Sermons preached, 110; address, 1; members received, 13; baptisms, 6; pastoral calls, 100; weddings, 2; funerals, 6. Salary, $305.60.

J. D. Dollar—Churches: Lanett and Noonday. Sermons preached, 107; addresses, 12; members received, 48; baptisms, 33; pastoral calls, 470; weddings, 5; funerals, 22. Salary, $1,577.65.

H. M. Gray—Churches: Hillside, East La Grange, Richland. Sermons preached, 99; addresses, 8; members received, 19; baptisms, 10; pastoral calls, 100; weddings, 2; funerals, 2. Salary, $1,273.38.

T. W. Gray—Church: Carver's Grove. Sermons preached, 65; addresses, 10; pastoral calls, 25; wedding, 1; funerals, 5. Salary, $75.00.

C. W. Hanson—Churches: First (La Grange), Oak Grove. Sermons preached, 155; addresses, 10; members received, 68; baptisms, 47; visits, 300; weddings, 11; funerals, 35. Salary, $1,250.00.

H. R. Heard—Churches: Columbus and North Highland. Sermons preached, 85; addresses, 6; members received, 16; baptisms, 7; pastoral calls, 80; funerals, 4. Salary, $223.75.

Neil McQuarrie—Church: Rose Hill. Sermons preached, 30; addresses, 3; members received, 3; pastoral calls, 98. Salary, $300.00.

A. H. Sheppard—Churches: Antioch, Rock Stand, Bethany. Sermons preached, 75; members received, 14; baptisms, 12; pastoral calls, 250; weddings, 2; funerals, 4. Salary, $343.96.

Myron Tyler—Retired. Sermons preached, 12; addresses, 4.

E. B. Smith—Licentiate. Sermons preached, 34; prayer meetings, 23.

CHURCH STATISTICS—GEORGIA AND ALABAMA CONFERENCE.

CHURCHES.	PASTORS.	SECRETARIES AND ADDRESSES.	Members Reported Last Year.	Present Membership.	Conference Apportionments.	Amount Paid on Apportionments.	All Benevolences.	Paid on Pastor's Salary.	Buildings and Equipment.	All Other Expenses.	TOTAL.	Value of Church Property.
Ambrose	W. C. Carpenter.	J. M. Dees, Brookfield, Ga.	62	61	$ 55.00	$ 44.00	$ 356.73	$ 300.00	$ 375.00	$ 231.00	$ 921.00	$ 15,000
Baulah	T. J. Dean.	S. C. Graddy, Phenix City Ala.	123	99			18.77	305.60	46.25	42.00	411.00	
East La Grange	H. M. Gray.	W. L. Jarrill, 401 Hines St., LaGrange, Ga.	34	25				175.80		27.50	203.00	2,500
Enigma	W. C. Carpenter.	C. C. Little, Enigma, Ga.	52	56	55.00	15.00	27.50	94.87	75.00	17.00	229.37	1,500
First, La Grange	C. W. Hanson.	F. P. Landreth, 817 Forrest A., La Grange.	300	309	160.00			1000.00	764.54	227.12	2,091.66	20,000
Hill Side	H. M. Gray.	M. J. W. Nelson, 405 Jefferson, La Grange	48	60	50.00			842.35		59.00	901.35	3,000
Lanett	J. D. Dollar.	Mrs. T. F. Roqumore, Lanett, Ala.	280	294	160.00	62.25	20.00	1299.00	600.00	109.00	2,070.25	25,000
North Highland	H. R. Heard.	Alma Goodwin, 305 10th St., Columbus Ga	103	110			12.41	223.75	23.50	26.14	285.80	4,000
Oak Grove	C. W. Hanson.	Julian Floyd, ...ley, Ga.	187	202	110.00	29.55		250.00	83.73	11.00	374.28	4,000
Providence	G. H. Veazy.	T. L. Bishop, Richland, Ga.	36	39		25.00		160.00		75.00	260.00	800
Richland	G. D. Hunt.	J. C. Tarr, Richland, Ga.	45	48	50.00	50.00	31.52	253.11	5.00	20.00	359.53	12,000
Rose Hill	Neil McQuarrie.	Elizabeth Haughton, Columbus, Ga.	71	45		7.00		82.09		155.13	244.00	11,000
Vanceville	W. C. ...tor	Bill ...Mn, R. 7, Tifton, Ga.	80	91	55.00	31.66	490.35	143.00	95.50	414.50	1,341.66	2,500
Totals			1421	1439	$ 695.00	$ 264.46	$ 987.28	$5129.57	$2071.52	$1514.39	$ 9,692.90	$101,300

SUNDAY SCHOOL.	NAME AND ADDRESS OF SUPERINTENDENT.	Number of Officers and Teachers.	Total Enrollment.	Total Amount Raised for Year.
Ambrose	T. J. Holland, Ambrose, Ga	8	119	$ 150.00
Beulah	E. C. Bankston, Girard, Ala	6	46	114.09
East La Grange	W. L. Jarriel, 401 Hines St., La Grange, Ga	13	153	8.00
First La Grange	Roy Whaley, 506 Park Ave., La Grange, Ga	6	100	130.00
Hill Side	H. A. Gibson, 402 Linkan St., La Grange, Ga	17	244	57.97
Lanett	S. W. Seymour, Lanett, Ala			
Rose Hill	No Report			
Vanceville	W. A. Hand, Brookfield, Ga	6	84	104.00
Totals		56	746	$ 564.06

Proceedings of Thirty-second Annual Session of the Alabama Christian Conference

and the

FIRST SESSION OF THE JOINT CONFERENCE OF THE CONGREGATIONAL AND CHRISTIAN CHURCHES.

NOON DAY CHRISTIAN CHURCH, WEDOWEE, ALA.
OCTOBER 14-16, 1930.

FIRST DAY—MORNING SESSION.

Conference called to order by Vice-President Rev. C. W. Carter. President Rev. G. D. Hunt was detained because of a funeral. Scripture lesson by Rev. C. W. Carter. Prayer by Rev. G. Staley Hunt.

Welcome addresses by Mr. J. W. Payne and Rev. J. D. Dollar. Response by Dr. F. P. Ensminger.

Enrollment of ministers and delegates:

ENROLLMENT.

Ministers—C. W. Carter, J. H. Hughes, G. D. Hunt, G. S. Hunt, W. T. Meacham, G. H. Veazey.

Licentiates—G. R. Walker, W. H. Archer.

Churches and Delegates.

Antioch—Z. A. Kitchens, W. K. Hood, G. C. Brown, J. F. Beaird, Mrs. S. J. Hood, Mrs. C. J. Birdsong, Mrs. Mollie Kitchen.

Bethany—Mrs. A. H. Sheppard, Miss Mattie Sheppard.

Beulah—G. R. Walker, Mrs. Iola Walker, Mrs. G. D. Hunt.

Caver's Grove—D. B. Boyd, Mrs. Ollie Boyd, Misses Eris, Era and Ethel Boyd.

Christiana—M. M. Ingram, J. M. Ingram, Mrs. J. M. Ingram, Miss Groff Fuller.

Corinth—C. G. Knight, J. H. Carlisle.

Cragford—J. R. Wilson, Carter Mitchell.

Dingler's Chapel—J. G. Waldrep, W. D. Willingham, John Carter.

Forest Home—Mr. Polie Sikes, Mrs. Polie Sikes, Mrs. J. E. Almon.

Lowell—Miss Cumi Waldrep, Mr. Hoyt Waldrep, Mrs. Emily Williams, Mrs. Emma Philpot, Mrs. Lena Chase.

McGuire's Chapel—By letter.

Mt. Zion—J. B. Still, W. C. Morris, J. H. Morris, Peirce Keable, M. L. Jones.

New Harmony—W. F. Clifton, Mrs. Hattie Clifton.

New Hope—C. W. Stevens, L. H. Liles, Miss Alene Liles, Miss Leila Mae Hill.

Noon Day—S. W. Carpenter, Mrs. Annie Green, Mrs. A. B. Sikes, C. O. Sikes, Grady Nix, Woodrow Amerson, Miss Cloie Sikes, Mrs. Moazena Traylor.

Pisgah—A. T. Strickland.

Pleasant Grove—I. D. Harris.

Roanoke—W. L. Stewart, V. E. Kitchens, E. M. Hood, Miss Clyde Dollar, Miss Jessie Pinkard.

Rock Springs—Milford Austin, Mitchell Waldrep, Miss Winnie Mae Broach, Miss Eula Mae Austin.

Rock Stand—A. R. Kirby, E. D. Kirby, W. B. Weathers.

Shady Grove—Not represented.

Spring Hill—O. H. Orr.

Wadley—Mrs. G. L. Stevens, J. T. Gibson.

The following officers were re-elected:

President—Rev. G. D. Hunt.

Vice-President—Rev. C. W. Carter.

Secretary—Rev. G. H. Veazey.

Assistant Secretary—Rev. G. S. Hunt.

Treasurer—J. W. Payne.

The tentative program was adopted as the order of business.

The following persons were seated some time during the sitting of this body as honorary members: Dr. F. P. Ensminger, Miss Marguerite Davison, Revs. Chas. W. Smith, R. A. McKay, J. P. Bean, E. W. Butler, A. C. Nelson, J. E. Each, M. L. Thrasher, M. L. Hargraves, M. D. Morgan, H. T. McKay, N. A. Long, Walter Curl, C. S. Brooks, Dr. Henry B. Mowbray, Dr. Frank E. Jenkins, Miss Dora Brackin, of the Congregational Church, with thirty-five lay members; Revs. H. M. Gray, J. D. Dollar and A. H. Sheppard, of the Georgia and Alabama Christian Conference; J. E. Amason, of the Congregational-Methodist Church; L. P. Martin, of the M. E. Church, South.

Rev. C. W. Carter was elected to deliver the annual address. Communion was held following the sermon. This was conducted by Rev. C. W. Carter.

Adjourn for lunch. Benediction by Rev. R. A. McKay.

FIRST DAY—AFTERNOON SESSION.

Conference called to order by President Rev. G. D. Hunt. Prayer by Rev. G. H. Veazey.

REPORT OF EXECUTIVE COMMITTEE.

We, your Executive Committee, submit the following report:

We have had no business of any consequence to come before us this year, except to make a program for this session of Conference.

G. D. HUNT, *Chairman.*

Adopted.

REPORT OF COMMITTEE ON MORAL REFORM.

Be it resolved:

1. That the Alabama Christian Converence here assembled register its hearty approval of every effort to preserve the Holy Sabbath Day for the uses warranted to be made of it by the examples and teachings of Christ.

2. That we disapprove violently every practice of individual or organized life that tends toward the lowering of moral standards.

3. That we register our continued approval of the eighteenth amendment to the Constitution of the United States and of the Volstead act, and plead with every voter of our constituency to exercise his or her full power in selecting for office men whose life, example and moral conviction and courage commit them openly to the enforcement of these and all other laws of our statute books.

4. We sincerely believe prohibition is coming, not going; it is winning, not losing. The clamor we hear is the clamor of the defeated, and is not the voice of America.

5. We heartily favor the eighteenth amendment without modification. It is a law of the United States, and should be observed by all of us. In our opinion, it has been of untold benefit to our young people as well as to the women and men of our great nation in improving the living conditions and making the nation more progressive.

6. The liquor traffic has always been the incredible foe of the home, the Church, and the State. Its record has always been one of degradation and death. It forces those septic sins against society that poison life. Rotton politics, commercialized gambling and organized prostitution are its diseased offspring. To license such an immoral menace is to sanction it, and to sanction a sin is equivalent to participating in the outrage it perpetrates. Prohibition does not abolish the drink habit altogether, but it does make the liquor traffic an outlaw.

7. That we endeavor to provide such wholesome social opportunities for our youth that the lure of commercialized amusements may be abated and its baneful results averted.

8. That the leadership of our brotherhood seek to know so thoroughly the way and will of Christ that they may represent Him aright, both in word and example.

9. That we endeavor to keep before our youth such lofty ideals as will be most fruitful in character.

W. T. MEACHAM,
V. E. KITCHENS,
D. W. SHEPPARD,
Committee.

Adopted.

REPORT OF COMMITTEE ON SUPERANNUATION.

Nothing has claimed our attention since last Conference. The widows of the late C. M. Dollar and J. W. Elder are receiving help from this source.

C. W. CARTER, *Chairman.*

Adopted.

Ministerial reports were read. All our ministers reported except one licentiate.

Church reports were read. All our Churches reported except one.

The following message from Mr. C. D. Johnston, superintendent of the Christian Orphanage, Elon College, N. C., was read and discussed by Rev. G. D. Hunt:

To the Alabama Conference:

Dear Folks,—I regret very much that circumstances prevent me from attending your Conference this year. I have always enjoyed attending the Conferences in Georgia and Alabama so much that it is a source of much regret that I cannot be with you in this session. I would have been delighted to have had an opportunity to present the Orphanage claims during the sitting of your Conference, but while I am not present in person I am with you in spirit and pray that the Lord will be with you during the sitting of your Conference and richly bless every member thereof.

On behalf of the Christian Orphanage, I want to say that we want to appeal to you from the bottom of our heart to put forth your greatest effort in the Thanksgiving offering this fall, and make them as liberal as it is possible to do. We have had a very hard year financially this year, and it is the first year in fourteen years of our service here that we have had to borrow money with which to pay our bills, and it almost breaks our heart because circumstances have placed us in that position. But by the united efforts on the part of all our Churches and Sunday Schools, we have faith to believe that, through our Thanksgiving offerings, we will receive the amount borrowed and will accumulate a surplus on which to start off the next year.

I want to say we have from your two Conferences in Georgia and Alabama seven children, three of them are nearly grown. One of the girls from your Conference will reach the age limit the first of the year, and we are going to place her in a hospital to take training to be a nurse. I hope within the next three years to send her back to you a graduate nurse to help nurse your sick people back to health again. We hope that by the training she has received here and will receive in this hospital she will be amply prepared to be a real asset to you on her return. Of course, the others will be looked after as they reach the age limit and placed where we think it will be the best for them.

I hope every Church in the Alabama Conference will make a Thanksgiving offering this year to help us in this work of love and charity.

Again expressing my regret to not be able to be present with you, I beg to remain, as ever,

CHAS. D. JOHNSTON, *Sup't.*

A resolution of respect to Rev. H. W. Elder was presented by Rev. G. D. Hunt, and testimonies were made by most of the ministers present.

RESOLUTION.

In memory of Rev. Hilliard Walter Elder, who departed this life August 30, 1930.

Bro. Elder was, from young manhood, a faithful minister in the Christian Church. For more than forty years he was a very prominent minister of the Christian Church in Georgia and Alabama.

Most all the Churches in the Georgia Conference were either built or rebuilt by him. He organized more Churches and built more houses of worship than any other man in the South. There are very few homes in this beautiful Southland that he has not visited. His appearance and fellowship was so gentle and sweet that even the children found in him a companion and friend.

Bro. Elder was afflicted for more than three years and could not preach with his voice, but he preached with his life. No man ever lived among us who was more universally loved, and none has departed from us who will be more universally missed; but our loss is his eternal gain. Earth is poorer for his going; heaven is richer for his coming. Life is more lonely for us since his departure, but heaven and glory will be so much sweeter to him, that our sorrow and grief will be turned into joy.

Let us, brethren of the ministry, close up the rent in our ranks. Let us seek to emulate the many noble virtues of our fallen comrade. Let us continue to give to the lost of the earth, and to the sorrowing and suffering the same salvation and comfort that he preached.

G. D. HUNT.

Adopted.

A Committee on Resolutions was appointed, composed of G. H. Veazey, C. W. Carter, J. H. Hughes.

Report of the Woman's Board was given by Mrs. G. L. Stevens.

Rev. E. M. Carter was granted a transfer from this Conference to the Eastern North Carolina Christian Conference.

Conference adjourned, and the Congregational brethren held session of their Conference the balance of the afternoon and evening.

SECOND DAY—MORNING SESSION.

Conference called to order by President. Minutes of yesterday's session were read and approved.

Moved and carried that the Congregational brotherhood supply a man for the 11 o'clock sermon today.

A Committee on Church Union was appointed, composed of Revs. G. D. Hunt, C. W. Carter, J. H. Hughes.

REPORT OF COMMITTEE ON FOREIGN MISSIONS.

1. Let us, as pastors and laymen, raise our voices in prayer, that the Saviour may bless and multiply our missionary efforts of this year.

2. Let us express our appreciation for the great work of the Woman's Missionary Society by co-operating to a greater extent with them in their work.

3. Let us preach missions, teach missions, and practice missions for the sake of Him who died for all.

G. STALEY HUNT, *Chairman.*

Address by G. Staley Hunt. Adopted.

REPORT OF HOME MISSION BOARD.

Our Board has been greatly handicapped this year. Owing to the great financial depression all over our country, we have been able to do but a small part of what we had planned to do. We have had, jointly with the Georgia and Alabama Conference, a field worker employed this year. We had pledged from both Conferences almost enough money to pay the salary of the field worker, but since times have been so hard with our people, only a small amount of these pledges have been paid.

Our field worker has visited all the Churches in our Conference and has conducted revivals at many of our Churches in both Conferences, with good results. We are sure that this work should be continued, and the joint board should work out some plan to finance the work.

Our Board contributed one hundred dollars to the salary of the field worker and twenty-six dollars on expenses of delegates to the Southern Christian Convention at Raleigh, N. C. We appropriated five dollars to Rev. A. H. Sheppard for a trip to Shady Grove Church.

We are urging our Churches in and around Cragford to locate a pastor at Cragford for the group of Churches in that locality. We hope this can be done, and the Board should assist them in every possible way.

We ask that our Conference raise next year for Conference Home Missions the sum of —————.

We also approve the plan of getting our Conference Home Mission work lined up with the work or plan of the Congregational work of the State.

We ask our pastors to provide for at least one missionary rally at all their Churches next year.

G. D. HUNT, *Chairman.*

Address by chairman. Adopted.

REPORT OF COMMITTEE ON EDUCATION.

The purpose of our denominational colleges is chiefly to teach Christian education. In order to do this, we must have Christian teachers, in order to create the right kind of atmosphere in which students are to do their work. There is no force coming from the institutions of the Church as strong for building character as our educational institutions, supervised and supported by the Church.

There are various forces which enter into Christian education, with their corresponding values, and no Church can be worth while that does not sense the situation of the hour and adjust its educational work as to curricula, teaching force and material equipment to meet the needs of this hour.

Your own Piedmont Junior College was organized for the purpose of preparing for Christian leadership, and the very urgent needs of the hour are friends and money. We are depending upon the loyal support of the Alabama Christian Conference, and shall be extremely disappointed if we do not get it. Therefore, we would recommend the following:

1. That we give our loyal support to our denominational schools and colleges.

2. That all our people who feel themselves called of God to preach the gospel, train for work in one of our Church schools.

3. That we approve of the methods used by Dr. Jenkins for securing funds for Piedmont Junior College—$25,000 for current expenses and $35,000 for completing, equipping and beautifying the campus and freeing the college of all indebtedness.

4. That the Alabama Conference accept as its share from Sunday School offerings $150.00.

5. That the usual offering of $100.00 be taken for Piedmont Junior College by the Alabama Conference during the Conference session, and that all money subscribed by the Sunday Schools be applied on the $100.00 to be raised by fifth-Sunday offerings, and all money raised or pledged by missionary societies, Christian Endeavor Societies, Churches or individuals be applied on the interest on the endowment note.

6. That every Church of the Conference observe "Piedmont Junior College Day" with a suitable program this Conference year.

7. That a suitable person be chosen by each Church in the Conference to look after the interests of education and Piedmont Junior College as to publicity, students and finances.

8. That all our Churches send representatives to our Summer School of Religious Education at Wadley.

9. That we express our appreciation to Dr. Frank E. Jenkins for what he has already done for Piedmont Junior College, and pledge our loyal support to him in all his future plans and endeavors in his work for building up Piedmont Junior College.

10. That we will do our best as a Conference to raise the interest on the endowment note of $12,500 held by the college from the Alabama Conference, which is $625, and approve of having the interest amount apportioned to the Churches of the Conference.

S. L. BEOUGHER, *Chairman.*

This report was read by Rev. G. S. Hunt. Discussions by Dr. Frank E. Jenkins, Rev. C. W. Carter, Rev. G. D. Hunt.

While this report was pending, an offering was taken for Piedmont Junior College, amounting to $123.00 in cash and pledges.

Adopted.

Sermon by Dr. Frank E. Jenkins.

Miss Sallie Poore was licensed as a probationer of Christ to preach the gospel wherever the Holy Spirit may direct.

Adjourned for lunch. Benediction by Rev. G. D. Hunt.

SECOND DAY—AFTERNOON SESSION.

The Woman's Joint Board met and held short session.

Conference called to order by President.

Devotional by Rev. C. W. Carter.

Report of committee to look after some property in Clay County, Ala., belonging to the Christian Church. The committee was continued, with power to dispose of said property as they deem wise.

REPORT OF COMMITTEE ON RELIGIOUS LITERATURE.

Realizing the importance of good literature, and its affect on our lives, we therefore recommend *The Christian Sun* and *Congregationalist and Herald of Gospel Liberty* to our people.

J. H. HUGHES, *Chairman.*

Adopted.

REPORT OF SUNDAY SCHOOL AND CHRISTIAN ENDEAVOR COMMITTEE.

Great interest has been shown in our Sunday School and Christian Endeavor work during the past year. Our Convention was held at Rock Springs Church, June 28-29. It was a great success.

The Summer School of Christian Education at Piedmont Junior College was well attended by our young people.

Your committee recommends:

1. That our pastors put forth a special effort to understand the needs of our youth and prepare themselves to work co-operatively with the youth of their respective Churches in all their undertakings.

2. That each Sunday School give one Sunday's offering to missions and one to the Orphanage each month.

3. That each Sunday School give every fifth Sunday's offering to Piedmont Junior College, and if possible one offering each month to the same. (Each Sunday School may decide for itself as to the advisability of this.)

4. That each Sunday School and Christian Endeavor Society arrange to send two or more representatives to the Summer School of Christian Education at Piedmont Junior College.

5. That each Sunday School endeavor to put on regular programs that will increase interest in the work.

G. STALEY HUNT, *Chairman.*

Adopted.

REPORT OF COMMITTEE ON APPORTIONMENTS.

We, your Committee on Apportionments, wish to make the following apportionments for the next Conference year:

Antioch	$ 50.00	New Harmony	30.00
Bethany	20.00	New Hope	40.00
Beulah	20.00	Noon Day	37.50
Corinth	20.00	Pisgah	35.00
Christiana	17.50	Pleasant Grove	30.00
Cragford	25.00	Roanoke	40.00
Caver's Grove	12.50	Rock Spring	25.00
Dingler's Chapel	15.00	Rock Stand	35.00
Forest Home	17.50	Shady Grove	10.00
Lowell	30.00	Spring Hill	15.00
McGuire's Chapel	15.00	Wadley	50.00
Mt. Zion	40.00		

We wish to recommend further that the funds collected at this session be divided on the following basis:

Conference Missions ....40 per cent
Conference Funds ....10 per cent
Convention Funds ....50 per cent

J. W. PAYNE, *Chairman.*

Adopted.

The Treasurer was ordered to pay G. H. Veazey $15.00 for his services as Secretary.

REPORT OF COMMITTEE ON MEMORIALS.

In memory of the departed members of the various Churches of the Alabama Christian Conferences who have passed from labor to reward since our last annual session.

Antioch—Mrs. Mary Brown, died January 27, 1930; Mrs. Viola Royston, died March 22, 1930; Mrs. Jane Fincher, died April 28, 1930.

Christiana—W. A. Jennings, died ——— 29, 1930.

Forest Home—Mrs. J. D. Barfield, died December 21, 1929.

Mt. Zion—One member; name not given.

New Harmony—Mrs. J. O. Peek, died June 4, 1930.

New Hope—Mrs. Mary Stevens, died October, 1930; Raymond Sands, died October 13, 1930.

Noon Day—Mrs. Arizona Fincher, died November 1, 1929.

Pisgah—Mrs. Farmer, died December, 1929.

Roanoke—H. L. Kitchens, died March 29, 1930.

We recognize the providence of God in removing from this earth the ones mentioned above, and that we bow in submission to His will. They will be lovingly remembered by us. We feel that their going has made the Church-militant poorer, but the Church-triumphant is made richer.

C. W. CARTER.

Adopted.

REPORT OF COMMITTEE ON NOMINATIONS.

We, your Committee on Nominations, make the following report:

For Home Mission Board—O. L. Royston, C. J. Hester, C. H. Allen, Leon Payne. (Allen and Payne were elected.)

For Sunday School and Christian Endeavor—Verna Chrisler, John Tom Birdsong, Eunice Stevens, Cloie Sikes. (Stevens and Sikes were elected.)

Adopted.

RESOLUTION OF THANKS.

Be it resolved that we extend unto the members of this Church and community our heartfelt thanks for their generosity and hospitality in so splendidly entertaining this body.

J. H. HUGHES.

Adopted by rising vote of both bodies.

Report of Joint Committee on Union of the Congregational and Christian Conferences, read by Dr. F. P. Ensminger.

President C. W. Smith called the Congregational Conference into joint session with ours. The Constitution and By-Laws were read and each item discussed separately, then the vote was taken to adopt same. The Christian representatives voted first. Each body voted unanimously. All stood and sang "Blest Be the Tie That Binds." Prayer was led by Rev. G. D. Hunt.

Rev. G. D. Hunt was elected Moderator of this joint session.

The United Church, at Phenix City, invited the first session of the United Conference to meet with them on the second Tuesday morning in November, 1931. The invitation was accepted.

The Treasurer made his report, as follows:

Report of Treasurer.

HOME MISSIONS.

1929.	*Receipts.*	
Oct. 15.	Balance in treasury	$ 295.76
	Received from Churches	186.20
	Rev. W. T. Meacham, sale of ANNUALS	3.00
16.	Rev. G. D. Hunt, sale of ANNUALS	3.25
1930.		
Mar. 10.	Rev. G. H. Veazey, sale of ANNUALS	3.00
May 19.	Overlooked in checking up after Conference	.50
Oct. 13.	J. W. Payne, for ANNUALS	1.25
	Total	$ 492.96

1929.	*Disbursements.*		
Oct. 18.	N. D. Burson, painting Noon Day Church	$200.00	
	W. C. Edge, Treas., Board of Evangelism	100.00	
Nov. 26.	E. H. O'Neal, painting Caver's Grove Church	37.50	
27.	E. H. O'Neal, bal. painting Caver's Gr. Church	37.50	
1930.			
Mar. 7.	Central Publishing Co., for ANNUALS	50.00	
May 6.	Rev. G. D. Hunt, expense to S. C. C	26.00	
July 16.	Rev. G. D. Hunt, exp. of Rev. A. H. Shepherd	5.00	
Oct. 14.	To balance in treasury	36.96	
			$ 492.96

CONFERENCE FUND.

1929.	*Receipts.*	
Oct. 15.	Balance in treasury	$ 32.20
	Received from Churches	53.19
	Total	$ 85.39

1929.   *Disbursements.*

Oct. 16. To Rev. G. H. Veazey, Secretary................$ 15.00
     17. To J. W. Payne, Treasurer 10.00
     19. To Rev. G. H. Veazey, expenses to G. V.........   25.00
Dec. 4. To Roanoke Leader, for printing...............   7.00
      5. To Dr. S. L. Beougher, exp. to Congretional Con.   5.00
1930.
May   6. To Dr. S. L. Beougher, exp. to S. C. C..........   10.00
          To Miss Waldrep, exp. to S. C. C...............   8.85
          To balance in treasury 4.54
                                                          ——— $ 85.39

CONVENTION FUND.

1929.   *Receipts.*
Oct. 15. Received from Churches .... $ 292.58

1929.   *Disbursements.*
Oct. 21. To Dr. W. C. Wicker, Treas. S. C. C................. $ 292.58

                                        J. W. PAYNE, *Treasurer.*

NOTE: There has been $279.70 of this year's apportionments paid.

The President appointed the following standing committees for the Alabama Christian Conference:

Executive—G. D. Hunt, S. L. Beougher, C. W. Carter.

Education (Schools and Colleges)—S. L. Beougher, G. S. Hunt, and Frank E. Jenkins.

Sunday School and Christian Endeavor Board—L. H. Huey, Klien Hood (one year); Eunice Steven, Cloie Sikes (two years).

Religious Literature—J. H. Hughes, G. H. Veazey, G. R. Walker.

Moral Reform—W. T. Meacham, C. G. Knight, C. H. Mitchell.

Home Mission Board—W. C. Edge, M. L. Hamlin (one year); C. H. Allen, Leon Payne (two years).

Superannuation—C. W. Carter, J. H. Hughes, W. T. Meacham.

Foreign Missions—G. S. Hunt, Mrs. V. E. Kitchens, Mrs. O. H. Orr.

Apportionments—J. J. Carter, E. C. DeVaughan, W. D. Willingham.

Nominations—D. W. Sheppard, A. I. Landers, S. W. Carpenter.

The following Nominating Committee was appointed for the United Conference: Revs. E. W. Butler, J. E. Each, M. L. Thrasher, C. W. Carter, G. H. Veazey.

Conference adjourned.

Young people held session. Discussion group led by Miss Marguerite Davison, followed by a picnic supper in the woods nearby, with vesper service around a bonfire.

Reassembled at the Church at 7 o'clock.

Devotional service led by the young people of Roanoke Church. Reports were given by the young people of the various Churches of their societies.

Addresses by Miss Dora Brackin and Prof. W. C. Edge.

Adjourned.

THIRD DAY—MORNING SESSION.

Congregational Conference called to order by President Rev. Chas. W. Smith. Record kept by N. A. Long.

N. A. Long went home at 10:30 o'clock.

A resolution of thanks for the invitation and entertainment while here was voted by the Congregational brethren.

The following addresses were made: "Reviving Rural Churches," Rev. A. C. Nelson; "The Church Budget," Rev. E. W. Butler; "Our Educational Institutions," Rev. R. A. McKay; "The Church and Young People," Rev. J. E. Each; "The Work of the Pastor," Rev. M. L. Thrasher; "The Sunday School Institute," Rev. M. L. Hargraves; "The Church House," Rev. Chas. W. Smith.

Adjourned for lunch.

THIRD DAY—AFTERNOON SESSION.

Conference called to order by Rev. G. D. Hunt, Moderator of the United Conference, at 1:30 o'clock.

Report of Miss Marion Fairbanks, librarian of Thorsby Institute, was read.

Moved and carried that this body endorse the movement of Thorsby Institute to become a junior college.

Moved and carried that this Conference convey to Dr. Frank E. Jenkins its appreciation of his heroic and sacrificial work for our junior colleges.

Moved and carried that we endorse the celebration of the fiftieth anniversary of Christian Endeavor.

Moved and carried that we send greetings to the United Church, in Birmingham, and exhort it to make plans to assume a position of leadership in the Alabama Conference of Congregational and Christian Churches.

That this Conference endorse the project of a United Church at Alexander City, and ask the boards of both Churches to give consideration to the project.

RESOLUTION.

That we send a letter of condolence to the widow of the late Geo. W. C. Waites.

Adopted.

Rev. E. W. Butler was asked to write this letter.

Moved and carried that we adopt November 16, 1930, as "Loyalty Sunday," and exhort all our Churches to observe it.

A statistical report of the Congregational Churches was given by Miss Marguerite Davison.

We recommend that the East Alabama Association come into as close relation as possible with the Alabama Christian Conference. Adopted.

Moved and carried that the Alabama Christian Conference send fraternal members to the East Alabama Association of Congregational Churches at Wesley's Chapel.

REPORT OF TREASURER OF CONGREGATIONAL CHURCHES.

From August 1 to October 16, 1930.

1930.

Aug. 1.	Balance on hand	$	73.20
Sep. 1.	Adv. Thorsby Institute in State Minutes		2.50
Oct. 15.	United Church, Phenix City		5.00
	Wesley's Chapel, Delta		4.60
	Bethel, Millerville		4.25
	Clio		7.80
	Midland City		4.40
	Fairview, Hackleburg		3.30
	Union Grove, Haleyville		.70
	Total	$	105.75

1930.   DISBURSEMENTS.

Aug. 10.	Telephone	$	.50
	State Minutes		40.25
	Distributing State Minutes		1.75
Oct. 1.	Programs for State meeting		8.00
	Postage		1.00
			51.50
	Balance in treasury	$	54.25

E. W. BUTLER, *Treasurer.*

Moved and carried that the Registrar-Treasurer be allowed $25.00 for services and expenses.

Moved and carried that the Superintendent and Associate Superintendent have our minutes printed as they see fit.

Conference adjourned till 7:30 o'clock.

THIRD DAY—EVENING SESSION.

Sermon by Dr. Newell, president of Piedmont College, at 7:30.

Adjourned, to meet with the United Church, Phenix City, Ala., the second Tuesday in November, 1931, at 10 o'clock A. M.

REV. G. D. HUNT, *Moderator.*
REV. G. H. VEAZEY, *Secretary.*

P. S.: The time and place of the next session of the Alabama Christian Conference is left to the Executive Committee. It is the United Conference that will meet at Phenix City.

MINISTERIAL REPORTS.

S. L. Beougher—Church in charge: Wadley. Sermons preached, 60; special addresses, 20; members received, 4; visits, 100. Salary, $166.10.

C. W. Carter—Churches in charge: Christiana, Corinth, Spring Hill. Sermons preached, 43; members received, 9; visits, 42; weddings, 2; funerals, 6. Salary, $117.32.

E. M. Carter—Churches in charge: In Eastern N. C. Conference. Sermons preached, 139; special addresses, 3; members received, 38; pastoral visits, 413; wedding, 1; funerals, 16. Salary, $1,375.

C. Carl Dollar—Church in charge: Haw River, in Eastern N. C. Conference. Sermons, 36; special addresses, 5; visits, 10; funeral, 1. Salary, $175.

J. H. Hughes—Church in charge: Pisgah. Sermons preached, 31; members received, 8; weddings, 2; funeral, 1. Salary, $160.

G. D. Hunt—Field worker for Alabama and Georgia and Alabama Christian Conferences. Sermons, 172; special addresses, 25; weddings, 4 ;funerals, 29. Salary, $900.

G. Staley Hunt—Churches in charge: Beulah, Cragford, New Hope, Pleasant Grove. Sermons preached, 70; special addresses, 5; members received, 8; visits, 25. Salary, $296.

W. T. Meacham—Churches in charge: Dingler's Chapel, Lowell, New Harmony. Sermons preached, 70; special addresses, 14; members received, 22; visits, 326; weddings, 4; funerals, 6. Salary, $325.

G. H. Veazey—Churches in charge: Roanoke, Rock Springs, Providence Chapel (Ga. & Ala. Conference). Sermons, 80; special addresses, 12; members received, 17; visits, 250; weddings, 2; funerals, 6. Salary, $885.

LICENTIATES.

W. H. Archer—Sermons preached, 8; special addresses, 6.

G. Roy Walker—Sermons preached, 12; salary, $34.

J. Y. Vickers—No report.

CHURCH STATISTICS—ALABAMA CONFERENCE.

CHURCHES.	PASTORS.	SECRETARIES AND ADDRESSES.	Members Reported Last Year.	Present Membership.	Number Families Represented.	Conference Apportionments.	Amount Paid on Apportionments.	Paid on Pastor's Salary.	Amount Raised for Missions.	All Other Benevolences.	All Other Purposes.	Total Amount Raised.	Value of Church Property.
Antioch	A. H. Sheppard	Steva Hood, R. 1, Roanoke, Ala	141	134	40	$100.00	$18.15	$225.00			$88.95	$313.95	$1,500
Bethany	A. H. Sheppard	W. J. Harry, Glenn, Ga	35	37	35	40.00	8.00	61.90			30.00	99.90	1,000
Beulah	G. S. Hunt	J. D. Hall, R. 3, Wadley, Ala	126	102	30	50.00	20.00	64.00				84.00	2,000
Caver's Grove	T. W. Gray	Clara Miles, Wedowee, Ala	56	55	16	35.00	5.00	75.00				80.00	1,200
Christiana	C. W. Carter	Hiram Duck, R. 2, Dadeville, Ala	68	67	35	40.00		58.25				58.25	1,500
Corinth	G. H. Veazey	Barbara Melton, R. 4, Wadley, Ala	81	82	22	50.00		26.50			36.19	62.69	1,500
Cragford	S. L. Beougher	F. W. Mitchell, Cragford, Ala	34	34	21	40.00	21.00	62.00				83.00	2,000
Dingler's Chapel		Ione Young, Lineville, Ala	35	30	11	25.00	1.00	32.50				33.50	1,000
Forest Home	H. M. Gray	Bradley Houze, R. 2, Roanoke, Ala	49	53	15	40.00	3.20	93.90	$3.20	$12.00		112.30	1,200
Lowell	W. T. Meacham	Cumi Waldrep, Roanoke, Ala	135	132	86	50.00	11.10	228.45	9.20		23.50	272.25	Union
McGuire's Chapel	G. R. Walker	M. L. Vickers, R. 2, Daviston, Ala	109	86		35.00							1,000
Mt. Zion	W. T. Meacham	Homer Morris, R. 1, Roanoke, Ala	170	187		100.00	7.50	79.00			50.45	136.95	2,500
New Harmony	W. T. Meacham	J. W. Devaughan, R. 1, Lineville, Ala	63	62	25	60.00	3.00	56.25		4.00	75.00	138.25	2,000
New Hope	G. S. Hunt	J. N. McCollough, R. 1, Roanoke, Ala	176	175		100.00	25.00	125.00	2.83	32.48	7.25	192.56	2,000
Noon Day	J. D. Dollar	T. W. Garner, Wedowee, Ala	120	149	72	75.00	31.75	216.45			35.40	283.60	2,900
Pisgah	J. H. Hughes	Mrs. Delia Callahan, Pisgah, Ala	109	116		50.00	5.50	160.00			80.00	245.50	3,000
Pleasant Grove	G. S. Hunt	W. T. Hill, R. 3, Lafayette, Ala	96	90	67	60.00		54.15	3.85			58.00	2,800
Roanoke	G. D. Hunt	Mrs. V. E. Kitchens, Roanoke, Ala	80	80	35	75.00	35.00	600.00	10.00	152.00	384.00	1,181.00	5,000
Rock Springs	G. H. Veazey	Milford Austin, R. 4, Roanoke, Ala	98	88	41	50.00	9.00	125.00		8.00	144.76	286.26	1,100
Rock Stand	A. H. Sheppard	W. B. Weathers, R. 4, Roanoke, Ala	64	70	23	75.00		75.75				75.75	1,400
Shady Grove			56										1,000
Spring Hill	G. R. Walker	Hubert Phillips, Lineville, Ala	42	64	15	40.00		32.50	10.00			42.50	350
Wadley	S. L. Beougher	C. L. Stevens, Wadley, Ala	93	83	37	100.00	36.00	186.00	20.00		21.60	263.60	2,800
Totals			2036	1976	626	$1270.00	$240.20	$2637.60	$59.08	$208.48	$968.10	$4,103.75	$40,750

SUNDAY SCHOOL STATISTICS—ALABAMA CONFERENCE.

SUNDAY SCHOOL.	NAME AND ADDRESS OF SUPERINTENDENT.	Number Officers and Teachers.	Number of Classes.	Number Pupils Enrolled.	Average Attendance.	Total Amount Raised.
Antioch*	J. F. Beaird, Roanoke, Ala.	6	6	96	50	$ 20.40
Bethany*	Marvin Burgess, Rock Mills, Ala.	6	3	58	30	17.98
Beulah	J. D. Hall, R. 3, Wadley, Ala.					11.00
Caver's Grove	W. O. Narred, Wedowee, Ala.	5	4	40	25	24.54
Christiana*	Mrs. Willie Duck, R. 2, Dadeville, Ala.	6	4	80	40	12.00
Corinth*	J. H. Carlisle, R. 4, Wadley, Ala.	5	4	35	20	16.40
Cragford*	C. H. Mitchell, Cragford, Ala.	4	4	19	15	35.00
Forest Home	L. H. Houze, R. 2, Roanoke, Ala.	7	4	50	40	
Lowell (Union)	J. L. Dudley, Roanoke, Ala.	11	8	270	100	55.00
Mt. Zion*	J. B. Still, R. 1, Roanoke, Ala.	6	4	53	35	18.36
New Harmony*	E. C. Devaughan, R. 1, Lineville, Ala.	6	4	52	35	14.32
New Hope*	C. W. Stevens, R. 1, Roanoke, Ala.	6	4	68	45	64.52
Noon Day	O. Z. Messer, R. 2, Lamar, Ala.	12		100		62.00
Pisgah*	W. C. Warren, Pisgah, Ala.	8	7	124	75	26.00
Pleasant Grove*	W. T. Hill, R. 3, Lafayette, Ala.	9	6	69	50	141.31
Roanoke*	C. J. Hester, Roanoke, Ala.	9	6	80	50	34.30
Rock Springs*	J. F. McCulloch, R. 1, Roanoke, Ala.	8	4	70	40	30.00
Rock Stand*	E. B. Kirby, R. 4, Roanoke, Ala.	6	6	65	40	27.11
Spring Hill*	L. B. Cockerel, Lineville, Ala.	6	3	37	25	107.94
Wadley*	J. J. Carter, Wadley, Ala.	7	5	45	30	
Totals		123	86	1,711	740	$708.18

*Use our denominational literature.

NAME OF CONFERENCE.	Members Reported Last Year.	Present Membership.	Conference Apportionments.	Paid on Conference Apportionments.	Amount Raised for Missions.	All Other Benevolences.	Amount Paid on Pastors' Salaries.	Amount Paid for Other Purposes.	Total Amount Raised during Year.	Value of Church Property.
Virginia Valley Central Conference: B. J. Earp, Pres., Winchester, Va. A. W. Andes, Secy., Harrisonburg, Va....	2,598	2,558	$ 1,680.00	$ 1,240.55	$ 1,026.83	$ 524.68	$ 5,140.55	$ 2,847.41	$ 10,780.02	$ 96,767.00
Eastern Virginia Conference: H. S. Hardcastle, Pres., Suffolk, Va. I. W. Johnson, Secy., Suffolk, Va....	10,680	10,777	10,235.00	8,318.00	12,552.00	11,067.00	46,681.00	91,266.00	169,958.00	1,336,550.00
Western North Carolina Conference: T. J. Green, Pres., R. D., Ramseur, N. C. J. H. Harden, Secy., Graham, N. C....	3,662	3,854	2,695.00	1,506.61	3,779.21	6,532.72	9,124.60	7,556.10	28,499.24	176,235.00
North Carolina and Virginia Conference: C. H. Rowland, Pres., Greensboro, N. C. S. C. Harrell, Secy., Durham, N. C....	6,703	6,961	8,265.00	2,875.74	3,782.44	5,720.26	17,590.41	20,389.85	50,359.70	278,200.00
Eastern North Carolina Conference: W. C. Wicker, Pres., Elon College, N. C. L. L. Vaughan, Secy., W. Raleigh, N. C....	4,997	5,044	2,765.00	1,208.10	2,032.82	1,907.66	11,372.81	5,918.70	22,440.00	318,850.00
Georgia and Alabama Conference: J. D. Dollar, Pres., Lanett, Ala. Mrs. J. O. Mabry, Secy., West Point, Ga....	1,441	1,439	695.00	264.46	....	987.28	5,129.57	3,585.91	9,692.90	101,300.00
Alabama Conference: G. D. Hunt, Pres., Wadley, Ala. G. H. Veazey, Secy., Roanoke, Ala....	2,036	1,976	1,270.00	240.20	59.08	208.48	2,637.60	968.10	4,103.75	40,750.00
Totals..	32,117	32,609	$27,605.00	$15,653.66	$23,262.38	$26,948.08	$106,884.73	$130,917.68	$ 295,833.70	$ 2,348,652.00

Joint Annual Meeting of the Alabama Christian and Congregational Conferences

Noonday Christian Church, 4½ Miles N. E. of Wedowee, Ala.
October 14-16, 1930.

FIRST DAY—EVENING SESSION.

Devotional exercises by Rev. N. A. Long, Midland City.

A survey of the mission work of the world by Conference Superintendent F. P. Ensminger.

Sermon: "Rightly Faced" (Heb. 11:10), by Rev. Henry B. Mowbray, Demorest, Ga.

SECOND DAY—MORNING SESSION.

Enrollment of members and delegates, as follows:

ENROLLMENT.

Ministers—M. D. Morgan, E. W. Butler, J. E. Each, R. A. McKay, A. C. Nelson, J. P. Bean, H. T. McKay, C. W. Smith, N. A. Long, Walter Curl, M. L. Hargraves.

Honorary—F. P. Ensminger, Miss Marguerite Davison, Dr. H. B. Mowbray, Miss Dora Brackin, Dr. F. E. Jenkins.

Churches and 'Delegates.

Antioch—J. A. Adams, Monroe Adams, Lavonia Bayson, Mrs. M. L. Thrasher.

Blackwoods—Audrey Kelley, Pera Johnson, Mrs. B. F. Johnson, O. L. Johnson.

Christian Hill—Mrs. E. L. Long, L. A. Boutwell.

Clio, New Hope—Lilla V. Long.

Fairview—Levy Hall.

Friendship—Clem Hays.

Mt. Grove—Alex. Clark, Howard Thomas.

Mt. Moriah—M. M. Patterson, S. B. Norwood.

New Home—Annie Garrison, Coreta Barrow, Mr. Garrison, Mrs. Mary R. Garrison.

Oak Grove, Trinity—Dan Price.

Phenix City—Mrs. L. A. Smith, Vera Saunders, Martha Appleby, George Smith.

Rock Springs—Dewey McBroom.

Thorsby—Miss Fairbanks.

Union Grove—O. O. Wamsly.
Union, Mt. Creek—I. C. Johnson, Mrs. I. C. Johnson.
Watson Chapel—Marion Dopson.
Wesley Chapel—J. T. Mise.
Wright's Chapel—Ruth Best, DeWitt Kelley.

Voted that all members of Christian Conference in attendance be made honorary members.

Voted that program, as printed, be accepted, with such changes as may be necessary.

Voted that a committee of three be appointed to confer with similar committee of Christian Conference to consider further plans of union. Committee: E. W. Butler, F. P. Ensminger, J. E. Each.

Voted that Rev. M. L. Thrasher be made honorary member.

SECOND DAY—EVENING SESSION.

Joint meeting of both bodies, Rev. G. D. Hunt in chair.

Dr. Ensminger presented the Constitution, and following changes noted:

CONSTITUTION CHANGES.

Article 3. Change: Licentiates of the constituent bodies who are not elected delegates shall be considered honorary members, and shall be expected to attend the Conference.

Article 4. Change: Omit "or trustees"; add, "These officers shall be the Executive Committee of the Conference."

Article 6. In sentence 2, leave out "Board of Directors." Change: This Conference shall meet in the month of November. If need demands, the time and place of meeting shall be named by the Executive Committee.

Article 7. May be amended by two-thirds vote of Conference, provided such amendment be filed with Registrar at least sixty days ahead.

BY-LAWS.

Article 1. Conference begins on second Tuesday A. M. in November.

Article 2. Conference preacher and alternate shall be elected at Conference for previous year. Vacancies may be filled by Executive Committee.

Constitution, as a whole, unanimously adopted by both Congregationalists and Christians.

United Church, Phenix City, invited the next session of Conference, and it was so voted.

Voted that matter of arranging minutes of both bodies and united body be referred to superintendent and associate, with power.

THIRD DAY—MORNING SESSION.

Devotionals led by Marion Dopson.

Voted that Rev. Zenas Bean and Miss Dora Brackin be seated as honorary members.

Program, as printed, gone into.

Voted that Miss Davison be asked to contribute regularly to *The Christian Sun*, telling of her work.

Program changed and business session held at 9:50 o'clock.

Report of Nominating Committee adopted as read.

Moderator—Rev. G. D. Hunt.

Assistant Moderator—Rev. Samuel Long.

Superintendent and Registrar—F. P. Ensminger.

Auditor—Rev. C. W. Smith.

Associate Superintendent—Rev. G. D. Hunt.

Conference Preacher—Rev. C. W. Carter; alternate, Rev. W. H. Tillman.

Delegates to National Council—Dr. S. L. Beougher, Geo. D. Hunt; alternates, Rev. C. W. Smith, C. P. Lunsford.

Voted that Executive Committee be given power to arrange program for next Conference and work out details of activity.

Minutes of the Thirty-ninth Annual Session of the Eastern Virginia Christian Missionary Association

First Christian Church, Norfolk, Va.—December 9, 1930.

MORNING SESSION.

Called to order at 10:30 o'clock by President Rev. H. C. Caviness.
Devotional services by Rev. W. H. Garman.

Welcome address by Rev. J. E. McCauley. Response by Rev. R. E. Brittle.

The printed program, as prepared by the committee, was adopted as the order of the day, with such changes as may be necessary.

The following answered, with their dues, in response to the roll call:

Berea, Nansemond—Church, $10; Sunday School, $10; Ladies' Aid, $10; Women's Class, $10; R. B. Odom, $10; Mrs. H. B. Harrell, $5; Mrs. R. B. Odom, $5—total, $60.

Berea, Norfolk—Sunday School, $10; Adult Bible Class, $10; M. W. Hollowell, $10—total, $30.

Bethlehem—Star Bible Class, $10; Ladies' Aid, $10—total, $20.

Christian Temple—Church, $10; Sunday School Mission Treasurer, $10; Sunday School, $10; Temple Men's Class, $10; Twiddy Class, $10; Dorcas Class, $10; Ladies' Aid, $10; Missionary Society, $10; T. E. Brickhouse, $10; J. W. Manning, $10; A. M. Johnson, $10; L. E. Smith, $10; Mission Treasurer, $10; Mrs. T. E. Brickhouse, $5; Mrs. J. E. Harrell, $5; Mrs. L. E. Smith, $5; Mrs. L. W. Stagg, $5; Mrs. J. A. Eley, $5; Mrs. R. B. Wood, $5; Mrs. R. C. Rawls, $5; R. C. Rawls, $10; Mrs. W. L. Cooper, $5; F. M. Brewer, $10—total, $190

Elm Avenue, Portsmouth—Men's Bible Class, $10; Ladies' Bible Class, $10; Missionary Society, $10; Sunday School, $10; Ladies' Aid, $10; T. N. Lowe, $10; Mrs. J. W. Felton, $5; Mrs. T. J. Hendricks, $5—total, $70.

First, Norfolk—Rev. J. E. McCauley, $10; Friend's (Women's) Bible Class, $10; Geo. H. Frey, $10; Mrs. Geo. H. Frey, $5—total, $35.

First, Portsmouth—Rev. H. C. Caviness, $10; C. E. Society, $10; J. F. Brothers, $10; Mrs. W. J. Etheridge, $5; Church, $10; Men's Class, $10; H. E. Rountree, $10; Ladies' Aid Society, $10; Mrs. S. P. Gort, $5; Caroline Gort, $5; Woman's Missionary, $10; J. C. Ellis, $10; Sunday School, $10; Ruth Curling, $5; A Friend, $5; Young People's Missionary, $10; Mrs. J. S. Wright, $5; Mrs. J. C. Ellis, $5; Geo. W. Haywood, $10; Mrs. C. F. Rudd, $5—total, $160.

Greater Norfolk S. S. Ass'n—Three memberships, $30.

Franklin—Mrs. J. B. Gay, $5; Mrs. E. P. Jones, $5; Mrs. J. A. Williams, $5; Miss Mary Lee Williams, $5; Miss Dolly Williams, $5; Rev. J. W. Fix, $10; J. W. Fix, Jr., $5; J. A. Williams, $10; Norfleet Bible Class, $10; Ladies' Aid, $10; Sunday School, $10; Berta Rowland Class, $10; L. R. Jones, $10— total, $100.

Holland—W. J. Holland, $10; Olive Branch Class, $10; Sunday School, $10; Church, $10; Mrs. W. J. Holland, $5; Ladies' Bible Class, $10; Ladies' Aid, $10; J. P. Dalton, $10; Dr. J. G. Holland, $10; Mrs. J. G. Holland, $5; Brotherhood Class, $10; Berta Rowland Society, $10; Mrs. G. G. Holland, $5; Mrs. J. T. Jones, $5; Mrs. R. T. Ridel, $5; A. J. Jolly, $10; Mrs. A. J. Jolly, $5; Woman's Missionary Society, $10—total, $150.

Holy Neck—Philathea Class, $10; B. D. Jones, $10; Baracca Class, $10; Church, $10; First Bible Class, $10; R. C. Norfleet, $10; J. T. Rawls, $10; Mrs. J. T. Rawls, $5; Dr. N. G. Newman, $10; Mrs. H. L. Worl, $5; E. T. Holland, $10; Mrs. E. T. Holland, $5; Mrs. S. R. B. Howell, $5; Missionary Society, $10; Mrs. J. J. Gummer, $10; Darden Oberry Bible Class, $10; Church Society, $10; Mrs. J. K. Jones, $5—total, $155.

Liberty Springs—Rev. I. W. Johnson, $10; Mrs. E. B. Rawls, $5; Mrs. H. E. Savage, $5; Mrs. F. F. Brinkley, $5; Baracca Class, $10; Philathea Class, $10; Berta Johnson Class, $10; I. T. Byrd, $10; Church, $10; Joel E. Harrell, $10; Mrs. Joel E. Harrell, $5; Park C. Brinkley, $5; Sunday School, $10— total, $105.

Newport News—Sunday School, $10; R. L. Baker, $10; Mrs. R. L. Baker, $5; Ladies' Bible Class, $10; Mrs. F. W. Vaughn, $5; Mrs. W. B. Baker, $5; Miss June Joy Hyatte, $5; Ladies' Aid, $10; Ladies' Missionary Society, $10; Church, $10; Rev. M. F. Allen, $10; Mrs. M. F. Allen, $5; Choir, $10; C. D. West, $10; Paul H. Allen, $5; J. G. Irby, $10; Men's Bible Class, $10; W. L. Riles, $10—total, $150.

Oakland—Sunday School, $10; Forward Movement Bible Class, $10— total, $20.

Ocean View—Church, by Rev. J. H. Warren, $10.

Old Zion—Ladies' Bible Class, $10; Morning Star Bible Class, $10; Men's Bible Class, $10—total, $30.

Rosemont—Men's Bible Class, $10; J. F. Morgan, $10; Mrs. B. F. Gibson, $5—total, $25.

South Norfolk—Ladies' Aid, $10; Sunday School, $10; Ladies' Bible Class, $10—total, $30.

Suffolk—Sunday School, $20; Ladies' B. & S. Union, $20; Philathea Class, $20; Woman's H. & F. Missionary Society, $10; Baracca Class, $10; Junior Philathea Class, $10; Girls' Missionary Society, $10; Aiming High Class, $10; J. E. West, $10; E. E. Holland, $10; Mrs. C. A. Shoop, $10; O. S. Smith, Sr., $10; B. D. Crocker, $10; Dr. J. E. Rawls, $10; J. E. Vincent, $10; H. H. Holland, $10; W. S. Beamon, $10; Dr. W. W. Staley, $10; Mrs. M. C. Riddick, $10; Mrs. B. D. Crocker, $5; Mrs. J. D. Luke, $5; Mrs. I. W. Johnson, $5; Miss Susie Holland, $5; Mrs. A. T. Holland, $5; Mrs. G. W. Nurney, $5; Mrs. J. M. Darden, $5; Mrs. C. B. Duke, $5; Mrs. A. D. Brinkley, $5; Mrs. Bessie Creekmore, $5; Mrs. J. D. McClenny, $5; Miss Margaret West, $5; Mrs. Annie S. Calhoun, $5; Mrs. W. V. Leathers, $5; Mrs. W. H. Jones, $5; Home Department, $10; Miss Jamie Felton, $5; Church, $10; C. W. Truitt, $10—total, $330.

Waverly—Church, $10; Victor Bible Class, $10; Acorn Bible Class, $10; Sunday School, $10; Rev. F. C. Lester, $10; Judge J. F. West in memoriam, by Sunday School, $10; Mrs. Gray's Bible Class, $10; Mrs. F. A. Epps, $5—total, $75.

Windsor—Mrs. J. W. Roberts, $5.

REPORT OF TREASURER.

1929.		RECEIPTS.	
Dec.	2.	Balance in bank	$ 132.79
	4.	Deposits	1,835.00
	9.	Miss Hattie Savage	5.00
		C. A. Piland	5.00
1930.			
Mar.	10.	Miss Jamie Felton	5.00
		Total	$1,982.79

1929.		DISBURSEMENTS.	
Dec.	11.	Paid L. E. Smith (Temple)	$1,000.00
		Paid O. D. Poythress (So. Norfolk)	250.00
		Paid J. W. Felton (Elm Avenue)	200.00
		Paid C. J. Heath (Portsmouth)	480.00
		Paid J. F. Morgan, printing programs	1.85
		Paid J. E. McCauley, postage	.75
1930.			
Jan.	11.	Paid N. G. Newman, reimbursed check	10.00
Dec.	3.	Balance in bank	40.19
			$1,982.79

B. D. JONES, *Treasurer*.

The report was referred to the Finance Committee.

The President appointed the following special committees:

Resolutions—Mrs. I. W. Johnson, Revs. W. H. Garman, and J. H. Warren.

Nominations—Dr. L. E. Smith, M. W. Hollowell, Rev. H. S. Hardcastle.

Place of Next Meeting—Dr. N. G. Newman, Mrs. C. F. Rudd, Rev. W. M. Jay.

Address: "The Quest for Happiness," by Rev. C. E. Gerringer.

Adjourned for lunch. Benediction by Dr. L. E. Smith.

AFTERNOON SESSION.

Called to order at 1:30 o'clock by President Caviness.

Prayer by Rev. H. S. Hardcastle.

REPORT OF FINANCE COMMITTEE.

We, your Committee on Finance, submit the following:

We have examined the Treasurer's report and find the same to be correct.

Collections today amount to $1,815.00

We recommend the paying of the following bills:

To J. E. McCauley, for printing and postage.......$	4.00
To H. C. Caviness, for printing and postage........	5.00
To Central Publishing Co., printing	3.00
Total ....$	12.00

Respectfully submitted,
E. T. HOLLAND,
T. N. LOWE,
F. C. LESTER,
M. W. HOLLOWELL,
J. E. McCAULEY,
Committee.

Report adopted.

Round-table discussion was led by Rev. H. S. Hardcastle on the subject, "How to Make Our Association More Effective." During the discussion, a number pledged themselves to get new members for next year.

REPORT OF COMMITTEE ON PLANS.

We recommend the following appropriations: Waverly, $500; First Church, Portsmouth, $400; Elm Avenue, Portsmouth, $200; South Norfolk, $100; Christian Temple, $630, making $9,080 on the $10,000 to the Temple (the Temple to get as much more than the $630 as the finances will permit, with a reserve of $25 for expenses).

Respectfully submitted,
J. E. WEST,
MRS. L. W. STAGG,
E. T. HOLLAND,
R. B. ODOM,
C. J. HEATH,
J. F. BROTHERS,
Committee.

Report adopted.

REPORT OF COMMITTEE ON PLACE.

Your committee has had two invitations—First Church, Portsmouth, and Waverly. We recommend that we meet next year with the Waverly Church.

N. G. NEWMAN,
W. M. JAY,
MRS. C. F. RUDD,
Committee.

Report adopted.

REPORT OF COMMITTEE ON RESOLUTIONS.

We submit the following resolutions:

1. Resolved, That this Association express, by standing vote, our sincere appreciation and thanks to the pastor and members of First Christian Church, Norfolk, for the kind and hospitable entertainment of this day.

2. We congratulate the membership of the Association for the splendid financial report rendered, evidencing a splendid sacrificial loyalty to our Lord Jesus Christ.

MRS. I. W. JOHNSON,
J. H. WARREN,
Committee.

Report adopted.

REPORT OF NOMINATING COMMITTEE.

Your committee makes the following nominations:
President—Rev. H. C. Caviness.
Vice-President—Rev. R. E. Brittle.
Financial Secretary—Rev. J. W. Fix.
Recording Secretary—J. F. Morgan.
Treasurer—B. D. Jones.

L. E. SMITH,
M. W. HOLLOWELL,
H. S. HARDCASTLE,
Committee.

Report adopted.

It was moved and carried that we have the minutes printed in THE ANNUAL, as usual.

E. T. Holland was authorized to deliver the money to the Treasurer, B. D. Jones, who is absent on account of illness.

The President appointed the following standing committees:

Plans—Col. J. E. West, R. B. Odem, Mrs. L. W. Stagg, and E. T. Holland.

Field—Revs. H. S. Hardcastle, I. W. Johnson, J. E. McCauley, Mrs. J. A. Williams, and J. W. Felton.

Finance—Rev. O. D. Poythress, M. W. Hollowell, Rev. F. C. Lester, and T. H. Lowe.

Executive—Revs. H. C. Caviness, J. E. McCauley, J. F. Morgan, J. W. Fix, and B. D. Jones.

Program—Revs. H. C. Caviness, J. E. McCauley, J. F. Morgan, and W. H. Garman.

Membership Campaign—J. M. Darden, C. D. West, Col. J. E. West, Revs. W. H. Garman, L. E. Smith, W. C. Hook, M. F. Allen, E. B. White, J. M. Roberts, R. E. Brittle, W. D. Harward, C. C. Ryan, C. E. Gerringer, Mrs. E. T. Holland, Mrs. C. J. Heath.

The Association adjourned, to meet with the Waverly Christian Church on Tuesday after the first Sunday in December, 1931, at 10:30 A. M.   Benediction by Dr. W. W. Staley.

H. C. CAVINESS, *President.*

J. F. MORGAN, *Recording Sec'y.*

Minutes of Third Annual Session of Virginia Valley Central Woman's Missionary Conference

ANTIOCH CHURCH—AUGUST 1, 1930.

MORNING SESSION.

Conference called to order by President Mrs. R. A. Larrick. Hymn, "Come, Thou Almighty King." Rev. B. J. Earp led in prayer. Mrs. A. S. Turner read a selection of Scripture, and Mrs. Larrick led in prayer. Minutes of Board meeting were read and approved.

Roll of Churches was called, and the following were represented: Antioch 15, Bethel 1, Bethlehem 1, Christian Chapel 2, Linville 9, Mt. Olivet (R) 3, New Hope 4, Winchester 7, Woods' Chapel 9.

The following Board members answered to their names: Mrs. R. A. Larrick, Mrs. B. F. Frank, Miss Verdie Showalter, Miss Ella Pickering, Miss Ora Scott, and Mrs. A. W. Andes.

The Winchester Woman's Society gave a pageant, "The Three Boxes."

Miss Treva Senger, teacher of expression, gave a reading, which was also enjoyed.

The congregation joined in the song, "Jesus is All the World to Me."

Rev. R. L. Williamson, pastor of Winchester Christian Church, preached a strong missionary sermon, based on Christ's talk with His disciples when He said, "Whom do men say that I am?" his subject being, "My Church."

Rev. W. B. Fuller led in prayer. An offering was taken, amounting to $9.30.

The following committees were appointed:

Nominations—Mrs. Roy Hosaflook, Mrs. B. R. Richards, Mrs. A. S. Turner, Miss Olive Showalter, Rev. W. B. Fuller.

Place of Next Meeting—Miss Ora Scott, Miss Winifred Anderson, Miss Ella Pickering and Mrs. A. W. Andes.

Resolutions—Rev. Joe French, Rev. B. J. Earp, Mrs. J. A. Kagey.

Goals—Mrs. R. L. Williamson, Mrs. B. F. Frank, Miss Ann Amelia Seabright, Miss Annie Laura Hensley.

Hymn, "Thine for Service, Lord."

Rev. Mr. Fuller, pastor of the Church, announced dinner on the grounds for all, and called on Rev. Mr. French to pronounce the benediction.

AFTERNOON SESSION.

Devotional services were conducted by Miss Ora Scott.
The Winchester Society gave a pageant, "Books and Books."

REPORT ON GOALS.

WOMEN'S SOCIETIES.
Goals Reached.

Mt. Olivet (R) 60%
Bethel 40%
Bethlehem 75%
Dry Run 40%
Leaksville 60%
Linville 80%
Winchester 80%
Woods' Chapel (new society)....20%

YOUNG PEOPLE'S SOCIETIES.
Goals Reached.

Antioch 70%
Bethel 40%
Timber Ridge 70%

Two societies reached 80 per cent of their goals; others less.

The Treasurer read her report, which was adopted, as follows:

REPORT OF TREASURER.

1929. RECEIPTS.

Aug. 1. Amount in treasury for Conference Contingent Fund.... $ 8.30
Amount carried over from last year................... 9.88

Women's Societies.

Bethel ....$ 1.70
Bethlehem 30.00
Dry Run 11.54
Leaksville 42.70
Linville 81.10
New Hope 14.85
Winchester 86.53
                                                                    268.42

Young People's Societies.

Antioch ....$ 24.31
Bethel 3.00
Bethlehem 3.00
Timber Ridge 10.60
Winchester 54.27
                                                                     95.18

Cradle Roll Societies.

Antioch ....$ .60
Bethlehem 2.61
Linville 8.30
Winchester 2.50
                                                                     14.01

Rally Offerings.

Bethel ....$ 5.06
Mayland 3.75
Mt. Olivet (G) 10.50
Winchester 2.50
Woods' Chapel 4.57
                                                                     26.38

Miscellaneous.

Mt. Olivet (R) Ladies' Aid....................\$ 12.40	
Mt. Olivet (R) C. E. 5.00	
Offering, Leaksville W. Con. 12.51	
Offering, 1929 "Conference Night" 20.26	
	50.17

Total receipts .... $ 472.34

DISBURSEMENTS.

1929.

Aug.	1.	To Mrs. B. F. Frank, postage ....\$	2.29	
Sep.	9.	To Mrs. Hardcastle	85.40	
1930.				
Jan.	6.	To Burk & Price, bond	2.50	
	13.	To Mrs. Hardcastle	94.29	
Apr.	15.	To Mrs. Hardcastle	62.67	
July	16.	To Mrs. Hardcastle	218.78	
				465.93

Aug.	1.	Amount in treasury for our own use................... $	6.41
		Received after closing book—Leaksville Women.........	1.50
		Leaksville Cradle Roll	5.75
		Balance in treasury .... $	13.66

MISS VERDIE SHOWALTER, *Treasurer.*

A letter from Mrs. J. A. Williams, President of Southern Woman's Board, was read, suggesting a change in time of our annual Conference meeting to late in September or first of October, as that would help us close our year's work with the four other Conferences in the Southern Convention. A motion prevailed that this change be made, leaving the exact date to the Woman's Board.

A motion passed to pay the following bills: Secretary, for postage, $1.00, and to Mrs. Earp, for printing of rally program, $1.50.

Life memberships was discussed. Any society raising $10.00 special can count this on their goal and select one of their number to a life membership.

The Winchester Society gave an interesting dialogue, "Every Grain of Corn."

Committee on Place decided in favor of Dry Run for next year.

Committee on Goals made the following report:

REPORT OF COMMITTEE ON GOALS.

POINTS OF EXCELLENCE.

1. An average attendance at meetings equal to one-half of membership.···	20%
2. Ten per cent of membership at mid-year mission rally.··············	20%
3. (a) Ten per cent of membership reading 1 or more missionary books.·	10%
(b) One hundred missionary articles read························	10%
4. Quarterly reports sent promptly by 1st of Oct., Jan., Apr. & July·····	20%
5. Thanksgiving service held	20%
	100%

FINANCIAL GOALS.

Women's Societies.

Bethel	$ 5.00	Mt. Olivet (G)	$ 10.00
Bethlehem	30.00	New Hope	15.00
Dry Run	15.00	Winchester	85.00
Leaksville	85.00	Mt. Olivet (R) L. A.	15.00
Linville	85.00	Woods' Chapel	20.00

Young People's Societies.

Antioch	$ 85.00	Timber Ridge	$ 30.00
Bethlehem	10.00	Mt. Lebanon	5.00
Bethel	2.50	Mt. Olivet (R) C. E.	5.00
New Hope	5.00	Winchester	35.00

Cradle Roll Societies.

Antioch	$ 7.50	Mayland	$ 1.00
Bethel	.75	Whistler's Chapel	.75
Bethlehem	4.50	Winchester	2.50
Leaksville	4.00	Dry Run	.75
Linville	5.00		

MRS. R. L. WILLIAMSON,
MRS. B. F. FRANK,
MISS A. A. SEABRIGHT,
MISS A. L. HENSLEY,
Committee.

Committee on Nominations reported, as follows:

REPORT OF COMMITTEE ON NOMINATIONS.

Your Committee on Nominations reports as follows:

President—Miss Ora Scott.
Vice-President—Mrs. A. W. Andes.
Secretary—Mrs. B. F. Frank.
Treasurer—Miss Verdie Showalter.
Superintendent Spiritual Life—Miss Amy Louderback.
Superintendent Women's Societies—Mrs. R. C. Myers.
Superintendent Young People's Societies—Mrs. A. F. Kite.
Superintendent Literature and Mite Boxes—Miss Ella Pickering.
Superintendent Cradle Roll Societies—Mrs. E. Lena Rothgeb.

MRS. ROY HOSAFLOOK,
MRS. BOYD RICHARDS,
MRS. A. S. TURNER,
MISS OLIVE SHOWALTER,
W. B. FULLER,
Committee

Committee on Resolutions reported, as follows:

REPORT OF COMMITTEE ON RESOLUTIONS.

It is with pleasure and profit that we have spent the day at Antioch in the study of our Lord's great commission and in preparation to better observe its precept and His example. Let us, then, resolve:

1. That we express our appreciation to Antioch for entertainment.
2. That we express our regret at the absence of Rev. A. W. Andes.
3. That we express our thanks to the Winchester Society for the pageants given today.

4. That we pledge our support to the officers in their efforts to extend the kingdom work.

5. That we promise our Lord to be more active and useful in His kingdom work.

JOE FRENCH,
B. J. EARP,
MRS. J. A. KAGEY,
Committee.

Rev. Mr. Earp, President of Conference, announced meeting of Conference next week at Newport.

Miss Treva Senger gave several readings.

The meeting was then brought to a fitting close by singing "Showers of Blessings." We felt that we had had showers of blessings upon us for being in this missionary gathering; also because, at this very moment, we were having a drenching rain on the thirsty earth about us. Rev. Mr. Earp made the closing prayer.

MRS. R. A. LARRICK, *President.*
MRS. B. F. FRANK, *Secretary.*

Minutes of the Eighteenth Annual Session of the Eastern Virginia Woman's Missionary Conference

CHRISTIAN TEMPLE, NORFOLK, VA.—OCTOBER 24, 1930.

Theme: "Shall We Be Witnesses?"

MORNING SESSION.

The Eastern Virginia Woman's Missionary Conference met in its Eighteenth Annual Session, and was called to order by the President, Mrs. J. M. Harris, at 10 o'clock. Devotional service was led by Mrs. H. C. Caviness.

Reports of District Superintendents:

Waverly—Miss Louise Pittman: Societies, 19; enrollment, 219; offering, $637.02.

Franklin—Mrs. W. D. Harward: Societies, 15; enrollment, 249; offering, $800.79.

Nansemond—Mrs. B. D. Jones: Societies, 32; enrollment, 961; offering, $3,619.14.

Norfolk—Mrs. H. C. Caviness: Societies, 30; enrollment, 754; offering, $1,673.68.

Reports of departments:

Spiritual Life—Mrs. W. H. Andrews. Report showed a decided increase in the spiritual tone of the entire department.

Life Membership and Memorials—Mrs. O. S. Mills: Life Memberships, 5; memorials, 3.

Conference Editor—Mrs. J. W. Fix: Societies sending items for publication, 28. (In the absence of Mrs. Fix, this report was given by Rev. J. W. Fix.)

Young People—Mrs. R. T. Bradford: Societies, 47; enrollment, 991; offering, $2,287.64.

Cradle Roll—Mrs. F. M. Nelson: Societies, 20; enrollment, 413; offering, $143.88.

Reports adopted.

President's greeting, "How Our Conference Has Witnessed."

Recognition service. The four districts were well represented. Ministers present, 18.

Report on literature. Mrs. J. E. Cartwright presented the study books, helps and pageants for the year.

Report of Treasurer was read and adopted, as follows:

REPORT OF WOMAN'S HOME AND FOREIGN MISSION BOARD.

WOMEN'S SOCIETIES.

	Members.	Offering.		Members.	Offering.
Antioch	15	$ 72.57	Hopewell	12	23.70
Berea, Nansemond	24	173.40	Isle of Wight	15	62.50
Berea, Norfolk	20	57.00	Liberty Spring	55	224.10
Bethlehem	29	164.31	Mt. Carmel	23	92.34
Christian Temple	87	443.50	Newport News	37	52.84
Cypress Chapel	24	104.20	Oakland	16	81.80
Damascus	13	78.70	Old Zion (new)	20	38.80
Dendron	13	81.65	Rosemont	25	196.62
Elm Avenue	16	70.80	Suffolk	150	927.00
First, Portsmouth	28	125.75	South Norfolk	20	99.00
First, Norfolk	30	165.60	Wakefield	18	96.00
First, Richmond	14	82.20	Waverly	15	100.00
Franklin	37	223.60	Windsor	25	113.80
Holland	26	221.80	Ocean View (new)	8	1.00
Holy Neck	35	310.50			
			Totals	850	$4,485.08

YOUNG PEOPLE'S SOCIETIES.

	Members.	Offering.		Members.	Offering.
Antioch	18	$ 17.00	Liberty Spring	36	79.75
Berea, Oakland	39	40.10	New Lebanon	18	51.95
Burton's Grove	22	40.20	Newport News	10	7.70
Bethlehem	31	119.50	Mt. Carmel	22	20.20
Christian Temple	23	140.30	Old Zion (new)	23	15.60
Cypress Chapel	55	41.80	Rosemont	15	36.60
Dendron (new)	18	21.50	South Norfolk	33	42.10
First, Norfolk	30	14.00	Suffolk	53	366.45
First, Portsmouth	20	66.00	Spring Hill	20	19.60
Franklin	25	117.50	Waverly	6	20.00
Holland (B. Rowland)	22	161.00	Windsor	21	14.05
Holland (Barrett)	10	43.05	Union, Surry	18	20.00
Holy Neck	17	74.80			
Hopewell	12	14.40	Totals	617	$1,605.15

WILLING WORKERS' SOCIETIES.

	Members.	Offering.		Members.	Offering.
Berea, Nansemond	28	$ 27.82	Liberty Spring	15	25.50
Bethlehem	20	32.25	Mt. Carmel	14	25.40
Christian Temple	36	69.40	Newport News	10	33.20
Cypress Chapel	14	25.40	Old Zion (new)	5	12.50
Elm Avenue	7	12.00	Rosemont	20	22.00
First, Norfolk	15	7.00	South Norfolk	17	26.00
First, Portsmouth	24	25.50	Suffolk	35	78.50
Franklin	17	73.50	Windsor	17	21.90
Holland	28	73.90	Spring Hill	10	2.00
Holy Neck	25	68.50	Waverly	10	18.97
Hopewell	7	1.25			
			Totals	374	$ 682.49

CRADLE ROLL SOCIETIES.

	Members.	Offering.		Members.	Offering.
Antioch	30	$ 2.00	Hopewell	11	1.65
Berea, Nansemond	17	4.16	Liberty Spring	17	4.00
Bethlehem	18	4.80	Mt. Carmel	5	1.00
Christian Temple	45	14.00	Newport News	40	6.02
Cypress Chapel	8	3.30	Old Zion (new)	10	2.00
Damascus	18	3.65	Rosemont	25	10.00
First, Norfolk	19	2.00	South Norfolk	37	3.00
First, Portsmouth	11	3.50	Suffolk	28	5.00
Franklin	22	15.00	Windsor	17	4.90
Holy Neck	17	42.00			
Holland	18	12.00	Totals	413	$ 143.88

SUMMARY.

Women's Societies	$4,485.08
Young People's Societies	1,605.15
Willing Workers' Societies	682.49
Cradle Roll Societies	143.88
Rally offering	72.56
Offering Young People's Conference	26.45
Offering Woman's Annual Conference	71.78
Remainder of $500.00 gift of J. M. Darden	216.80
Grand total	$7,304.19
Balance brought forth from last year	178.48
Total	$7,482.67
Disbursements	7,227.43
Balance in bank December 1, 1930	$ 255.24

NOTE: Mr. Darden paid in $283.20 which was credited to the various societies raising the 10 per cent increase, according to his offer, making the total paid in by him, $500.00.

Respectfully submitted,

MRS. W. V. LEATHERS, *Treasurer.*

At the request of Mrs. W. V. Leathers, Treasurer Eastern Virginia Woman's Home and Foreign Mission Board, I beg to hereby certify that she has on deposit in the Farmers Bank of Nansemond the balance as shown by her report.

A. H. HARGRAVE, *Ass't Cashier.*

The President appointed the following committees:

Nominations—Mrs. I. W. Johnson, Mrs. J. P. Dalton, Mrs. M. J. W. White.

Resolutions—Mrs. W. H. Yates, Mrs. E. L. Beale, Mrs. J. F. Morgan.

Place of meeting was voted to be left in the hands of the Executive Committee.

Offering, $71.87.

Vocal solo: "Resignation," by Mr. Maudaunt Etheridge.

Address: "Modern Miniatures," by Mrs. Ray Clarke Tillinghast, New York City.

AFTERNOON SESSION.

Called to order at 2 o'clock. A telegram was read from Dr. J. O. Atkinson, who was attending a meeting of the General Board, in Wisconsin, expressing his regret in not being able to attend this Conference.

Vocal duet by Revs. J. F. Morgan and O. D. Poythress.

Address: "The Passion Play—A Witness," by Dr. L. E. Smith.

Memoirs: Mrs. I. W. Johnson conducted a reverent service in memory of the following members of the Conference who died during the past year: Mrs. M. J. Lee, Mrs. Corinne Griggs, Mrs. Mitt Darden, Mrs. W. H. Rountree, Mrs. N. H. Bradshaw, Mrs. Annie Luke, Mrs. Howard Luke, Mrs. Nettie J. White, Mrs. M. E. Gordon, Mrs. Barsha Duke, Miss Mary Brinkley, Miss Alice Turlington.

Mrs. J. A. Williams, President of the Woman's Mission Board of the Southern Christian Convention, spoke on distribution of our funds and points on which the Conference banner is won.

Banners were presented by Mrs. J. M. Harris, as follows: Women, Holy Neck; Young People, Berta Rowland Society of Holland; Willing Workers, Franklin; Cradle Roll, Holy Neck won for the third consecutive year, and keeps the banner.

The attendance banner was won by the Young People's (Barrett) Society, of Holland, and the Young People of Cypress Chapel. Each will keep the banner for six months of the year.

One hundred per cent societies: Women—Holland, Christian Temple, First (Portsmouth); Young People—Bethlehem, Franklin, Holy Neck; Willing Workers—Holland, Windsor, Holy Neck.

Honor Roll Churches: Berea (Nansemond), Bethlehem, Christian Temple, Cypress Chapel, First (Portsmouth), Franklin, Holland, Holy Neck, Liberty Spring, Mt. Carmel, Old Zion, Rosemont (South Norfolk), Suffolk.

It was moved and carried that the price of the Conference lunch be increased from 35 cents to 45 cents.

The following recommendations were read and accepted:

RECOMMENDATIONS.

1. That the goal for the year be $7,500.

2. That we work in harmony with the General Board relative to the distribution of our funds.

3. That three-fourths of the membership of all Women's Societies subscribe to *The Christian Sun*.

4. That the women and young people pay 10 cents each into Literature and Contingent Fund, and the Willing Workers be released.

5. That all societies strengthen their program of information.

MRS. J. M. HARRIS, *Pres.*
MRS. L. W. STAGG, *Sec'y.*

The President explained that, owing to the absence of Dr. Atkinson, it had not been decided just how the annual thankoffering would be placed.

On behalf of the Conference, Mrs. J. M. Harris was presented with a lovely piece of silver in recognition of the splendid services rendered. The presentation was made by Mrs. L. W. Stagg.

Mr. J. M. Darden spoke a few words of appreciation of the retiring President, and presented her with a gold coin.

REPORT OF COMMITTEE ON NOMINATIONS.

Your committee reports the following nominations:

President—Mrs. R. T. Bradford.
Vice-President—Mrs. O. M. Cockes.
Treasurer—Mrs. W. V. Leathers.
Secretary—Mrs. L. W. Stagg.
Superintendent Literature—Mrs. J. E. Cartwright.
Superintendent Young People—Mrs. E. L. Beale.
Superintendent Cradle Roll—Mrs. F. M. Nelson.
Superintendent Life Membership and Memorials—Mrs. O. S. Mills.
Superintendent Spiritual Life—Mrs. W. H. Andrews.
Conference Editor—Mrs. W. M. Jay.

MRS. I. W. JOHNSON,
MRS. M. J. W. WHITE,
MRS. J. P. DALTON,
Committee.

Report adopted.

The report of the Committee on nominations for the Young People's Conference was also adopted, as follows:

REPORT OF COMMITTEE ON Y. P. NOMINATIONS.

President—Miss Mary Lee Williams.
Vice-President—Miss Carolyn Gort.
Secretary—Miss Sarah Norfleet Brinkley.
Assistant Secretary—Miss Rachael Brinkley.

REPORT OF COMMITTEE ON RESOLUTIONS.

We, the members and visitors of the Eastern Virginia Woman's Missionary Conference, in its Eighteenth Annual Session, feel that, in these times of depression, we have been blessed with health and life's necessities, and while our goal has not quite been reached, let us not be discouraged; but be it resolved:

That we go back to our societies inspired to do more than ever for our Master's cause.

That we express our thanks to the committee who arranged this splendid program, and to all who contributed to its success; especially Mrs. Ray Clarke Tillinghast, of New York, for her most inspiring and enlightening address, and Dr. L. E. Smith for his wonderful message on the "Passion Play."

That we give a rising vote of thanks to the ladies of the Temple for their hospitality and delicious lunch.

MRS. W. H. YATES,
MRS. E. L. BEALE,
MRS. J. F. MORGAN,
Committee.

Report adopted.

At this time the retiring President presented the new President, Mrs. R. T. Bradford, who responded briefly to the welcome extended her.

The Conference adjourned, to meet Friday before the Eastern Virginia Conference, in 1931. Benediction by Rev. H. C. Caviness.

MRS. R. T. BRADFORD, *President*.
MRS. L. W. STAGG, *Secretary*.

Minutes of the Twelfth Annual Session of the North Carolina Woman's Missionary Conference

LIBERTY (VANCE) CHRISTIAN CHURCH—OCTOBER 17, 1930.

MORNING SESSION.

The Twelfth Annual Session of the North Carolina Woman's Missionary Conference met with the Christian Church at Liberty, Vance County, on October 17, 1930. Called to order by the President, Mrs. C. H. Rowland. Mrs. R. J. Newton, of the Liberty Church, led the devotional service.

Greetings from the District Superintendents were as follows:

Alamance—Mrs. J. W. Patton.
Guilford—Mrs. O. H. Paris.
Halifax—Mrs. Alfred Hayes.
Durham-Wake—Mrs. Grady Leonard.
Franklin-Vance-Warren—Miss Margaret Alston.
Randolph—No report.
Chatham—Mrs. R. L. Ross.

The Secretary of the Conference made her report. The same was adopted.

Mrs. Stanley C. Harrell, Superintendent of Young People's Work, made report and explained the program she had outlined, based on "The Star of India." The report was adopted.

Mrs. Boshart, of Raleigh, read the report of Mrs. R. M. Rothgeb, Superintendent of the Cradle Roll Department. The report was adopted.

Mrs. W. H. Carroll, Superintendent of Spiritual Life, made report. She recommended that our societies study Romans this year. The report was adopted.

Mrs. W. T. Scott read the report of the Literature Superintendent, Mrs. J. J. Henderson. The same was adopted.

The Treasurer, Mrs. W. R. Sellars, reported, as follows, and it was adopted:

REPORT OF TREASURER.

WOMEN'S SOCIETIES.

Amelia	$ 9.60	Berea	3.80
Antioch	4.60	Burlington	916.58
Bethlehem	8.07	Catawba Springs	26.10
Bethlehem Aid	5.00	Chapel Hill	50.00

Caraleigh	5.60	New Hope	6.60
Danville	10.00	Palm St., Greensboro	10.00
Durham	277.77	Parks Cross Roads	2.80
Elon College	304.00	Pleasant Grove	30.00
Fuller's Chapel	7.20	Pleasant Hill	23.40
Grace's Chapel	10.85	Pleasant Ridge	56.00
Graham	30.00	Piney Plains	30.00
Greensboro	351.50	Providence Memorial	30.00
Haw River	9.05	Raleigh	150.00
Hebron	10.00	Ramseur	55.00
Henderson	100.00	Randleman	9.60
High Point	13.15	Reidsville	125.00
Howard's Chapel	10.00	Sanford	127.70
Ingram	21.95	Shallow Well	75.00
Liberty (Va.)	10.00	Shiloh	15.65
Liberty, Vance	100.00	Turner's Chapel	53.00
Long's Chapel	5.00	Union Ridge	40.00
Lynchburg	25.65	Virgilina	69.51
Monticello	25.10	Wake Chapel	85.00
Mt. Auburn	90.00	Youngsville	15.30
Mt. Zion	7.00		
New Lebanon	8.30	Total	$3,465.43

YOUNG PEOPLE'S SOCIETIES.

Bethlehem	$ 3.79	Henderson	5.00
Burlington	250.00	Long's Chapel	2.00
Burlington Junior	100.91	Pleasant Hill	10.00
Durham	50.76	Ramseur	5.00
Elon College Junior	25.00	Turner's Chapel	4.00
Graham	8.09	Wake Chapel	1.00
Greensboro	90.00		
Greensboro Junior	15.00	Total	$ 570.55

WILLING WORKERS' SOCIETIES.

Bethlehem	$ 1.15	Greensboro	25.00
Burlington	51.11	Reidsville	15.00
Durham	35.00	Virgilina	12.30
Durham Junior	20.30		
Elon College	25.00	Total	$ 184.86

CRADLE ROLL SOCIETIES.

Bethlehem	$ .60	Park's Cross Roads	4.25
Burlington	25.00	Piney Plains	5.00
Durham	30.00	Raleigh	10.00
Elon College	25.00	Ramseur	3.16
Greensboro	15.00	Sanford	3.53
High Point	2.00	Turner's Chapel	3.00
Liberty, Vance	5.00	Wake Chapel	10.00
Long's Chapel	1.00		
		Total	$ 142.54

DISTRICT MEETINGS.

Alamance	$ 16.00	Randolph	5.00
Guilford	14.00	Vance, Warren	5.00
Halifax	5.30		
Lee, Chatham	7.00	Total	$ 52.30

SUMMARY.

Women's Societies $3,465.43
Young People's Societies 570.55
Willing Workers' Societies 184.86
Cradle Roll Societies 142.54
District Meetings 52.30
Conference Offering 27.42

Total receipts $4,443.10

1930.	*Disbursements.*	
Jan. 14.	Paid Mrs. H. S. Hardcastle, Treas............$	523.23
Apr. 14.	Paid Mrs. H. S. Hardcastle, Treas............	1,303.35
July 15.	Paid Mrs. H. S. Hardcastle, Treas............	852.16
Sep. 9.	Paid Mrs. H. S. Hardcastle, Treas............	10.00
Oct. 21.	Paid Mrs. H. S. Hardcastle, Treas............	1,754.36

$4,443.10

1929. CURRENT EXPENSE FUND.

Nov. 20. Balance brought from last year .... $ 64.22
1930.
Oct. 17. Amount received, refund from Mrs. J. J. Henderson..... 2.00

Total receipts .... $ 66.22

1929.	*Disbursements.*	
Nov. 20.	Paid A. D. Pate Co., for printing...............$	2.25
29.	Paid W. P. Fowler, expense of Board meeting.....	3.45
Dec. 2.	Paid Mrs. C. H. Rowland, for stamps...........	2.00
	Mrs. J. J. Henderson, for stamps...............	2.00
	Mrs. W. H. Carroll, for stamps.................	2.00
	Paid Miss Mulholland, for stamps..............	2.00
	Paid Miss Cotton, for stamps..................	2.00
1930.		
Jan. 7.	Paid A. D. Pate Co., printing goals 1930.........	10.15
7.	Paid Mrs. W. R. Sellars, for stamps.............	2.00
Mar. 1.	Paid A. D. Pate, printing 3 receipt books........	4.50
Apr. 14.	Paid Mrs. W. R. Sellars, for stamps.............	2.00
May 27.	Paid Mrs. R. N. Rothgeb, for stamps...........	1.00
Sep. 3.	Paid A. D. Pate, printing paper for Mrs. Rothgeb.	2.35
24.	Paid Mrs. A. M. Shepherd, for stamps..........	2.50
Oct. 2.	Paid Mrs. W. R. Sellars, for stamps.............	2.00
22.	Paid Central Publishing Co., for programs.......	3.75

45.95

Balance .... $ 20.27

MRS. W. R. SELLARS, *Treasurer.*

Mrs. S. C. Harrell reported on life memberships and memorials. Three new members were added during the year.

The President reported that she had visited a number of Churches and had organized seven societies, attended five of the seven district meetings, and aided the work in whatever way she could.

The ministers present were given recognition. Rev. Stanley C. Harrell gave an inspiring address. He used as a subject, "His Word Magnified."

The President announced the following committees:

Nominations—Mrs. C. H. Stephenson, Mrs. J. P. Barrett, Mrs. J. A. Kimball.

Resolutions—Mrs. Boshart, Mrs. R. L. Ross, Mrs. Alfred Hayes.

Place—Mrs. Fred Howard, Mrs. W. M. Paris, Miss Nonie Moore.

Banner—Mrs. J. J. Henderson, Mrs. George McCullers, Mrs. Charles Aldridge.

Finance—Mrs. J. P. Avent, Mrs. W. R. Sellars.

An offertory solo was rendered by Mrs. H. B. Harward.
Roll call of Churches, and twenty-two responded.
Mrs. W. H. Boone led in a meditation entitled, "His Will Obeyed."
Miss Virginia Harward sang "Have Thine Own Way."
Adjourned for lunch.

AFTERNOON SESSION.

Mrs. W. T. Scott presented the study books. Miss Graham Rowland gave an address, "His Work; Our Task."

The Committee on Nominations reported, and those nominated were elected, as follows:

President—Mrs. C. H. Rowland.
Vice-President—Mrs. S. C. Harrell.
Secretary—Mrs. J. P. Barrett.
Treasurer—Mrs. W. R. Sellars.
Superintendent of Spiritual Life—Mrs. W. H. Carroll.
Superintendent of Literature—Mrs. W. T. Scott.
Superintendent of Young People—Miss Lucile Mulholland.
Superintendent of Cradle Roll—Mrs. R. M. Rothgeb.

The Committee on Resolutions reported. Report adopted.

The Committee on Place for Next Session reported that Elon College had been selected.

The banner was awarded to the society at Elon College, Mrs. J. W. Patton presenting it and Mrs. W. P. Lawrence accepting it for the society.

The Finance Committee reported that the goal for the year would be five thousand dollars. A message was sent to the Mission Secretary, Dr. J. O. Atkinson, who could not be present.

After a closing service of consecration, the Conference adjourned.

MRS. C. H. ROWLAND, *President.*
MISS LUCILE MULHOLLAND, *Secretary.*

Minutes of Sixth Annual Session of Woman's Missionary Convention of Alabama Christian Conference

New Hope Christian Church—October 12, 1930.

MORNING SESSION.

Called to order by President Mrs. V. E. Kitchens at 11 o'clock.
Song, "When the Roll is Called Up Yonder."
Scripture lesson read by Miss Cumi Waldrep (Rom. 10:11-18).
Prayer by Mrs. G. L. Stevens.

Enrollment—Churches and Delegates.

Antioch—Mrs. O. L. Royston, Miss Steva Hood, Miss Annie Laura Landers.
Lowell—Mrs. O. W. Chase, Mrs. Jewel Clark, Miss Cumi Waldrep.
Mt. Zion—Mrs. W. C. Morris, Mrs. J. B. Still, Mrs. J. B. Swann.
New Harmony—Mrs. Ross McCormick, Miss Eva McCain.
New Hope—Mrs. J. M. Richards, Mrs. S. Stevens, Mrs. Gus Pinkard.
Roanoke—Mrs. J. H. Chrisler, Mrs. S. B. Dollar.
Wadley—Mrs. V. L. Carter, Miss Cloie McCormick, Miss Verla Barnett.

Reports of group leaders:

Wadley Group—One Woman's Society, 1 Young people's, 1 Willing Workers', and 1 Cradle Roll.
Roanoke Group—One Woman's Society, 1 Young People's, 1 Willing Workers', and 1 Cradle Roll.
New Hope Group—Four Women's Societies, 2 Willing Workers' Societies.
Lineville Group—No report, but they have two Women's Societies.

Report of Superintendent of the Young People by Mrs. V. L. Carter.
Report of Superintendent of Willing Workers by Mrs. Paul Beaird.
Report of Superintendent of Cradle Roll by Mrs. A. I. Landers.
Report of Superintendent of Literature by Mrs. L. H. Liles.

The President read a letter from Mrs. A. M. Johnson, who sent $10.00 for a life membership for Mrs. G. D. Hunt to the Woman's Missionary Conference. The Conference gave a rising vote of thanks to Mrs. Johnson and instructed the Secretary to write her a letter of appreciation.

The Treasurer's report was read and adopted, as follows:

REPORT OF TREASURER.

Amount from last year .... $ 40.00

Receipts.

Women's Societies.

Antioch	7.85
Cragford	5.00
Forest Home	2.50
Lowell	10.00
New Hope	50.00
Pisgah	9.00
Roanoke	20.00
Wadley	44.64

Young People's Societies.

Roanoke	15.00
Wadley	25.00

Willing Workers' Societies.

Roanoke	9.00
Antioch	1.75

Cradle Roll.

Roanoke	6.00

Offerings at Rallies.

Corinth	3.12
Forest Home	3.57
New Harmony	3.40
Noon Day	4.86

Total .... $ 260.69

Disbursements.

To B. B. Brannon, for ledger ....$	1.00
To A. D. Pate, for printing goals	4.00
To Mrs. H. S. Hardcastle, for dues	10.30
To Mrs. G. L. Stevens, for postage	1.25
To Mrs. Kitchens and Mrs. Swint, railroad fare to rally	3.92
To W. C. Edge, for Rev. G. D. Hunt	19.95
To Mrs. Kitchens, expense to the S. C. C.	9.00
To W. T. Orr, for taxie fare to Noon Day Rally	5.00
To Mrs. H. S. Hardcastle, for regular fund	32.18
	86.60

Balance in treasury .... $ 174.09

Mrs. J. H. Swint, *Treasurer.*

The President delivered the annual message, "Foundations for the New Day."

Song, "Since Jesus Came Into My Heart."

An offering of $4.51 was taken.

The following committees were appointed:

Nominations—Mrs. S. W. Elder, Mrs. J. H. Chrisler, Mrs. O. W. Chase.

Place of Next Meeting—Mrs. O. L. Royston, Mrs. W. C. Morris.

Resolutions—Miss Cumi Waldrep, Mrs. V. L. Carter, Mrs. S. B. Dollar.

Short talks were made by Mr. C. W. Stevens and V. E. Kitchens.

Adjournment, and benediction by Mrs. J. H. Swint.

AFTERNOON SESSION.

Called to order by President at 1:30 o'clock.

Song, "Blessed Assurance."

Young people's program, led by Mrs. V. L. Carter.

Song, "If Jesus Goes With Me."

The 23rd Psalm was recited in unison.

Prayer, Miss Cumi Waldrep.

Song, "Jesus Calls Us."

"What Missions Mean to Young People," Mrs. V. L. Carter.

"What Missions Mean to Young People in Study and Service," Miss Cloie McCormick.

"The Task is Ours," Mrs. V. L. Carter.

"Necessity of Prayer in the Christian Life," Miss Annie Laura Landers.

"His Christ in Gethsemane," Miss Verla Barnett.

Prayer, Mrs. V. L. Carter.

"Shall We Work Together," Miss Marguerite Davison.

Song, "We'll Work Till Jesus Comes."

Address: "The Unavoidable Challenge," Rev. G. H. Veazey.

Address: "Jesus and the Five Thousand," Rev. G. S. Hunt.

Reports of committees.

The following officers were re-elected:

President—Mrs. V. E. Kitchens.

Vice-President—Miss Mary Jenkins.

Secretary—Mrs. G. L. Stevens.

Treasurer—Mrs. J. H. Swint.

Young People's Superintendent—Mrs. V. L. Carter.

Willing Workers' Superintendent—Mrs. Paul Beaird.

Cradle Roll Superintendent—Mrs. O. L. Royston.

Literature Superintendent—Mrs. L. H. Liles.

Life Membership Superintendent—Mrs. O. H. Orr.

The next session of this Conference will be held at Roanoke, the date to be announced later.

REPORT OF COMMITTEE ON RESOLUTIONS.

Although we realize we have worked under some hardships this year, we are not satisfied with the year's work, and do hereby resolve:

1. To put forth a greater effort than ever before to send the message of our Master to all parts of the world.

2. We recommend that each Church study missions, so as to know more of its real worth to the Church and community.

3. We wish to thank the people of New Hope Church and community for their hospitality today.

> Miss Cumi Waldrop,
> Mrs. V. L. Carter,
> Mrs. S. B. Dollar,
> *Committee.*

Adopted.

Mrs. W. H. Floyd spoke in behalf of the Church and Missionary Society of their pleasure in entertaining this Conference.

Conference adjourned, to meet with the First Christian Church at Roanoke, 1931. Benediction by Mrs. W. C. Morris.

> Mrs. V. E. Kitchens, *President.*
> Mrs. G. L. Stevens, *Secretary.*

Ministerial Directory

Alexander, W. S................4712 Foster Ave., Brooklyn, N. Y.
Allen, M. F.............2301 Roanoke Ave., Newport News, Va.
Allred, J. M....................Route 1, Asheboro, N. C.
Andes, A. W........................Harrisonburg, Va.
Apple, J. F..........................Elon College, N. C.
Atkinson, J. O.......................Elon College, N. C.

Barrett, D. P.........................Ponce, Porto Rico
Bennett, S. A......................Elon College, N. C.
Beougher, S. L.........................Wadley, Ala.
Brady, E. C...............................Hemp, N. C.

Carden, J. S.................906 Shepherd St., Durham, N. C.
Carpenter, W. C....................Brookfield, Ga.
Carter, C. W.........................Wadley, Ala.
Carter, E. M......................Youngsville, N. C.
Caviness, H. C..........12 North Elm Ave., Portsmouth, Va.
Clem, W. M.....................West Mansfield, Mass.
Crowder, W. T..............604 Park Ave., LaGrange, Ga.
Crutchfield, G. C...........5338 Fort Ave., Lynchburg, Va.
Crutchfield, H. E.............R. F. D., Henderson, N. C.
Cummings, J. C.........................Hemp, N. C.
Coulter, Roy D......................Elon College, N. C.
Cutchin, J. N......................South Norfolk, Va.

Dawson, T. B......................Elon College, N. C.
Dean, T. J...........................Girard, Ala.
Denison, W. H................C. P. A. Bldg., Dayton, Ohio
Denton, J. A....................Route 3, Raleigh, N. C.
Dixon, F. C.........................Anderson, S. C.
Dollar, J. D..............4 Collins St., Lanett, Ala.
Dollar, Jesse H.....................Reidsville, N. C.

Earp, B. J.........................Harrisonburg, Va.
Edwards, W. J.............211 Ward St., High Point, N. C.
Elder, W. W.............Chaplain U. S. N., Postmaster, San Francisco, Calif.

Fix, J. W..............................Franklin, Va.
Fleming, P. H..........................Burlington, N. C.
Flowers, A. R.............................Sims, N. C.
Foster, J. L.......................Elon College, N. C.
Fogleman, J. U......................Graham, N. C.
Franks, J. E....................Route 4, Raleigh, N. C.
French, Joe....................Route 1, Broadway, Va.
Fuller, W. B..........................Linville, Va.

Garman, W. H................1303 W. 27th St., Norfolk, Va.
Gerringer, C. E.......................Wakefield, Va.
Gray, H. M................406 Jefferson St., LaGrange, Ga.
Gray, H. T..................40 McGee St., LaGrange, Ga.

Gray, T. W. ....800 Elm St., LaGrange, Ga.
Green, G. J. ....Morrisville, N. C.
Green, T. J. ....Ramseur, N. C.

Hanson, C. W. ....817 Forest Ave., LaGrange, Ga.
Hardcastle, H. S. ....Suffolk, Va.
Harrell, Stanley C. ....Durham, N. C.
Harward, W. D. ....Windsor, Va.
Hayes, W. H. ....Seagrove, N. C.
Heard, H. R. ....Avondale, Ala.
Hilliard, H. C. ....Mt. Auburn, N. C.
Hook, W. C. ....Winchester, Va.
Howard, B. J. ....Chapel Hill, N. C.
Hughes, J. H. ....Pisgah, Ala.
Hurst, A. P. ....Elon College, N. C.
Hurst, A. W. ....Elon College, N. C.
Hunt, G. D. ....Wadley, Ala.
House, Robert Lee.......................Duke University, Durham, N. C.

Jay, W. M. ....Holland, Va.
Johnson, I. W. ....Suffolk, Va.
Johnson, J. Lee......................................Fuquay Springs, N. C.
Jones, Ellwood W. ....Havre de Grace, Md.

Kirbye, J. Edward. ....Raleigh, N. C.
Klapp, P. T. ....Elon College, N. C.

Lankford, G. O. ....Burlington, N. C.
Lassiter, L. L. ....Seaboard, Va.
Lester, F. C. ....Waverly, Va.
Long, D. A. ....Florence, S. C.
Lowe, T. N. ....Portsmouth, Va.

Madren, S. E. ....Fancy Gap, Va.
Martin, W. C. ....Candor, N. C.
McCauley, J. E. ....129 Hardy Ave., Norfolk, Va.
McQuarrie, Neil (Congregationalist) ....Columbus, Ga.
Meacham, W. T. ....Wadley, Ala.
Moffitt, D. R. ....Coleridge, N. C.
Moore, W. C. ....Dover, Del.
Morgan, J. F. ....Route 3, Norfolk, Va.

Neese, J. L. ....Route 2, Greensboro, N. C.
Newman, C. E. ....Virgilina, Va.
Newman, J. U. ....Elon College, N. C.
Newman, N. G. ....Holland, Va.

Orr, J. B. ....Gilmer, Texas

Patton, J. W. ....Elon College, N. C.
Pearce, G. A. ....306 N. King Ave., Dunn, N. C.
Poythress, O. D. ....South Norfolk, Va.
Pollard, M. A. ....Liberty, N. C.

Rainey, E. H. ....Atwood, Ill.
Riddle, O. B. ....Bethesda, Md.
Roberts, J. M. ....Windsor, Va.

Rountree, H. E.....................Chaplain, Navy Yard, Charleston, S. C.
Rowland, C. H.....................315 N. Edgewood St., Greensboro, N. C.
Ryan, C. C..............................3206 Grove Ave., Richmond, Va.

Scholz, H...Macon, N. C.
Scott, W. T...Salisbury, N. C.
Scotten, A. K...Coleridge, N. C.
Sheppard, A. H.......................................Route 2, Glenn, Ga.
Short, C. E...Chipley, Ga.
Smith, H. S..............................Yale Station, New Haven, Conn.
Smith, L. E...........................272 E. 39th St., Norfolk, Va.
Sorrell, M. T..........................117 Motley Ave., Danville, Va.
Spence, D. M..
Staley, W. W..Suffolk, Va.
Stephens, H. S...Dover, Del.
Stephenson, W. J.....................................Merry Oaks, N. C.
Sutcliffe, M. W...Camden, N. J.
Sutcliffe, W. R...Philadelphia, Pa.

Taylor, Herman C.......................................Dover, Del.
Tyler, Myron...............................Route 1, Blackshear, Ga.

Underhill, G. D..St. Johnsville, N. Y.
Underwood, G. R.......................................Pittsboro, N. C.

Veazey, G. H...Roanoke, Ala.

Warren, John H...Ocean View, Va.
White, E. B...Windsor, Va.
White, T. E...Elon College, N. C.
Whitten, R. A...Reidsville, N. C.
Wicker, W. C...Elon College, N. C.
Williamson, R. L.......................................Winchester, Va.
Wisner, R. L..Pisgah, Ala.
Wright, T. F..Sanford, N. C.
Wyrick, L. L..Elon College, N. C.

LICENTIATES.

Archer, W. N...Lineville, Ala.

Brittle, Richie Irvin.....................................Cypress Chapel, Va.

Chadwick, J. B..Wyoming, Del.
Coble, R. H...Route 5, Burlington, N. C.
Cox, H. V...Ramseur, N. C.

Dickens, J. M...Elon College, N. C.
Dollar, Carl C..Elon College, N. C.

Fogleman, J. D..Liberty, N. C.

Grissom, Raymond T....................................Elon College, N. C.

Harrod, J. T..
Henderson, John W.....................................Shenandoah, Va.
Huber, Lester Ellsworth...........................Belgian Congo, Africa
Hunt, G. S...Wadley, Ala.

Lowdermilk, B. H..Ramseur, N. C.

Mann, Alton B...Lanett, Ala.
McKenney, D. T...Lillington, N. C.

Nash, D. D..Hopewell, Va.

Parsons, D. F...........................Room 53, Gates Hall, Chicago, Ill.
Poore, Miss Sallie...Roanoke, Ala.

Shepherd, V. D...High Point, N. C.
Smith, E. B.....................................416 Lee St., LaGrange, Ga.
Smith, R. O...Bennett, N. C.
Smith, W. S...Glenwood, N. C.

Tally, George M..Corbinton, N. C.
Taylor, John...Rocky Mills, Ala.
Terrell, W. B...Elon College, N. C.

Underwood, I. T...............................Route 2, Altamahaw, N. C.

Vickers, J. Y..Wadley, Ala.

Walker, G. R..Wadley, Ala.
Willingham, W. W...........................Box 203, Phoenix City, Ala.
Wilson, S. B..Elon College, N. C.

Ministers 123

Licentiates 31